the ^Smart Approach to
new
home
decorating

CRE▲TIVE
HOMEOWNER®

the ^ new Smart Approach to

home decorating

CREATIVE HOMEOWNER®, Upper Saddle River, New Jersey

Editorial Director: Timothy O. Bakke
Production Manager: Kimberly H. Vivas

Editors: Fran J. Donegan, Kathie Robitz
Associate Editor: Lynn Elliot
Contributing Writers: Megan Accardi, Laura M Alovosus, Jane Cornell, Lynn Elliot, Alison Murray Morris, Kathie Robitz, and Joanne M. Sill
Assistant Editor/Photo Researcher: Sharon Ranftle
Assistant Editor: Jennifer Ramcke
Copy Editor: Megan Accardi
Proofreader: Paul Rieder

Senior Designer: David Geer
Illustrator: Vincent Alessi
Front Cover Photography: Mark Samu

Printed in the United States of America

Current Printing (last digit)
10

The New Smart Approach to Home Decorating, Second Edition
Library of Congress Control Number: 2002110575
ISBN: 1-58011-143-2

CREATIVE HOMEOWNER®
A Division of Federal Marketing Corp.
24 Park Way
Upper Saddle River, NJ 07458
www.creativehomeowner.com

ACKNOWLEDGMENTS

For the wealth of information and guidance they have provided, thank you to the American Society of Interior Designers (ASID), the International Society of Interior Designers (ISID), the International Furnishings and Design Association (IFDA), the National Kitchen & Bath Association (NKBA), the National Association of the Remodeling Industry (NARI), and the Color Association of the United States.

CONTENTS

INTRODUCTION 8

CHAPTER ONE
THE BASICS OF DESIGN 12
• Understanding Your Space • Creating a Plan • Decorating Room by Room • A Gallery of Smart Ideas

CHAPTER TWO
ADDING COLOR AND TEXTURE 32
• Working with Color • Introducing Pattern • Adding Texture • Creating a Design • A Gallery of Smart Ideas

CHAPTER THREE
THE RIGHT LIGHT 52
• Natural Light • Types of Artificial Light • Selecting Light Levels • Types of Bulbs • Determining Lighting Needs • Lighting Fixtures • The Role of Lighting in Architecture • A Gallery of Smart Ideas

CHAPTER FOUR
FLOORING OPTIONS 74
• Choices in Wood • Laminate Flooring • Vinyl Sheet and Tile Flooring • Ceramic Choices • Natural Stone • Carpeting and Rugs • Picking a Flooring Material • A Gallery of Smart Ideas

CHAPTER FIVE
WALL AND WINDOW TREATMENTS 92
• Assessing Your Walls • Decorative Paint Techniques • Painting Walls and Trim • Selecting Wallcoverings and Borders • Window Treatments • A Gallery of Smart Ideas

CHAPTER SIX
DISTINCTIVE TOUCHES 120
• Elements of Style • Special Details • A Gallery of Smart Ideas

CHAPTER SEVEN
THE FACTS ON FURNITURE 140
• Furniture for Your Home • Making Choices • Furniture Styles • Judging Quality • Recycling Your Furniture • A Gallery of Smart Ideas

CHAPTER EIGHT
THE ROOMS IN YOUR HOME 162
• Foyers and Hallways • Living Room • Family Room • Dining Room • Kitchen • Bedrooms • Children's Rooms • Bathrooms • Working with Professionals • A Gallery of Smart Ideas

CHAPTER NINE
CREATING A KITCHEN DESIGN 190
• Set Priorities • Basic Kitchen Layouts • Choosing Cabinets • Countertop Options • Selecting Fixtures • A Galley of Smart Ideas

CHAPTER TEN
CREATING A BATHROOM DESIGN 220
• Set Priorities • Basic Layouts • Types of Bathrooms • Shopping for Bath Products • Fixtures • Storage for the Bath • Serviceable Surfaces • What's Your Style • A Gallery of Smart Ideas

CHAPTER ELEVEN
OUTDOOR LIVING AREAS 250
• Decorating Sunrooms and Porches • Patios, Decks, and Gazebos • Tips on Landscaping • A Gallery of Smart Ideas

APPENDIX 268

RESOURCE GUIDE 276

GLOSSARY 278

INDEX 282

CREDITS 286

INTRODUCTION

Most people don't realize it, but there is an interior designer in them waiting to get out. The problem is that many of us are too afraid to take the steps that will give our creative persona its freedom. How often have you looked at a magazine or visited the home that was decorated by a professional or decorated by someone who seems to have a flair for it, and been intimidated—convinced you could never get those kinds of results on your own? What those folks have that you may not is a knowledge of the basics of design. They know how to manipulate the architecture of a room and then go about adding colors, textures, patterns, lighting, and furniture to make the space truly unique. In *The New Smart Approach to Home Decorating,* you will learn those basics and more.

Because so much of what you do (or hesitate to do) to your home is a matter of confidence, *The New Smart Approach to Home Decorating* explains everything you need to know to make educated decisions about decorating projects. It starts with an easy explanation of space—how to analyze it and work with what you have. Simple instructions for creating your own floor plan, along with furniture templates at the back of the book, let you try out different layouts. A chapter on color, pattern, and texture gives you the inside information you will need to design flawless schemes with paint and fabric. And you'll learn how to select the perfect wall, window, and floor treatments to pull together one cohesive look. If you're debating about whether to buy new furniture or reuse existing pieces, you'll find the answer in the chapter on furniture. Besides describing furniture styles, it offers important advice for judging quality in a piece and when it pays to refinish rather than buy new items.

The New Smart Approach to Home Decorating also addresses the special concerns of kitchen and bath design. So that you can make these rooms efficient *and* handsome, you'll find space-planning guidelines from the National Kitchen & Bath Association, as well as a rundown on the latest in cabinetry, fixtures, fittings, and finishing materials. You may also have questions about decorating as it pertains to specific rooms of the house. The chapter on decorating room by room comes with tips from professional interior designers who offer their advice about foyers, living rooms, family rooms, dining rooms, bedrooms, kitchens, and baths—and how to make each one special. And because today's living extends beyond the front and back doors, *The New Smart Approach to Home Decorating* takes you outside with ideas for giving outdoor living spaces, such as patios, decks, and porches, the same consideration as indoor rooms. To help you with the overall process, Smart Steps in every chapter take you through each phase of the decorating process. There is also a portfolio of inspirational designs in each chapter.

As the renowned celebrity decorator Billy Baldwin once said, "The first rule of decorating is that you can break almost all the rules." *The New Smart Approach to Home Decorating* shows you how to make up your own rules with style and flair.

Clockwise (from left): Period furniture sets the tone for this country-style dining room. A sunroom is outfitted with a nautical theme that is a favorite of the owners. A great room combines kitchen and living areas that flow into one another. A variety of fabrics add color and texture to this seating area in a formal living room. A child's room has bright colors and a fun layout; the stairs lead to a loft play area. Don't forget about outdoor spaces when decorating.

THE BASICS OF DESIGN

UNDERSTANDING YOUR SPACE ■
CREATING A PLAN ■ DECORATING
ROOM BY ROOM

Professional designers always begin a project by first analyzing the space with which they will be working. Things they look at include the size, shape, and intended use of the room. They also pay careful attention to any architectural features, such as molding, windows, and fireplaces before considering colors, fabrics, and furniture. This chapter will help you think like a professional designer. You will learn about the conceptual nature of space and how to examine your own.

You'll also learn how to manipulate space to make it more functional—small rooms will feel larger, and grand spaces will seem more intimate and cozy when you learn a few easy tricks that can alter your perception of the size and shape of a given space. Selecting and arranging furnishings will be less frustrating, too, because you won't have to do it by trial and error. Your understanding of scale and proportion, two fundamental concepts relating to space, will take the guesswork out of buying something that might otherwise be too big or too small for a particular room. Your eye for creating pleasing arrangements on walls, shelves, and tabletops will become more sophisticated as well, as you discover how to apply your new knowledge to the technique of putting together flawless groupings of art or other interesting objects.

Later in this chapter you'll learn how to take accurate measurements as well as how to sketch your ideas on paper just as professional interior designers do. Furniture templates, which you can find in the Appendix, will help you try out different ways to arrange your floor plan. But your first challenge as your own designer will be to become familiar with the basics of design.

UNDERSTANDING YOUR SPACE

Most of the time homeowners decorate by intuition, and practice makes perfect—sometimes. There are no strict rules to follow; however, every serious student of design begins by learning several fundamental principals relating to space that are always useful when applied practically. These principles include scale, proportion, line, balance, harmony, and rhythm.

SCALE AND PROPORTION

Scale and proportion work hand in hand. In decorating, *scale* simply refers to the size of something as it relates to the size of everything else, including people and the space itself. *Proportion* refers to the relationship of parts or objects to one another based on size—the size of the window is in proportion to the size of the room, for example. Good scale is achieved when all of the parts are proportionately correct relative to each other, as well as to the whole.

Although it is easy to see that something is too large or too small for its place, it takes a deliberate effort to achieve good proportion. Usually, it requires patience and experimentation with various objects and arrangements until something finally looks right, so just keep at it.

LINE

Next to consider is *line*. Simply put, line defines space. Two-dimensional space consists of flat surfaces, such as walls, floors, and ceilings, which are formed by intersecting lines. Adding depth, or volume, to a flat surface creates three-dimensional space such as a room. However, lines do more than define physical space; they also suggest various qualities. For example:

■ *Vertical lines* imply strength, dignity, and formality. A good example is a classical column, which always appears stately and strong.

■ *Horizontal lines*, on the other hand, convey relaxation and security, such as a restful bed or a sturdy platform.

■ *Diagonal lines*, such as a balustrade or a gable, express motion, transition, and change.

■ *Curved lines*, like those of a winding path, denote freedom, softness, and sensuality.

As you start to select the furnishings to include in your room's design, look for ways to incorporate a variety of lines into the plan. Most modern rooms are rectilinear. To relieve the repetition of the squares and rectangles inherent in the architecture and make them more interesting, introduce a few curves or diagonals with furniture and accessories.

BALANCE

Balance is another important concept related to space. It refers to the equilibrium among forms in a room. All of the furnishings, large and small, should be distributed evenly throughout the space, not just to one side of the room, for example. With balance, relationships between objects seem natural and comfortable to the eye. For instance, two framed pictures of relatively equal size and weight look appropriate hanging side by side on a wall, whereas the pairing of two pictures of unequal size and weight seems awkward and out of balance. Balanced relationships between objects can be either *symmetrical* or *asymmetrical*.

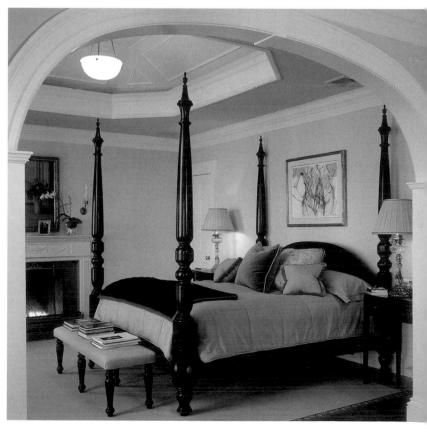

Clockwise (from above): Rather than add one large wall of glass to this high ceilinged room, the designer chose a pleasing arrangement of windows and doors of different shapes and sizes. The nook off of the landing on the stairs provides privacy in a large, open room. A generous arch softens the formal lines of this bedroom. An open switchback stairway fills the volume of this two-story-high foyer.

Left: Traditional furnishings harmonize with the style of this room, including the exposed beams, natural casings, and size, style, and shape of the windows.

Right: A door is balanced by the symmetry of the framed prints that seem to climb the wall beside it. Not only are the frames all the same, but the size of the images and the white spaces around them are also symmetrical.

Symmetry. This refers to the same arrangement of parts, objects, or forms on both sides of an imagined or real center line. A good example of symmetry is the placement of a chair and sconce on each side of a fireplace. For the arrangement to be pleasing, however, the chairs must be of equal size, as must the sconces, and placement must be identical. Anything that is even slightly off will be distracting. Because symmetrical arrangements appear formal, they look appropriate in a traditional setting.

Asymmetry. This refers to the balance between objects of different sizes as the result of placement. For example, picture a grouping of tall, slender candlesticks on one side of a mantelpiece and a short, wide vase on the other. As long as the scale is correct, asymmetry can be every bit as pleasing as symmetry. Because asymmetrical arrangements appear informal, they look at home in a contemporary setting.

HARMONY AND RHYTHM

Two other concepts, *harmony* and *rhythm*, concern creating patterns in space. Harmony is achieved in design when all of the elements relate to one another. In other words, everything coordinates within one scheme or motif. Matching styles, colors, and patterns are good examples. Rhythm refers to repeated patterns. You'll read more about these two concepts in Chapter Two, "Adding Color and Texture," on page 32. For now, keep in mind that harmony pulls a room together, while rhythm moves you around the room. The key to creating good harmony and rhythm is balance; always add at least one contrasting element for interest.

CREATING A PLAN

Chances are good there are some things you like about the existing space, as well as things you don't like. On the plus side, the windows may overlook a beautiful view, or the sunlight may stream into the room at the perfect hour of the day. However, there may be too many doorways and not enough solid walls for placing furniture, or the fireplace or some other large built-in feature, such as a bookcase, may be awkwardly situated. Maybe the room is too small for comfortable entertaining or too large to feel homey. Sometimes the space is oddly shaped; it may be long and narrow, for instance, or the ceilings may seem too high or too low.

Unless structural changes are an option, you'll have to work with the space you have rather than against it. In many cases, the negatives are not so much the structural aspects of the space but the scale of the objects chosen to fill it and how they have been arranged. Follow these Smart Steps to design functional as well as aesthetically pleasing space.

SMART steps | **ONE** Create a notebook. Use a loose-leaf binder to keep notes and any other information relating to your project, including your analysis of the existing space and your ideas and goals for it. Later on you can use it to hold paint chips, fabric and wallpaper samples, and pictures from magazines of rooms and furniture styles to which you may want to refer during this or a future decorating project. Begin by listing what you think are the best and worst features of the space. Call attention to important aspects, such as the orientation of the windows at various times of the day. Depending on when you typically use the space, you'll need to know whether it gets sunny in the morning (east-facing windows), at midday (south-facing windows), or in the late afternoon (west-facing windows). Alternatively, the space may get very little natural light (north-facing windows). If you routinely take a nap in the family room before dinner, think twice about positioning the sofa across from windows with a western exposure, for example. Also, take note of the view. Big, beautiful windows lose much of their allure when there isn't something pleasant outdoors to admire.

Next, look at the layout in terms of permanent features, such as doors and doorways, windows, stairs, and closets. Are there too few? Too many? Does the location of any them interfere with the layout? Are any shapes awkward? Consider adjacent spaces, too. Do they present problems concerning noise or privacy?

Jot down all of the different activities you expect the space to accommodate, along with any additional storage you may require.

Even if your budget is limited, make a list of all the possible solutions to your space problems. These might include enlarging the layout by building on or incorporating adjacent existing space, or adding, eliminating, or moving a wall, doorway, or window. Of course, structural changes such as these can be

Left: This window is the perfect spot to place a sofa or love seat. The floor-length curtains complement the high ceilings and, on a practical note, block out the late afternoon sun.

Right: Highlight the strong points of your room. Here the designer kept the exposed ceiling trusses in mind when selecting the furnishings and carpeting for this room.

costly and complicated and will require consultation with an architect or qualified remodeler. But the time for considering the possibility of making any one of them is during the early planning phases of your project, not after you've ordered new furniture based on the old layout.

TWO Walk the space. Go into the room, walk around it, spend time in it. It's a good idea to carry a clipboard and paper so that you can record information to add to your notebook later. Is there an easy flow from one area to another, or are the aisles tight or cluttered? Observe the traffic pattern from all entrances into the room. Notice the direction in which the doors swing. Is the furniture arrangement comfortable and attractive? Is there a focal point—one substantial element, such as a fireplace or a large piece of furniture— that anchors the space? If the space is large, there should be more than one focal point. Are activity areas clearly defined, or do they spill into one another? What's your overall impression? Does the room feel cozy or cramped? Airy or cavernous? Are the furnishings the right size? Remember, with space, everything is relative. The living room may not be too small; the sofa may be too big for the living room, for example. Sometimes it's the arrangement of furnishings that creates a problem. Pushing seating up against the walls isn't always the best placement. It's better to create small conversational groupings at opposite sides of a room if the space is large, or place one grouping in the center of a small space. Make sure you can move around these areas; traffic should never interrupt them. In

later chapters, you'll learn how color, pattern, and light also affect your perception of space.

THREE Measure up. Invest in a good steel measuring tape, and take careful, accurate dimensions of the space. If you can, ask another family member or a friend to help; he or she can hold the end of the tape in one corner while you measure the entire length of a wall in a single step. This eliminates the possibility of the cumulative error that often occurs when measuring a wall in increments. If a window or doorway breaks up the space, measure from one corner of the wall to the outer edge of the opening, and then proceed from the outer edge to the next corner.

Figure 1

Above: Begin with an informal sketch of what you want the room to look like.

Below: Transfer your design to graph paper. Be sure that measurements and furniture sizes are correct.

Figure 2

After obtaining the overall dimensions of the room, measure all the openings (doors and windows) and any other fixed features, such as a fireplace, staircase, closets, built-in bookcases, and cabinetry.

While you're at it, measure the existing furniture, too—even those pieces you may be thinking of replacing. With a few adjustments to the layout, you may decide to retain some of them. Later you can refer to these measurements when you're ready to add furniture to your plan.

Another reason to measure all of the furniture pieces at this point is so that you can compare their heights with those of the fixed features in the room. Keep in mind that when you draw your sketch and floor plan later, they will reflect only the widths of these objects. For visual interest, you'll want a pleasing balance of tall and short elements in the final design.

FOUR Make an informal sketch. As you walk through the space, make a free-hand drawing. Note all dimensions on the plan or in the margin, including the height of the ceiling. (See Figure 1, above.) Pencil in electrical switches and outlets, cable input, phone jacks, radiators, heat registers, air ducts, and light fixtures, as well. Indicate adjoining rooms or areas on the sketch, too. You don't want to block access to any of them.

FIVE Draw plans. Once you evaluate the existing space thoroughly, get ready to draw the layout to scale on $1/4$-inch graph paper. Each square will represent one foot. For example, if a wall measures 15 feet, the line you draw to indicate that wall will use 15 squares. To make straight lines and accurate corners, use a T-square; for the arch that symbolizes an open door, use a compass. If you don't have these tools on hand, be as careful as possible, and use any straight-edged instrument to draw your lines. You might invest in a handy ruler or yardstick.

Figure 3

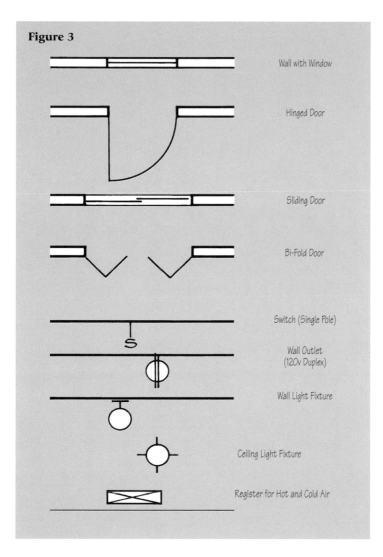

Wall with Window

Hinged Door

Sliding Door

Bi-Fold Door

Switch (Single Pole)

Wall Outlet (120v Duplex)

Wall Light Fixture

Ceiling Light Fixture

Register for Hot and Cold Air

but you should be precise on your final drawing. Although a $^1/_2$ inch here or there won't make any significant difference to your layout, it's best to use accurate measurements. For new furniture, refer to the manufacturer's spec sheet, which will include dimensions. Don't ever buy a piece of furniture you think looks like the right size. After paying for it and waiting weeks for its delivery, you don't want to find out your guess was wrong. If it's a custom order, you're stuck with it. Even with furniture you already own, don't assume standard size; measure it.

Use the standard furniture symbols in the Appendix to draw your templates. We've drawn each one to scale based on average dimensions, but you'll have to adjust the scale to your furniture's true size.

Left: Here are some standard architectural symbols that will come in handy when drawing up a plan. You will find additional symbols in the Appendix.

Below: Consider ways to get some use from wasted space. Here the designer turned an empty alcove that leads to the garden into a sunny seating area.

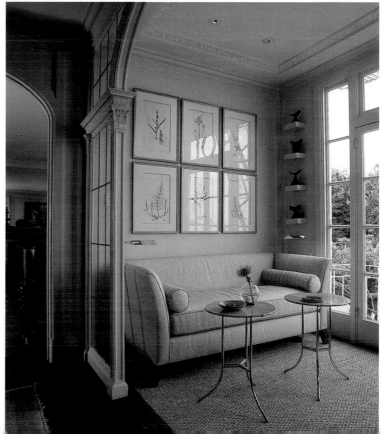

On your drawing, record the measurements the same way a design professional does: For 3 feet and 2 inches write 3'-2" and for 14 feet and $3^1/_4$ inches write 14'-3$^1/_4$". Figure 3, on this page, shows the symbols to use for the room's major features. When your drawing is complete, you'll have a good idea about how much and what size furniture will fit into the space.

SIX Create furniture templates. Next, make cutout templates of the furniture, using the same $^1/_4$-inch scale. Although you can refer to so-called standard sizes for furniture, be aware that there are variations. One manufacturer may make a 96-inch sofa, while another makes one that is $96^1/_2$ inches. It's okay to estimate for your rough sketch,

Cutouts to include in your template kit could be sofa beds, tables, chairs, free- standing bookcases, cupboards, or armoires, chests of drawers, and so on. If you are designing for the kitchen or bath, refer to those chapters and to the templates on pages 272–274 in the Appendix. Just remember that the appliances and fixtures in these two rooms cannot be moved as easily as pieces of furniture. There are technical considerations with regard to plumbing, electricity, and zoning regulations that affect placement. You may want to put your ideas on paper, but consult a kitchen or bath specialist or a licensed contractor before making actual changes.

DECORATING ROOM BY ROOM

With scaled templates in hand, you can move things around your scaled layout to see how to group pieces into different arrangements. Always note the traffic pattern in your floor plan when arranging furniture, however, and start by placing the largest, most important pieces first. For major aisles that will be used to move in and through the space, allow at least 3 feet if at all possible. Sometimes you can use furniture as a sort of boundary that prevents traffic through a work or conversation area—seating that is arranged around two or three sides of an area, for example. However, never place furniture in the middle of a major traffic lane.

If the shape of the space bothers you—it's too long, too narrow, too wide, too low, too tall—there are several simple tricks you can play on the eye to camouflage the problem visually. For example, if the room is

■ *Long,* divide the space by creating two separate, major groupings of furniture. Use area rugs to anchor each group in the divided space. You can also use square shapes, such as a square area rug, to "widen" the space.

■ *Narrow,* arrange furniture on the diagonal. In the bedroom, for example, place the bed catty-cornered. In the living room, angle the sofa between two walls. Again, introduce more squares, such as a square coffee table.

■ *Low,* add height with tall furnishings, such as bookcases, which will make the space feel grand. You might also consider tall lamps, such as torchères, or window treatments that extend above the window frame and hang from the area just below the ceiling to the floor. Use as many vertical lines in the room as possible, even on wall and fabric treatments. Vertical-stripe wallpaper or curtains are good examples. (See Chapter Two, "Adding Color and Texture," on page 32.)

■ *Tall,* lower the scale of the space by incorporating more horizontal lines in the room. Install molding one-half or three-quarters of the way up the walls to visually shorten them. Hang pictures lower on the wall. (See "Distinctive Touches," in Chapter Six, on page 120.)

FOCAL POINTS

There has to be one dramatic element in a room that draws your immediate attention. This is the focal point. If you're lucky, it may be a distinctive architectural element, such as a fireplace, a built-in cabinet, a handsome staircase or entry door in a foyer, or a spectacular window. If the room does not have one, create a focal point with furnishings. This could be a beautifully dressed bed; a large central seating group; dramatic window treatments on an otherwise undis-

Clockwise (from left): The tall cabinet, the curtains near the ceiling, the shelf along the upper part of the glass, and a variety of personal items all help turn a sunporch into a cozy informal dining area. Distinctive arched windows dominate this room, so the designer chose low, curved pieces that do not block the view. Tall windows are enhanced by the addition of full-height shutters.

SMARTtip   Clearing the Canvas

If you are having trouble creating a pleasing arrangement of furniture in a room, it can help to remove all of the contents and start from scratch. This is a good idea if you have trouble picturing things on paper or if you aren't going to buy a lot of new furniture and just need a fresh start. If at all possible, strip the room down completely, removing all of the furnishings, including window treatments, rugs, wall art, and accessories. This way you can observe the true architectural nature of the space without distractions that influence your perceptions. For example, minus the trappings of curtains, you can see that two windows may be slightly different sizes or installed too close to a corner. Other things you may notice might be odd corners, uneven walls, radiators or heating registers that are conspicuously located, or any other quirky features that are unique to your home.

Don't be in a rush to start filling up the room again. Live with it empty for a few days so that you can really get a sense of the space. Then slowly begin to bring things back inside, starting with the largest objects. You'll know immediately when you've crossed the line with something that doesn't belong. But you have to be willing to pull back and pare down.

tinguished window; a massive table, armoire, or cabinet; or wall art, particularly if it is highlighted. (See Chapter Three, "The Right Light," on page 52.) The focal point should be one of the first elements penciled onto your plan.

MULTIPURPOSE SPACE

No matter how much space we have, most of us complain about needing more. One way to get it is to use a room or an area for more than one purpose. For example, the kitchen may also serve as a home office or family room; a hallway is another spot that can double as an office; even a living room can serve more than one function, whether that of a part-time dining room, guest room, or study. Seemingly impossible spaces can be adjusted to accommodate more than one function as well. Furniture that folds up when not in use is helpful. One excellent example is a drop-leaf dining table that can be stored unobtrusively against a wall in the living room, then opened up when necessary. If you entertain overnight guests occasionally but not often enough to reserve a special room for the purpose, buy a convertible sofa. Keep extra linens in an antique trunk that can also act as a coffee table, or purchase a large ottoman with a hinged top that opens up to roomy storage. In a dining room/office, use a folding screen to hide electronic office equipment when not in use, and house stationery and other supplies in the bottom half of the china cabinet. Another option, when the home office is shared space with another room in the house, is to purchase an

Above and right: Many rooms must do double duty these days. The living room above is designed for conversation with visiting guests or enjoying the fire. But open the built-in cabinets and the focal point of the room changes. Behind the doors you will find a large-screen television as well as a collection of tapes and DVDs, turning the once formal parlor into an entertainment center.

armoire that features a fold-down desk, storage shelves, and accommodations for a computer, printer, and fax machine. Just close the doors when the work day is done.

You can also divide space with furniture. Remember: there is no rule that says all of it has to be arranged against a wall. Use tables or upholstered pieces to delineate separate functional areas of a room. Painting one wall a different color to visually separate one area from the other is another means of dividing space. If the front door opens directly into the living room, situate an open-shelving unit perpendicular to the door to create an entry area. If you've always wanted a quiet little getaway in your home but don't have

the extra room, use a landing or the end of a corridor. A comfortable chair, a small table, and a lamp are all you need for a little peace and quiet with a good book or a CD player and headphones. Use your imagination and try out other ways to make the most out of every square inch of space in your home.

As much as you may want to enlarge the functional capabilities of space by dividing it up into separate zones, don't overdo it with a series of stuffy little warrens, either. To keep the overall appearance of the space free-flowing and balanced, you'll have to provide at least one visual link that moves the eye along. There are a few different ways to do this. One is to use the same palette throughout. You may want to vary the intensity of the color from area to area, but sticking to the same basic hue creates a cohesive backdrop for everything. Another option is to "stretch" space by using the same floor treatment so that there is no separation as you move from one area to another.

FURNITURE PLACEMENT BY ROOM

There are recommended guidelines for clearances you should follow when arranging furniture. Just remember, they are not strict rules. You might try using them as starting points or to analyze an existing space. Then rework some things to suit your taste and lifestyle. The important thing is to make the room comfortable for the people who use it.

Left: Place furniture so that there are comfortable clearances around each piece. Note how the symmetry of the art on the wall helps anchor that part of the room.

Left: Master bedrooms are often thought of as personal retreats. Be sure to leave adequate clearances around the bed.

Opposite: A sun-filled space off the kitchen is perfect for a breakfast nook. These areas tend to get more use than formal dining rooms.

Below: A living room often contains a focal point that gives the rest of the room its decorating theme. Here it is the stone fireplace.

Living Rooms and Family Rooms. The kitchen may be the heart of a home, but the living room is where people can put their best foot forward. It's also the place, along with the family room, where many of us relax in front of the TV, listen to music, read, or just hang out. It's important, therefore, to have an attractive, comfortable arrangement of furniture in the living room, whether you use it only on occasion or everyday.

If you entertain often, rate the existing room's ability to accommodate large as well as small groups. Professionals recommend a distance of 4 to 10 feet between the sofa and chairs. Anything less is too cramped; anything more discourages easy conversation. For a comfortable amount of legroom, the coffee table should be positioned between 14 and 18 inches from the sofa.

When there's a large party, make sure there is space for guests to move around or break up into small groups. Most designers suggest one major seating area created by grouped upholstered pieces, plus several lightweight portable chairs located around the room. When company comes, these chairs can be moved around for socializing.

Do you watch TV in the room? If so, grab your measuring tape again. For optimal viewing, the distance between the TV monitor and the seating located opposite it should be three times the size of the screen. In other words, to comfortably watch TV on a 30-inch screen, you should sit 90 inches away from it.

Is there a focal point? All of the furnishings should take their cue from that important feature in terms of scale, proportion, and balance.

If you use the living room as a part-time home office, guest room, or dining area, look at how your existing arrangement is working now. Is the space organized in a way that keeps each function from interfering with another? Ideally, there should be a traffic lane that is at least 3 feet wide to move from one zone to another. If you don't have that much room, look for other ways to contain things. Your

plan may have to include an armoire or chest that can keep items such as extra pillows and blankets, office supplies, or files tucked away until you need them.

Dining Rooms and Kitchen Eat-in Areas. Certainly the table is the focus of any dining space, which could be a large formal room, a niche in the kitchen, or even a spot in the corner of the living room. When analyzing your existing dining space, your first question should be, "Is seating around the table comfortable?" Good space planning calls for suitable room to get up, down, and around easily. A seated adult occupies a depth of about 20 inches, but needs 12 to 16 inches more to pull back the chair and rise. Placing chairs at angles to the wall can save a few inches, but you'll need either a round or square table for this strategy. Rectangular tables require 24 inches per person and 32 to 36 inches of clearance between the table and the wall. On the serving side, the table-to-wall distance should be at least 44 inches.

Bedrooms. It may be your adult retreat, where you get away from the kids, or it may be your teenager's domain, where adults are off limits; nevertheless the bedroom is primarily the place one sleeps, so it's only logical to begin designing this space by placing the bed. For your comfort, as well as for safety, there are minimum clearances recommended for the space around the bed. When two people share the room, there must be an aisle that is spacious enough for either party to get in and out of bed easily and without bumping into an open door or having to climb over another person.

Begin by measuring the floor space on each side of the bed. The minimum clearance between the edge of the bed and the wall should be 24 inches. In addition, allow at least 36 inches between the edge of the bed and any door that opens into the room. If you place two beds side by side, maintain at least 18 inches between them. This will accommodate a small night table and a pathway for the average adult to swing out of bed and walk between the beds comfortably.

Now that you understand how to analyze and design comfortable, safe, attractive space, you're ready for the next chapter: how to use a designer's most powerful decorating tool—color.

a gallery of...

1 The use of area rugs and furniture group-ings can create sep-arate areas within a larger space. The furnishings here are in proportion to the dimensions of the room.

2 The uniform pattern of shelving around this doorway frames the adjoining room.

3 The lines of the drapes and table covering soften the harsh grids of the large door opening.

4 Two framed prints, a small lighting fixture, and a plant turn a small wall niche into a focal point at the end of a hall.

5 Casual dining areas, such as this break-fast nook, often have large windows to flood the area with natural light.

6 The narrow wall-covering border near the ceiling reinforces the horizontal line of the wallcovering panel near the floor.

...smart ideas

1 This massive fireplace needs a room with a high sloping ceiling or it will crowd the space.

2 The curve of the arch balances against the formal crown molding and the horizontal line of the wainscotting.

3 An open area near a door is the perfect spot for a bench. A wallpaper border caps sturdy bead-board to create a small mudroom.

4 Create a scene and a focal point by hanging a collection of photos or art above an attrac-tive cabinet.

5 Select furniture of the size and shape that best suit the dimen-sions of the area in which you want to place it.

CHAPTER 2

ADDING COLOR AND TEXTURE

**WORKING WITH COLOR ■
INTRODUCING PATTERN ■ ADDING
TEXTURE ■ CREATING A DESIGN**

The colors and textures you choose will set the tone for your home decor. If you are a traditionalist decorating a formal living room, you may find yourself drawn to a dove gray and cream color scheme. A kid's play room, on the other hand, may call for bright colors and bold patterns. Of course, the size of the room and its light levels will also play a part in your choices. They not only lead to color schemes but also help in selecting patterns and textures for the room. Pattern creates rhythm, a measured flow between a number of elements throughout a room. Texture is like a visual caesura, a pause that prevents the design from becoming predictable.

The trick in decorating is to create a harmonious balance between all of the elements. By investing some time in learning those theories behind the selection of color, pattern, and texture, you can begin to develop a mix that soothes your senses the way a pastoral piece of music does. The science of color is partly concerned with its precise measurement and the intricate chemistry of dyes and pigments. It also ventures into the more subjective realm of perception and psychology: exploring how colors relate to one another, how they affect the viewer, and how quantities, textures, and patterns alter the effects. A bit of color theory can provide a further foundation for the art of interior design.

WORKING WITH COLOR

Color is the most versatile tool a designer can employ. It is both the easiest way to improve space and an effective way to alter it. It is the most exciting decorating element. Yet many of us find the power of color intimidating and, fearful of stepping into new territory, stick with neutrals. The palette for walls is often white or cream—colors that work fine as a backdrop for more richly hued furnishings but are less successful in rooms with neutral-colored pieces. Aside from the strength of color itself, the enormity of color choices available in paints, wallpapers, fabrics, and flooring options can also overwhelm us, making us retreat to the safety of white for the walls and neutrals throughout. So how do you break the monotony and establish an exciting color scheme? First you'll have to overcome your fear of color, then narrow your choices. An explanation of the color wheel is a good place to begin.

HOW COLOR WORKS

Light reflected through a prism creates a rainbow, known as the color spectrum. Each band of color blends into the next, from red to violet. The longest band is red, then orange, yellow, green, blue, and violet. Modern color theory takes those bands from the spectrum and forms them into a circle, called the *color wheel*, to show the relationship of one color to another.

The color wheel includes *primary colors* (red, blue, and yellow), *secondary colors* (green, orange, violet), and *tertiary colors* (red-blue, blue-red, and so on). Secondary colors are made by mixing two primaries together, such as blue and yellow to make green. A primary color and a secondary color are mixed to make tertiary colors, such as blue and green to make turquoise.

Right: **Yellow walls not only brighten this small living room, they also serve as a backdrop for the many bold patterns in the space. Many of the fabric prints pick up the yellow of the walls.**

Intensity and Value. Colors, or hues, vary in their intensity—that is, the level of the color's purity or saturation. The primaries, secondaries, and tertiaries represent colors at their full intensity. There are several ways to lessen a color's intensity. You can lighten it with white to form a *tint*, darken it with black to create a *shade*, or add gray to arrive at a *tone*. In addition to changing the intensity of a color, these methods affect what is known as the color's value. *Value* is the lightness or darkness of the color. Tinting gives a color a lighter value, and shading, of course, makes it a darker value.

Color Wheel Combinations

The color wheel is the designer's most useful tool for pairing colors. Basically, it presents the spectrum of pigment hues as a circle. The primary colors (yellow, blue, and red) are combined in the remaining hues (orange, green, and purple). The following are the most-often used configurations for creating color schemes.

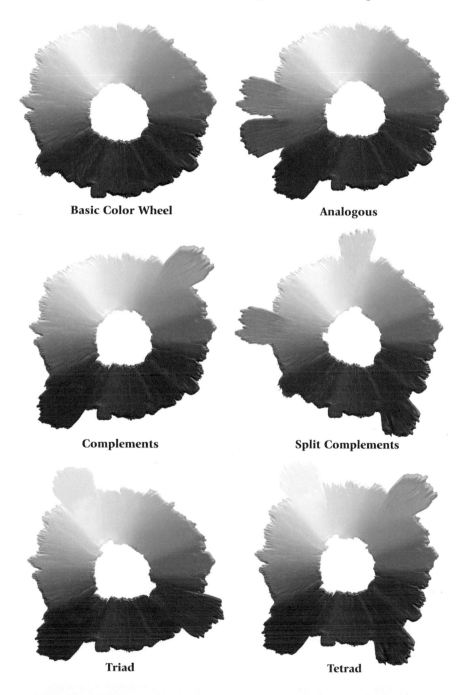

Basic Color Wheel

Analogous

Complements

Split Complements

Triad

Tetrad

PUTTING THE COLOR WHEEL TO WORK FOR YOU

Now that you've got it in front of you, use the color wheel to help you envision certain color combinations. An *analogous* scheme involves neighboring colors that share an underlying hue.

Complementary colors lie opposite each other on the color wheel and often work well together. What, you ask? A red and green living room? Well, yes, in full intensity that might be hard to stomach, but consider a rosy pink room with sage green accents. The same complements in varying intensities can make attractive, soothing combinations. A *double complementary* color scheme involves an additional set of opposites, such as green-blue and red-orange.

Alternatively, you could go with a *monochromatic* scheme, which involves using one color in a variety of intensities. That way your décor is sure to be harmonious. When developing a monochromatic scheme, lean toward several tints or several shades, but avoid too many contrasting values—that is, combinations of tints and shades. This can make your scheme look uneven.

If you want a more complex palette of three or more colors, look at the *triads* formed by three equidistant colors, such as red/yellow/blue or green/purple/orange. A *split complement* is composed of three colors—one primary or intermediate and two colors on either side of its opposite. For example, instead of teaming purple with yellow, shift the mix to purple with orange-yellow and yellow-green. Lastly, four colors equally spaced around the wheel, such as yellow/green/purple/red, form a *tetrad*. If such combinations sound a bit like Technicolor, remember that colors intended for interiors are rarely undiluted. Thus yellow might be cream, blue-purple a dark eggplant, and orange-red a muted terra cotta or whisper-pale peach. With less jargon, the color combinations fall into these two basic camps:

■ *harmonious*, or *analogous*, schemes, derived from near-by colors on the wheel—less than halfway around; and

■ *contrasting*, or *complementary*, schemes, involving directly opposite slices of the pie.

THE PSYCHOLOGY OF COLOR

Few of us get past kindergarten without acquiring a favorite color. Over the years our tastes change and we allow ourselves to appreciate more than one hue, but most of us can still name a preference when pressed. Picking out a few colors you like best—colors that make you feel happy—is as good a place as any to begin establishing your color scheme because it is largely an emotional decision. In narrowing down your choices and combining them with the preferences of those who will share the space, try to include both warm and cool colors. The warm hues—reds, yellows, oranges, peaches, and creams—are generally most effectively used in rooms where there will be a lot of activity because they make us feel livelier. Kitchens, office spaces, even bedrooms if you're a morning person, are all natural places for brighter, warmer, more uplifting hues. Cool colors tend to be more soothing and restful. You may want to reserve your blues, greens, and lilacs for the rooms where you go to unwind.

However, color responses are subjective and changeable. The pervasive use of green in schools and hospitals in decades past, for example, has prompted a visceral dislike of the color's "institutional" shades for many people. Some studies have suggested that red rooms may heighten blood pressure and yellow rooms make the occupants more argumentative.

Above: Because dining rooms aren't used as often as kitchens or family rooms, many people feel comfortable experimenting with bold color schemes for these spaces.

Sharp contrasts or schemes that feature bold colors can be fun in rooms used only occasionally, but they can become tiresome on a daily basis. Of course, these are general guidelines. Some people never tire of a favorite color— even if it is repeated in every room of the house.

Cultural Effects. We may be less aware of how our culture and era shape our color responses. In America and much of Europe, blue is a perennial favorite color, while red ranks first in other locales, such as Spain and Japan. Western brides dress in joyful white—a mourning color in some Far Eastern societies. Even within one culture, the accustomed palette changes. In the Victorian era, early Impressionist paintings shocked viewers, who saw them as garishly bright. Yet to our jaded eyes, the same paintings seem restfully pastel. Even closer to our own times, we might chuckle or wince at colors and combinations from a decorating guide dated 1955 or 1969—colors that struck the readers of the day as perfectly keen or groovy. And a few decades hence, our own most stylish efforts may suffer a similar fate.

The pull of comfortable, traditional colors and the push for novel, fashionable choices have shaped the American palette since the nation's early days. But the home decorator can hold to one constant: human beings seek variety in their surroundings. Light colors seem upbeat, clean, and lively but turn cold and monotonous if unrelieved. Dark colors are plush and enclosing but in excess can turn gloomy. Midtones are attractively comfortable, but a room decked completely in midtones can be dull and monotonous. Bright, saturated hues are eye-catching accents but uncomfortably demanding in quantity. In short, one could do worse than to follow the old decorating maxim, "Something dark, something light, something dull, something bright."

ALTERING SPACE WITH COLOR

As a designer, you can use warm colors and cool colors quite effectively to manipulate the way a room is perceived visually, as well as emotionally. For instance, you can cozy up a large room with warm colors. Because warm colors appear to advance, walls swathed in sunny hues seem closer together and make a room feel more intimate. Conversely, cool tones and neutrals appear to recede and can be used to open up a smaller space.

These color tricks can be employed more subtly as well. For example, suppose you've got your heart set on a cheery, predominantly yellow living room. But it's a smaller room and you'd also like to expand it visually as much as is possible. Do you have to switch your palette to blues and neutrals? Not necessarily. The less-intense version of a color will generally reduce its apparent

Left: Blue is a cool, soothing color and a good choice for a child's bedroom. Here the designer selected different shades of blue for the walls, furniture, and window treatments.

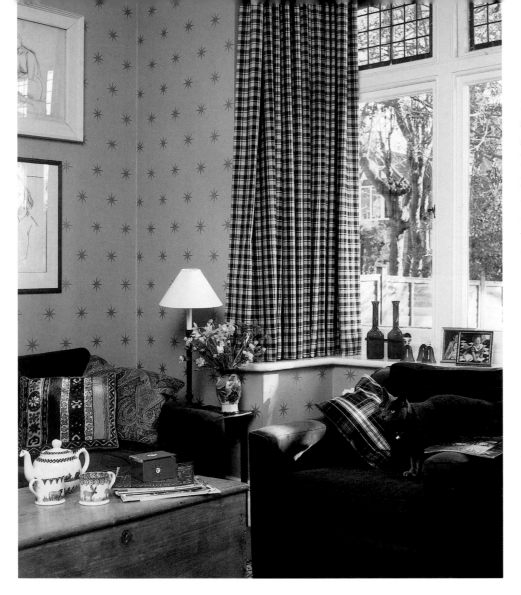

Light," on page 52.) Make sure you consider this when choosing a color. Paint some test samples on the wall, and watch how the colors change depending on the position of the sun. Do they need to be adjusted? Rooms with a northern exposure will be filled with bluer, cooler light, which weakens warm colors but intensifies cool hues. Ones facing south will have a warmer, yellowish light. That light can have the opposite effect on colors. All in all, colors interact in complex ways, so these generalizations are not absolute, but they're good starting points for making initial judgements.

INTRODUCING PATTERN

You can add pattern to a room in a variety of ways—wallpaper and fabric being the two most popular. Because pattern is largely a vehicle for color, the same rules that guide the selection of color effectively narrow the field when it comes to selecting a pattern or complement of patterns. The designer's old friend, scale, from Chapter One, is the other important consideration when picking patterns.

Above: Mix patterns the same way you mix colors—by looking for a connection. Here the designer chose small patterns for the wallcovering, curtains, and pillows.

tendency to advance or recede. Investigate the other intensities, the shades and tones of yellow, to see whether there's one that does the job.

Generally speaking, sharp contrasts have the same impact as a dark color, reducing perceived space. Monochromatic schemes enlarge space. Neutrals of similar value make walls retreat and can flow unobtrusively from room to room.

Light and Color. Lighting can change color dramatically as well. The quality of natural light changes through the course of the day, too. (See Chapter Three, "The Right

Large-scale patterns are like warm colors in that they appear to come toward you. They can create a lively and stimulating atmosphere and generally make a large space seem cozier. In a small space, handle a large-scale pattern with care or it can overpower the room. That doesn't mean rule it out completely, but perhaps use it sparingly. Small-scale patterns appear to recede, making small spaces seem larger. They can also be used effectively to camouflage odd angles or corners that you find in attic ceilings. Try a subtle, non-directional pattern for this kind of application. In a large room, the effect of a small pattern can be bland. From a distance, it may read as a single color. If you're using a small-scale pattern in a large space, pick one with vibrant colors.

How to Mix Patterns. Mixing patterns can be intimidating, in part because it's subjective to experimentation, judgement, and "eye." Responding to this fear, manufacturers provide an abundance of coordinated wallcovering and fabric collections, available through wallpaper books and in-store design services. Such collections, selected by professionals, can save you a lot of legwork and still leave scope for your own input. If you prefer to mix your own patterns, try to match the scale of the pattern to that of the area over which it is to be used. The general rule is to use large prints on large-sized furnishings, medium prints on medium pieces, and small prints on accent pieces. A sofa, for instance, looks better than a dining room chair with a large-scale pattern. A delicate stencil makes a better border for a tabletop than on a wall. But these rules are not hard and fast.

Another trick for mixing patterns is to provide links of scale, motif, and color. The regularity of checks, stripes, textural looks, and geometrics, particularly if small-scale and low-contrast, tends to make them easy-to-mix "neutral" patterns. A small floral can play off a thin ticking stripe, while a cabbage-rose chintz may require a bolder stripe as a same-scale foil. You may choose to use the same or similar patterns in varying sizes or develop a theme by focusing on florals, geometrics, or ethnic prints.

The most effective link is shared colors or a similar level of intensity between the prints. A solid-color companion that pulls out a hue shared by two prints provides another connection. Exact matches are the backbone of manufacturers' coordinated collections. But to arrive at your own personal mix, you can interpret the principle loosely, and experiment to see which pattern combinations work for you.

ADDING TEXTURE

Texture doesn't have the obvious impact on a room that color and pattern wield. But how a material feels, as well as how it looks, does influence room design. Incorporating a variety of textures in a room adds to its richness in a way that's most comparable to the subtle inclusion of the line varieties discussed in Chapter One. A mix of textures plays upon the senses and adds another layer of complexity and sophistication to a design scheme. As with every aspect of decorating, mixing textures involves a balancing act. To give a room a distinctive character, you might let one texture predominate the room, but the right contrast can make the scheme more intriguing.

Below: **Texture plays a subtle, often subjective, role in a decorating scheme. This sitting area contains a small print wallcovering, a voluminous window treatment, and a rich fabric for the chair and table covering.**

TYPES OF TEXTURE

The easiest way to incorporate texture into a design is with fabric. Brocades and damasks, *moirés* and chenilles, tweeds and chintzes—all conjure up different looks and sensations. Fabrics, however, are just the beginning. Tactile interest can emanate from any material or surface that is coarse or smooth, hard or soft, matte or shiny. Coarse and matte surfaces, such as stone, rough-hewn wood, stucco, corduroy, or terra cotta, absorb light and sound. Glossy and smooth surfaces, which range from metal and glass to silk and enamel, reflect light.

Spatial Effects. To start adding texture into your design, assess your room's needs. Does it lack warmth? Or does it feel too closed in? Texture affects a room spatially. Coarse or matte surfaces will make a room seem smaller and cozier. A living room of only glossy surfaces can seem cold and impersonal without a velvet slipcover on the sofa to add warmth and contrast. Smooth and shiny surfaces do the

Above: **This unusually designed room feels comfortable and intimate thanks to the selection of rich fabrics used on the comforter and furniture, and the distinctive wall treatment.**

reverse—they make a room look larger and brighter. A study that feels too stuffy, for instance, may benefit from the addition of a mirror or a glass-topped table. Light reflected off of either object will brighten the space.

Pattern and Color. Keep in mind that texture also affects pattern and color. With fabrics, texture can either soften or enhance a pattern. For instance, patterns are crisp on glazed chintz but are blurred on terrycloth. A coarsely textured surface tones down the intensity of a paint color, and gives the color subtle variations. High-gloss surfaces increase the intensity of a color. Think of how the gray color of a tweed jacket looks "heathered" and muted. On a silk shirt, however, the same gray color would look shimmery and more intense—a completely different effect. Every room has an existing element of texture—a stone fireplace, brass hardware, a gleaming hardwood floor, a stuccoed wall, or an iridescent tile border—that you may want to take into consideration when planning your design.

Relatively featureless rooms may be improved by adding contrasting textures. Wallpaper comes in a variety of textures—foils, flocks, embossed papers, and real fabric, to list a few. Paint can be applied in matte or gloss finishes and special painted effects, discussed in detail in Chapter Five, can add texture. Tile and other architectural embellishments, such as cornices and moldings, can also imbue a room with more tactile richness.

Window treatments are another natural outlet for texture. Fabric choices for draperies and curtains, as well as the fabrics and other materials available for blinds and shades, are enormous and varied. Texture can be enhanced by the way fabric is hung. Pleating, for example, creates a play of light and shadow. You can combine layers of fabric or fabric and blinds to show off different textures.

On the floor, carpets can be smooth, knobby, sculpted, or flecked for visual texture. Rugs, rush, coir, sisal, wood, or cork are warming texture options. Quarry tiles, ceramic tiles, marble, and slate make a room cooler. Varying the materials can make the effect more interesting. An Oriental rug over a varnished wood floor is a classic example.

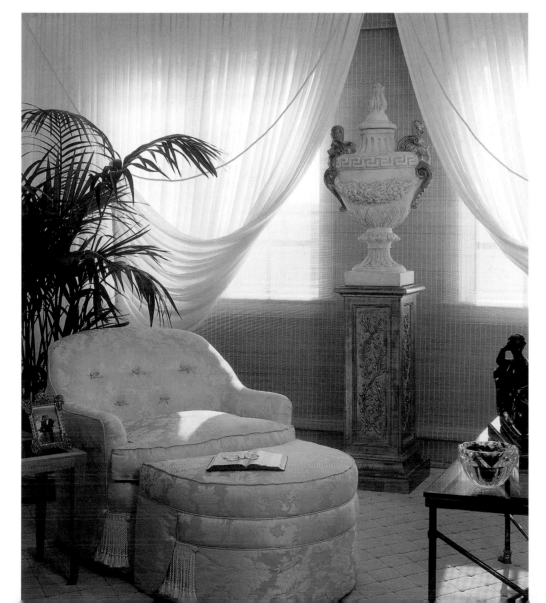

CREATING A DESIGN

You've analyzed your room, you've determined how you want it to function, and you'd like to make it restful and soothing. As luck would have it, blue is your favorite color. So now what? How do you get from there to choosing the "right" shade of blue, deciding where to use it, picking a coordinating wallpaper pattern, selecting fabrics for the furniture, and ensuring plenty of tactile richness to boot? Take it slowly, in steps—Smart Steps, that is.

Left: Think a neutral color scheme has to be boring? This room shows how adding texture—here it is the layering of different window treatments to create a certain mood—can completely change the look and feel of a space. Bright colors would be out of place here.

ONE Create a sample board. One way designers organize the colors, patterns, and textures that they plan to use in a room is to create a sample board. The white, foam-cored presentation board sold in art supply stores, measuring at least $8\frac{1}{2} \times 11$ inches, is ideal for this purpose. Attach to the board with rubber cement (or tack to it with removable sticky material) any swatches of fabric, wallpaper patterns, or paint color chips you're considering. Keep the swatches and other items in the same proportion on the board as they would be in the room. For example, a paint sample that you're considering for the walls will be quite large, whereas an accent color will take up far less space. The fabric you plan to use on the sofa should take up more space on the board than one you're thinking about for a small window treatment or footstool. As a general rule of thumb, designate about two thirds of the board for wall and ceiling treatments, and divide the remaining third between floors and furnishings. Add and remove things as you experiment with different looks, and be certain to look at the board in the room for which it's created at different times of day, under both natural and artificial lighting conditions.

TWO Develop your color scheme. Bringing to bear all you now know about color (how it affects mood, how it can seemingly expand or decrease space, what you like, and what your family likes), pick one. Frequently, you can establish your color based on elements already in the room that you don't plan to replace—an upholstered furnishing, a carpet, or even a favorite painting. Once you determine the main color, look at its complement or triad on the color wheel, and pick an accent or two. If you're painting your walls, go to the paint store and get sample chips of each

Above: Because the designer selected soft muted colors, the checkerboard design blends into the background rather than overpowering the room.

Design Materials

As you have likely gleaned from this discussion of color, pattern, and texture, designers rely on certain materials to carry various effects into a living space. Most design materials have specific functions and applications where they are preferable to other options in their category. In flooring materials, for example, ceramic tile may perform well in a kitchen setting but not as effectively in a living room. Within many categories, there are varying degrees of quality. Throughout this book, the appropriate applications of different materials and tips on how to judge the quality of some materials is addressed in pertinent chapters. In Chapter Four, for instance, you'll find an examination of flooring materials. Chapter Five contains an in-depth coverage of paints and wallpaper options. Here, because textiles are such integral players when it comes to delivering color, pattern, and texture, is a brief overview of some common decorating fabrics and their make-up.

Brocade: Often weighty fabric woven of silk, cotton, wool, or a combination. A raised, floral design (called a jacquard) is its distinguishing feature. Typically used for upholstery and draperies.

Cambric: A plain, tightly woven linen or cotton fabric with a sheen on one side. Curtain panels, pillows, and lightweight slipcovers can be successfully made from cambric.

Canvas: A course, woven cotton material, available in heavy or lighter gauges. Canvas is strong and inexpensive. Will hold up for upholstery, slipcovers, or draperies.

Chintz: Cotton fabric, often in floral or other all-over print, coated with a resin that gives it a sheen. Dry cleaning is necessary. Used for pillows, curtains, and some upholstery.

Cotton duck: A cream-colored cotton that comes in various weights. Ideal for no-sew curtains. See *canvas*.

Crewel: Plain woven, natural cotton fabric with wool embroidery. Traditionally used for upholstery and draperies.

Damask: Another jacquard material made of cotton, silk, wool, or a combination with raised satin design. Widely used for draperies and upholstery.

Gingham: Plain-weave cotton fabric woven in block or checked prints. Its crisp look makes this fabric popular for trim, curtain panels, draperies, tablecloths, and bedspreads.

Lace: Cotton or cotton-polyester blend material featuring open-work designs. Frequently used for curtains.

Linen: An unusually strong fabric made from processed flax. Works best when used simply, such as tab-topped curtains.

Moiré: A finish on a silk or acetate fabric intended to resemble watermarking. Washing removes the finish; dry-clean only. Depending on thickness, good for draperies and upholstery.

Muslin: A course, plain weave cotton in white or cream. It is often sheer, and not as heavy as canvas is. Used for sheeting, curtains, and light slipcovers.

Organdy: Light cotton washed in acid for a crisp finish. Used for trimming and curtains.

Satin: A silk, linen, or cotton weave with a glossy surface and dull back, sometimes with a *moiré* finish. Not particularly durable, but fine for draperies and light-use upholstery.

Silk: A soft, shiny fabric made from the fine fibers produced by silkworms. It is favored for swags and formal drapery.

Taffeta: Silk and acetate weave that appears shiny and maintains shape. Useful for trimmings and draperies.

Tapestry: A heavy, woven cloth that imitates handmade tapestries. Often used for upholstery, pillows, and wall hangings.

Toile de Jouy: An eighteenth-century cotton or linen fabric printed with pastoral scenes. First produced in the French town of Jouy. Used for curtains, upholstery, and pillows.

Velvet: Made from cotton, viscose rayon, or polyester, velvet features a smooth, iridescent-looking pile. Velvet is available in different piles. Finer velvets are good for draperies; heavier ones for upholstery.

of your colors in every intensity you can find. If you're planning to wallpaper, borrow the books with the kinds of patterns you like, and pore through them until you find something that works. Often you can pull your accent colors from the wallpaper pattern that you choose.

THREE Consider mixing fabric patterns. Most wallpaper makers offer fabrics to coordinate with their wallpaper patterns. Consider these, but also visit fabric stores to find other coordinating prints for upholstery and window treatments. Don't forget to check out ready-made slipcovers and window treatments, too. To experiment with mixing patterns, start simply. Geometric patterns often mix well together—stripes with checks or plaids or dots. It is always easier to mix patterns that contain one or more common colors. Two different patterns can be linked by color, fabric weight, texture, and degree of formality. You can mix patterns in different scales, but don't go overboard. Use a large pattern on a large element, such as a sofa, smaller prints for windows, and something smaller still for pillows. Same-size patterns fight for attention. As a general rule, a good mix includes small-, medium-, and large-scale prints. Checks with stripes, dots with plaids, florals with geometrics are all possibilities when coordinated tastefully. Designers develop a knack for picking eye-catching combinations—and through trial and error, you will, too. Look through magazines or wallpaper books for ideas. In any room where you're mixing patterns, it is important to give your eyes a place to rest. Be sure to add solid-color furnishings to the room as well.

FOUR Pick one print and stick with it. If mixing does not appeal to you and you prefer to use one bold print, make sure the scale is large enough to carry the room. Paint the walls a saturated color picked out from the fabric. Use a second color for other large upholstered pieces or window treatments. Then pick the sharpest, brightest hue from the pattern for accents. Add variety with textiles—a rug, for example. Balance the pattern throughout the room.

FIVE Customize your plan. Color schemes aren't one-size-fits-all. The most successful ones are custom-tailored for a particular space. In your clear-eyed assessment of your needs, here are some aspects to consider:

Clockwise (from above): **The owners of this room started with the white walls as a background and relied on the bedspread, furniture, and accessories to give the room a spark of color. A light-colored palette is enriched by the texture of the bedding, baskets, and other accessories. Patterns that have a common theme and a restrained use of color are the hallmarks of this formal living room. In this room, the eye is immediately drawn to the colorful pillows and the artwork on the wall.**

Physical Space. Consider not just whether the room is large or small but how the dimensions drive the plans. In a big room, would you rather scale down for a more intimate mood or emphasize the room's lofty spaciousness? In tight quarters, will you pull out every space-enhancing trick or bring on rich, deep colors to create a cozy "jewel box"? Is the space disjointed by doorways, windows, and jogs, asking to be unified in a smooth sweep of color? Or is it a bland box that begs for detail? There may be elements you want to downplay. What are the room's finer features—the ready-made focal points?

Is the room located in a suburban ranch, a town house, a clean-lined apartment, a country house, or a beach bungalow? The color scheme may reflect a distinctive architectural period or regional character. You don't have to listen to the house's suggestions—an East Coast apartment can have a Southwest flavor or a country house some big-city slickness—but playing against type takes more design ingenuity. Also consider the prevailing climate. If you face chilly, rainy winters, consider the psychological warmth of sunshiny tints and deep textures. In hot regions, smooth surfaces and light backgrounds seem particularly fresh and cool.

Lifestyle Concerns. Will the room be a high-traffic space, requiring washable, forgiving surfaces and colors? A space reserved for company occasions might be jazzed up with glamorous, less-practical choices. What activities take place in the room—reading, crafts, watching TV, or conversation? Is it a family space? A family space may need a color scheme that won't show dirt. Do family members have any strong opinions on color that you'd like to accommodate? If so, consider incorporating a favored color by using it as an accent or even as the base color for the entire scheme.

Will you spend long hours in the room or brief periods? Rooms you pass through briefly can usually carry off more-dramatic colors and patterns than rooms where you linger.

Atmosphere. What sort of mood would you like the room to project? Elegant? Homey? The room's purpose often prompts the color choices. You might, for example, lean toward an invigorating tint for a home office. The atmosphere should also relate to the room's purpose. You may, for example, need a soothing color for a bedroom.

Natural Light. The room's orientation can influence the palette, depending on whether you're trying to tone down or maximize the available light. In a true sunroom, dark or bright textiles, which are prone to fading, might be reserved for easily changed accents. Before tailoring a room for sunshine, make sure the artificial lighting also flatters the selection. The next chapter, "The Right Light," will take you through the process of creating a lighting plan, plus it will show you how light affects color and how it sets the tone of a room.

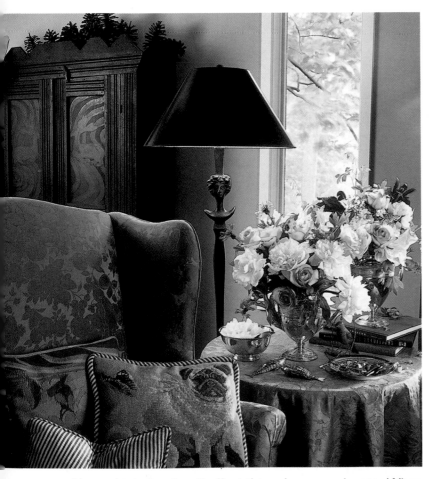

Above: Light levels will affect the colors you choose. When selecting paints, wallcovering, and furniture, be sure to view them in both natural and artificial light.

Right: The designer started with the fireplace as a focal point and then chose colors and patterns to create a homey living room in a traditional style.

a gallery of...

1

1 To complement the yellow walls, the owners chose blue upholstery for the chairs and blue stemware for the table.

2 Here is a classic traditional color scheme for the walls, reinforced by the area rug. The white woodwork brings out the beauty of the intricate molding.

3 If you tend to shy away from adding pattern or texture, begin by introducing small doses of pattern as in this room.

4 Despite the neutral color of the wall, the texture of the wicker furniture and the layering of color and fabric on the table bring this room to life.

5 Although both the sofa and the screen feature bold prints, they are similar enough so that they work together.

...smart ideas

1 A rich, warm color scheme tends to make a space seem smaller and more intimate. Cool colors have the opposite effect.

2 A neutral, yet textured, background is an ideal setting for black polished furniture and a glass-top table.

3 For those who shy away from mixing color and pattern on their own, wallcovering manufacturers offer entire lines in which they match wallcoverings with borders, as shown here.

4 Red accents set off the deep green used here.

5 Choose bright colors and bold patterns for a child's room.

6 The designer toned down the wall pattern by remaining in the same color family throughout the room.

7 When combining patterns in a room, make sure that there is a recurring color theme. Yellow and colors analogous to yellow are the theme here.

CHAPTER 3

THE RIGHT LIGHT

NATURAL LIGHT ▪ TYPES OF ARTIFICIAL LIGHT ▪ SELECTING LIGHT LEVELS ▪ TYPES OF BULBS ▪ DETERMINING LIGHTING NEEDS ▪ LIGHT FIXTURES ▪ THE ROLE OF LIGHTING IN ARCHITECTURE

A lighting plan plays a major role in any well-designed home. Not only is a well-lighted house safer and more functional, it also shows off colors, forms, and textures to their best advantage. A lighting plan should include the available natural light at different times of the day and the many different types of artificial light available.

The quality of the light we live with also affects our sense of well being. We learn more quickly and work better in bright, warm light. When we want to rest, dim light relaxes us. All of these considerations point to the importance of thoughtfully planning lighting for the home. Whether you decide to devise a lighting scheme yourself or call in a lighting specialist, remember: good interior designers take advantage of the transformational power of light and so can you. In this chapter, you'll learn how to use light to manipulate the perception of space, casting it up to make a low ceiling seem higher or washing the walls with it to make a small room appear spacious. You'll also learn how to use light in a painterly fashion to emphasize forms or objects. What could be more dramatic than the shadow play of leaves on a nearby wall or ceiling, produced by aiming a small spotlight upwards from underneath a bold, sculptural plant?

To make wise choices from among the wide variety of lighting types available, compare them on a level playing field. That's what lighting measurements can help you do.

You'll also need to learn about the types of lighting, the different kinds of bulbs and fixtures, in addition to the terminology. This will help you with planning, and will make you more effective when discussing ideas with experts and sales staff. For instance, many of us use the words "fixture" and "lamp" interchangeably, but when lighting professionals speak of "lamps" they are talking about "bulbs." Learn to speak the language.

Once you have prepared yourself, you can begin sketching out a plan that can cover areas within one room and to create a flow from one space to another.

NATURAL LIGHT

Any discussion about lighting your home has to begin with natural light. To the human eye, the desirable norm is sunlight. Part of its appeal is its variety. Consider the clear illumination on a cloudless mountaintop. Compare that to the diffused light on a misty morning or the intense brightness on a tropical beach. Then there's the changeability of sunlight between a cool rainy day, a clear winter afternoon, and a full summer blaze, or the contrast between the color of sunlight at noon and the way it appears as afternoon wears into evening.

The amount and quality of natural light a room receives depends on the size of its windows and its orientation with regard to the sun. South-facing windows get the lion's share of direct sunlight for most of the day. East-facing rooms benefit from early mornings, while rooms that face west are

Today, at the flick of a switch, you can illuminate your home inside—and out. You can program and store entire lighting schemes thanks to the latest technology. On command, create bright light for work, then change the mood to cozy when you want to relax, or adjust it all over again for TV viewing. Set your lights on timers for safety and security, or activate them by remote control.

For complicated situations, you may want to consult with a lighting design professional, or you may feel comfortable devising a plan yourself with the help of an electrician. In any case, you need to understand something of the basic science of light, how it is measured, and its effect on color.

sunny in the afternoon. Because its back is to the sun, a north-facing room receives only indirect natural light and tends to be cool and dim.

When you are renovating or redecorating a room, always look at the existing space and take the seasons, time of day, and orientation of the windows into consideration. Sometimes making a window bigger, or adding another one, doesn't make a room brighter. If the window's siting is toward the north, the room will just get colder. You can make a breakfast nook cheerier with a window that faces east, but don't try to take a late afternoon nap in a room with west-facing windows, unless you can control the light with shades, blinds, or lined curtains.

The natural light in the room will affect any tasks you perform as well. Never arrange furniture, such as a desk or worktable, so that you are facing directly into bright sunlight. But be careful about having your back to a window. This can create shadows on your work surface. Ideally, follow the old axiom that recommends "light coming from over the left shoulder." By charting the light, and arranging your room and selecting window treatments accordingly, you can avoid problems.

TYPES OF ARTIFICIAL LIGHT

Artificial light picks up where natural light leaves off. It is the illumination that you provide, and unlike natural light, you can also fine-tune it. In the daytime, artificial light augments natural light; after dark, it compensates for daylight completely. The key to devising a versatile plan that can change with each activity, as well as with the time of day or the weather, begins with knowing about the different types of artificial light. Here's a review:

Right: Choose artificial light sources to solve problems. Here a bedside lamp fills two needs: it provides general illumination and serves as a reading lamp.

AMBIENT LIGHT

Ambient, or general, light is illumination that fills an entire room. Its source is sometimes an overhead fixture, but the light itself does not appear to come from any one specific direction. Ambient light surrounds a room generally. An obvious example of ambient light is ceiling-hung fluorescent strips in the average office environment. A covering over the strips hides the source and diffuses the light throughout the room.

A wall sconce is another good example of ambient light. The fixture washes light up the wall for an overall glow. The wall reflects the light, which diminishes the appearance of a single source. While you can tell the light is coming from the sconce, the overall glow is diffused.

The key to good ambient lighting is making it inconspicuous. Ambient light is merely the backdrop for the rest of the room, not the main feature. It changes with the surrounding environment—always providing light but never becoming obvious. For example, ambient lighting used during the day should blend in with the amount of natural light entering the room. At night, you should be able to diminish the light level so that it doesn't contrast jarringly against the darkness outside.

TASK LIGHT

As its name implies, task lighting is purely functional. It illuminates a specific area for a particular job, such as chopping food on a kitchen counter, laboring over a woodworking project, or applying makeup.

Theatrical lighting around vanity mirrors is an excellent example of task lighting. It provides cross-illumination while avoiding the distorting shadows often seen with overhead lighting. Task lighting should always be included in any room where specific functions take place, but its use should be optional. In other words, you can turn it on when you need it and keep it off at other times. Task lights should not be on the same switch with the fixture that provides general illumination. Using both types simultaneously creates a harsh, too-bright effect.

ACCENT LIGHT

Often overlooked, but always the most dramatic, accent lighting draws attention to a particular element in the room, such as a handsome architectural feature or a work of art. Accent lighting makes a room come alive. It creates a mood. It shapes space. Lights recessed into a soffit above a handsome kitchen countertop cast a downward glow of illumination that offsets the counter without spilling light into the rest of the room. Cove lighting over a bathtub shimmers above the water and delineates a bathing area dramatically.

Without accent lighting, there may be light, but no focus, no character, no show business. With it, a design becomes exciting, theatrical, and rich.

DECORATIVE LIGHT

While accent lighting draws attention to another object or surface, decorative lighting draws attention to itself. It can be kinetic, in the form of candles or flames in a fireplace, or static, such as fixed wall candelabra. It is there to grab attention. It is lighting for the pure sake of lighting.

Because decorative lighting is compelling, it can be a device to indirectly attract or distract. You can use it to draw the eye upward toward a cathedral ceiling, for example. By capturing your eye, decorative lighting forces your focus away from anything else. It doesn't highlight anything, as accent lighting does. And it doesn't provide a great deal of illumination, as ambient lighting does. It is the device that most lighting designers love to use, the final stroke in a complex multilayered plan.

Some types of decorative lighting include candles, chandeliers, neon sculptures or signs, a strip of miniature lights—any type of light that is deliberate and contrived. Include it to unify a room—to strike a balance among the various types of lighting, including natural light from the sun and moon.

Clockwise (from above): **Backlighting draws the eye to the decorative objects on the shelves. Recessed ceiling fixtures wash the wall with light. The fixture over the pool table provides adequate task lighting for players. This hall contains both ambient light and accent lighting over the statue.**

CONTRAST AND DIFFUSION

Task lighting and accent lighting are examples of high-contrast lighting—they eliminate shadows and bring an object into sharp, crisp focus. Ambient lighting and decorative lighting are more diffused. They are softer, more forgiving lights that are comfortable and relaxing. Most rooms benefit from a combination of contrast lighting and diffused light, so incorporate both in your plan.

SMARTtip   Recommended Ranges of Light Levels

You can avoid eyestrain by having plenty of ambient light, thereby reducing the contrast to task lighting. Start by determining the level of light needed for the activity or task, and then relate it to the surroundings. (See "Determining Your Lighting Needs," on page 63 of this chapter.) Task lighting, lighting immediately nearby, and then the lowest lighting in the area (as in a room's corners) should range from no more than a ratio of four to one, preferably three to one near task lighting. You can compare watts and foot-candles cast by various light sources to determine the ratios or approximate them with your naked eye. The following table provides the recommended ranges of light levels for seeing activities in the home. The more intense the activity, the greater the light level should be.

ACTIVITY	EASY OR SHORT DURATION	CRITICAL OR PROLONGED
Dining	Low	Low
Entertaining	Low to high	Low to high
Grooming	Moderate	High
Craftwork *	Moderate	High
Kitchen/laundry chores	Low to moderate	High
Reading	Low to moderate	High
Studying	Moderate	High
TV viewing	Low to moderate	Low to moderate
Computer work	Moderate	High
Workbench *	Moderate	High
Tabletop games	Low to moderate	Moderate to high
Writing	Low to moderate	High

* Benefits from supplementary directional light.

SELECTING LIGHT LEVELS

Design professionals have established a set of ideal lighting levels for performing the various activities and tasks that take place in any house. Your own personal preferences should lie within the minimum and maximum levels they have established. Some people favor more light; others prefer less. Good lighting begins with taking the recommended levels of light into account and tempering them with your preferences and those of people with whom you live. In common spaces, such as the family room, living room, and kitchen, it is better to err on the side of brightness. Adapt lighting in private areas, such as a study, bedroom, or workshop, to individual needs. Consult the Smart Tip "Recommended Ranges of Light Levels," on page 58, as a starting point in establishing your own levels. Once you've determined the level of light you require for each task or activity, relate this light to the surroundings. You can avoid eyestrain by including plenty of ambient light, thereby reducing its contrast to task lighting. Task lighting, the general lighting immediately nearby, and the lowest lighting in the area (as in a room's corners) should not contrast sharply. The light you use to read by, for example, should only be two to three times as bright as the surrounding light in the room. Using a reading light in an otherwise dark room strains your eyes by forcing them to adjust frequently from light to darkness. The greatest range of light in any room should be a four-to-one ratio at most.

Direct Glare. Bare-bulb glare is obvious. You can avoid it by selecting the proper size shade, adjusting the angle of a fixture, or using a low-wattage bulb or one with frosting.

Lighting professionals caution against "glare bombs," fixtures that produce unavoidable, uncomfortable light. A common offender is the bathroom globe or strip light over the vanity; another is the exposed bulb in some ceiling fixtures; a third is an inferior fluorescent fixture that blasts you with bright direct light. In the first case, you might try replacing the bulbs with heavily frosted versions. If you plan to include track lights in your scheme, install baffles over the bulbs. They are devices that are designed to reduce spill light and glare. When you visit a lighting showroom, ask specifically to see bulbs and fixtures designed to reduce glare.

Left: Mix light sources for the best effects. Here a large chandelier provides lighting for diners. The designer filled out the lighting scheme with wall-hung fixtures and a roaring fire.

When you create a layout for your furniture arrangement, it's always wise to assess it for glare. For instance, if you situate the new family room sofa to face a game table, every time you flick on the suspended pendant light over the tabletop, you're creating glare for anyone seated on the sofa. Always check the field of vision from each seated, as well as each standing, position.

Indirect Glare. Any flat reflective surface can be the source of indirect glare. That includes shiny desktops, countertops, tables, mirrors and any other glass or metal surfaces, and TV and computer screens.

To determine reflected glare, simply place a mirror in front of or on top of any surface you suspect will reflect glare. The mirror will isolate reflected light glare. Place a temporary light where you plan to install a permanent source, and then do the glare check before making your final installation.

TYPES OF BULBS

Just changing the types of bulbs, or lamps as professional lighting designers call them, in your existing household fixtures can make a major difference in the way the room looks, functions, and feels. Does this mean you should go out and replace all of your fluorescent lamps with halogen fixtures and call off the rest of your remodeling plans? That might be exaggerating the power of the right light. But don't underestimate it, either.

Understanding the differences in lamps will help you select the right light sources for every area in your house. Most homes require the use of several different lamps. Light is like paint. You get different effects depending on the combinations you use. And color is nothing but the reflection of different types of light. When planning a lighting scheme, always consider the relationship between color and light.

Clockwise (from above): **The typical kitchen requires ambient lighting, such as that provided by the hanging fixture, and task lighting, such as that provided by the undercabinet fluorescent lights. The soft glow above the cabinets is a good example of accent lighting. The natural colors produced by incandescent lamps work well in bedrooms. Some recessed ceiling fixtures allow you to direct the light where you want it. The incandescent lamps over the desk work well, but halogen lamps and fixtures would also work.**

STANDARD MEASUREMENTS FOR COLOR

Scales used universally in lighting assess the color temperature the lamp gives off and how light from the lamp affects the objects it is lighting. We explored the concept of natural light and its effect on color in Chapter Two. Now let's look at warm and cool artificial lights and how they affect color. The term *color temperature* describes the appearance of light in terms of the warmth or coolness of its color. Fluorescent lamps, which do not emit a continuous spectrum of light, are assigned a *correlated color temperature* (CCT) value. Lamps, which range in color from red to orange to yellow to blue to

Right: **The designer of this kitchen chose incandescent lamps as task lighting for the island and fluorescent fixtures to light the working areas of the counter.**

blue-white, are ranked according to the Kelvin (K) temperature scale. This rating will help you to select lamps that are closely matched, and you can vary the coolness or warmth of lighting for specific situations. Generally, light sources below 3,000K are considered warm, while those above 4,100K are considered cool. Midrange light sources fall between 3,200K and 3,600K.

Color rendition describes how a light source affects the perception of the color of an object it illuminates. The Color Rendition Index (CRI) is a way of measuring a lamp's ability to render true color (the color of an object in sunlight). The color rendering capabilities of lamps are rated from 1 to 100 with true color at 100. If you want different lamps to light an object the same way, match and compare temperature (or CCT) and CRI. Check the temperature first, then the CRI.

TYPES OF BULBS

Most homes include a combination of warm and cool tones, so selecting bulbs that provide balanced lighting comfortably close to what appears normal to the eye is usually the most attractive choice. Experiment with various combinations of bulbs to create your own desired effect. Balance and layering are the two keys to success. Here is a brief description of the types of bulbs and their characteristics.

Incandescent. Like sunlight, incandescent bulbs emit *continuous-spectrum light,* or light that contains every color. Illumination from these bulbs, in fact, is even warmer than sunlight, making its effect very appealing in a room. It makes our skin tones look good, and even enhances our feeling of well-being. The drawbacks to incandescent bulbs are that they use a lot of electricity, are fragile, have a short lifespan, and produce a lot of heat.

They come in a variety of shapes, sizes, and applications. (One type features a waterproof lens cover that makes it

suitable for over a tub or inside a shower.) These bulbs usually are made of glass, and can be clear, diffuse, tinted, colored, or have a reflective coating inside.

Fluorescent. These energy-efficient bulbs cast a diffuse, shadowless light that makes them great for general illumina-

SMARTtip   Dimmer Switches

You can dim lights just slightly to extend lamp life and save energy, and there will be very little perceptible change in light level. For instance, dimming the light to 50 percent will be perceived as though the light were only dimmed to 70 percent. Therefore, there is no dramatic dilation or constriction of the eye due to light level change.

tion. The old standard fluorescents are very unflattering, however, making everything and everyone appear pale and bland. Newer fluorescent bulbs, called *triphosphor fluorescent lamps*, are warmer and render color that more closely resembles sunlight. Fluorescents are available both in the familiar tube versions and in newer, compact styles.

Because the life cycle of fluorescents is shortened when used for periods of less than three hours, place them in situations where the light will be left on for an extended period of time. For example, a fluorescent might not make sense in a storage area where light is only occasionally needed for a few minutes. On the other hand, installing a fluorescent fixture as your overhead kitchen light makes sense because it's likely to be on for hours at a time.

Halogen. This is actually a type of incandescent lamp that produces brighter, whiter light at a lower wattage and with greater energy efficiency. The disadvantages are a higher price tag and a higher heat output that requires a special shielding for fire prevention. Halogen lamps have a slightly different shape and thicker, heavier glass bulbs than incandescent bulbs. The low-voltage version of halogen bulbs produces a brighter light than a standard halogen, and is even more energy-efficient. Low-voltage halogens are typically used for creative accent lighting.

Fiber Optics. One of countless innovations gradually finding its way into the home, fiber-optic systems consist of one extremely bright lamp to transport light to one or more destinations through fiber-optic conduits. Used for accent lighting, fiber-optic lighting does not generate excessive heat, making it ideal for highlighting artwork.

Right: **If your lights don't seem bright enough, substitute existing bulbs, or lamps, with new ones that produce more lumens. The more lumens per watt, the more efficient the bulb.**

DETERMINING LIGHTING NEEDS

When a room isn't bright enough, most people just exchange low-watt bulbs for high-watt versions. Wattage, however, is simply a measurement of how much electricity a lamp consumes. The light output of a bulb is actually measured in lumens. If the bulbs you have been using aren't providing enough general light, substitute them with ones that have more lumens. The next time you shop for bulbs, read the packaging, which indicates the lumens per watt (lpw) produced by a bulb. The more lumens per watt, the more efficient the lamp. When looking for intensity produced by a lamp, refer to its candlepower (Cp). The more candela (units), the brighter the source.

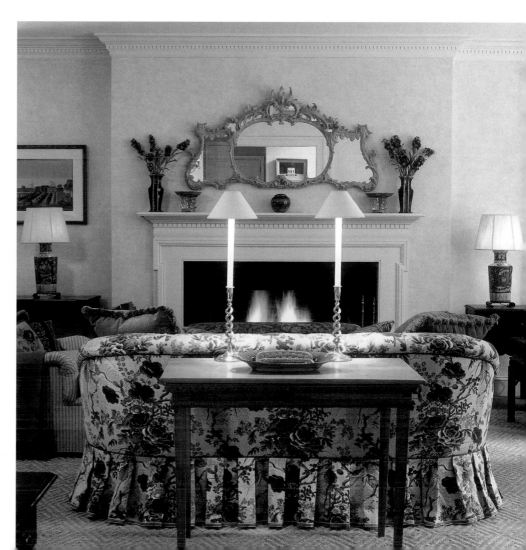

But when planning a suitable light design, you must take other factors into consideration. Besides the amount of natural light the room receives, consider how you will use it—to rest, work, dine, entertain, or a combination of activities. Next, assess the reflectance levels in the room, or the amount of light that is reflected from a colored surface, such as a tile floor or a painted wall. Light colors are reflective; dark colors are absorbent. For example, white reflects 80 percent of the light in a room, while black reflects only 4 percent of it. Surface texture also makes a difference—mirror-like surfaces can reflect as much as 90 percent. In practical terms, a room with satin or glossy white or pale walls requires less light than one with deep, jewel-toned walls.

Next, consider the size of the room. How high are the ceilings? High ceilings require brighter lights to dispel shadows. But you'll have to tone down the level of brightness in a room with low ceilings because light tends to bounce off low ceilings and walls. How many windows and skylights are there? Do they face the sunny south, or is their exposure to the north, or somewhere in between?

Designers typically determine lighting needs by using suggested foot-candle (Fc) levels for different activities and areas. Foot-candles, which refer to the amount of light that falls on a surface, are used primarily for directional lamps. To determine the foot-candle power you will need to adequately light an area, divide the candlepower (Cp) of the bulb you intend to use by the distance (D) from the fixture to the surface squared ($Fc=Cp \div D^2$).

Above: **Rooms with high ceilings require brighter lights to get rid of shadows. Note how the recessed ceiling fixture illuminates both the painting and the area near the ceiling.**

There are no perfect stock formulas. But by looking at how each of these factors affects the others, you can make educated choices when developing your light plan. Keeping in mind the science and technology involved in lighting will help you assess your own requirements for the room. Ideally, you'll want to incorporate a variety of options for various activities, to create ambiance, and for decoration. Use the following Smart Steps to get started.

SMART steps

ONE: Examine your activities. Above all, your lighting design should enhance the function of the room. Try preparing dinner with a new recipe or following a complicated sewing pattern without the right light. Make a list of all of the day and nighttime activities that may take place in room, such as TV watching, studying, cooking, and crafts.

TWO: **Sketch an informal plan.** Refer to the floor plan you drew of the room or make a new sketch. (See Chapter One, "The Basics of Design," on page 12.) Circle the activity centers—work tables, reading chairs, TV viewing spots, and so forth. Not everything you expect to do will require the same level of light.

Note each activity center with a "G" for general or ambient light, "T" for task light, "A" for accent light, and "D" for decorative light. In some places, you may want to indicate more than one type of light. An easy chair may be used at times for reading and at other times for TV viewing or even just rest, for example.

Place your general lighting first; then indicate where you'll need task lights. After you've noted every activity center for task lighting, decide where you want to install accent lighting. You might want some recessed fixtures over a countertop or piece of art. Maybe you want to highlight beautiful crown molding or hand-painted tile. If you want to use accent lighting but don't know where it should go, ask yourself what is the most interesting feature in the room. It may be something as simple as a wall-hung framed print, a collection of first-edition books on a shelf, or a bay window with a beautiful view.

You don't have to place decorative lighting into your plan unless it is a wired fixture, such as a neon sculpture or a track system of low-voltage halogens. But if you know you'll be using candles in the room, it is a good idea to indicate them, too. That way you can plan a place that will hold them safely.

THREE: **Check your local code.** Every municipality has its own codes regarding the placement of light and electricity around water. Before you purchase any light fixtures for the kitchen and bath, especially, check your local code with the building inspector or speak with your contractor.

Left: Match light levels to the area to be lighted. This small table lamp provides enough illumination for the hanging prints and the display on this hall table.

FOUR: Visit lighting showrooms. The best way to get ideas is to visit lighting showrooms and the lighting department in home centers. This will give you a chance to take an inventory of fixture types and styles currently on the market. Also, you can take advantage of the advice of lighting specialists employed at these stores. They can help you create the right plan and choose an appropriate style of lighting. Bring along your sketch and your list of activities, as well as the design materials you have compiled containing clippings, notes, sample plans, color charts, tile, paint, and fabric samples. The lighting designer can take it from there.

As you might already expect, some in-store advice is free. Ask about it. A few suggestions may be all you need to steer you in the right direction. Otherwise, you may want to con-

Right: The ambient lighting in this room is complemented by the accent lighting hidden in the cove near the ceiling. These lights produce a soft glow.

Below: The warm colors of this room seem to glow thanks to the light from the incandescent lamps. A hanging light highlights a treasured work of art.

sider an in-home consultation. Inquire about fees, which may be modest. Sometimes a small investment in professional advice pays off handsomely in the final result—and in the discount professional designers can offer on fixtures.

There are also systems that computerize a variety of lighting options. A lighting specialist can design an entire program that sets the lights throughout the room on a system devised for different moods and activities. Everything is pre-progammed and controlled by one central panel. However, these "smart systems" can be high-priced.

LIGHTING FIXTURES

There's practically an endless number of fixture styles on the market to match every decor and catch everyone's imagination. The past few years have proved to be a lighting designer's dream as fixtures have become more decorative and lighting schemes more varied and eclectic. From nostalgic reproductions to architecturally inspired designs and contemporary styles, there are models to suit any look in the form of table and floor models, wall sconces, chandeliers, strip lights, recessed canister lights, track lights, ceiling fixtures, and novelty types. The copious selection of finishes in all of these styles offers lots of excitement, too. Look for everything from ceramic, glass, and colored enamels to brass, chrome, pewter, nickel, and copper; brushed, matted, or antiqued, as well as dramatic designs in wrought iron and verdigris. For more interest, select fixtures with a combination of finishes, such as a verdigris with antiqued brass or copper paired with wrought iron.

For a sophisticated look, combine more than one fixture type and avoid matched pairs, such as two identical table lamps at either end of a sofa. In a bathroom, a ceiling fixture that includes a ventilating fan is especially practical. For accenting in any room, pair uplighting fixtures, such as wall sconces, with downlighting types: recessed lights or a ceiling-mounted unit, for example. Install track lighting to wash an entire wall with illumination. Do this when you want to call attention to a beautiful wallcovering, a special paint technique, or a mural.

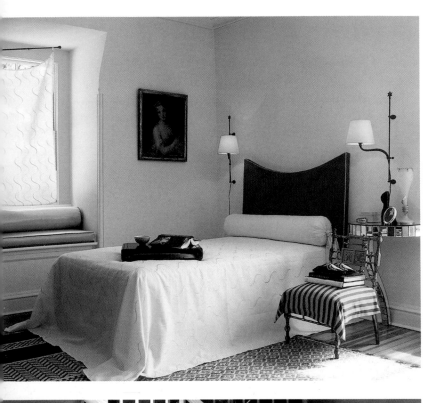

Finally, before you purchase a light fixture, ask to see it lit up in the store. That way you can be sure it produces the type of effect you desire.

THE ROLE OF LIGHTING IN ARCHITECTURE

Lighted coves, soffits (or cornices), and valances make the most of architectural features in a room. Fixtures designed for this purpose create dramatic reflective light. Coves distribute light upward. Soffits distribute light downward. Valances distribute light both up and down. A shield, usually made of a piece of wood or plaster molding, hides the light itself. Baffles, louvers, or diffusers direct light and reduce glare. Consider incorporating one of these ideas into your design if you want to make a big splash with lighting.

Be creative when thinking about architectural lighting. Install it along the top or bottom of cabinets or inside the cove of a raised ceiling. Integrate a lighted valance with a vaulted ceiling or a curtain sweep; vertically light a wall niche; and highlight molding. Whatever you decide, first analyze your architectural lighting needs. Ask yourself these questions:

■ Is the reflected wall or ceiling smooth enough to be attractive?

■ Can I alter the look of the lighting by tinting the surface upon which it reflects?

■ Can I increase efficiency by painting the interior of the valance, cove, or soffit white? (Remember, light-colored surfaces reflect light.)

■ Does the reflected light enhance the rest of the room's light or detract from it?

■ Is the ceiling high enough (at least 8 feet) to keep the light from spilling onto the walls? (The top of the cove should be at least 18 inches from the ceiling.)

Talk with your contractor to see what kind of architectural effects are feasible in your design. Once you have established your lighting plan, the next step is to choose flooring.

Clockwise (from below): Decorative objects on the shelves are lit up by a nearby floor lamp. A table lamp shows the patterns of a wall with a decorative painted finish. A unique chandelier draws the eye to this room's ceiling molding. For special effects, consider ways to light works of art and houseplants. Here the designer placed a light above a potted shrub to give its leaves a golden shimmer. The light fixtures contribute to the overall design of this bedroom.

a gallery of...

1 The designer created a scene and a mood with the selection of the two wall fixtures that flank the painting.

2 Standard incandescent bulbs, or lamps, reflect the richness of the wallcovering, furniture, and accessories.

3 There are a variety of bulbs available, but don't forget about the subtlety of candle-light. Arranged on a mantel or windowsill, candles make great accent lights.

4 Consider the size, shape, and use of the room when select-ing bulbs and fixtures.

5 Select lighting fixtures that match the room's furniture and overall design.

...smart **ideas**

1 Consider both natural and artificial light sources when designing your rooms. Note how the design of the wall fixture complements the ceiling light.

2 The fixtures in this bathroom not only provide adequate light for grooming, they also contribute to the style of the room.

3 Match the fixture to the room. The traditional style of this room cries out for the ornate cut-glass chandelier to be complete.

4 Careful placement of light fixtures can help you create distinct spaces within a larger area. The designer placed a hanging ceiling fixture over the table to define the dining space within the larger room.

CHAPTER 4

FLOORING OPTIONS

CHOICES IN WOOD ■ LAMINATE FLOORING ■
VINYL SHEET AND TILE FLOORING ■
CERAMIC CHOICES ■ NATURAL STONE ■
CARPETING AND RUGS ■
PICKING A FLOORING MATERIAL

Selecting a flooring material is one of the most important decisions you will make when decorating a room. The right material can enhance the color scheme and the overall look of the room, and flooring provides a unique tactile component to the design.

If you are are acting as your own designer, one of the first things you should do is learn about the various types of flooring—from wood to stone to vinyl—on today's market. The choices are myriad and innovations in technology have widened the range of finishes.

Like a professional, be sure to consider the principles of color, texture, and pattern, relating them to your selection and to the rest of the elements in the room. (See Chapter Two, "Adding Color and Texture," on page 32.) If the wallpaper features a big, bold design, for instance, you'll want to tone things down with a solid-color floor or one with a small pattern. If the room is large, you can make it cozy with a number of area rugs that define intimate furniture groupings. A country-style living room might benefit from a textured tile that has rustic appeal or from braided rugs. A formal entry hall will make a stately impression with an intricate parquet border or a checkerboard marble floor.

You'll also have to consider the function of the space that you are decorating before making a final decision. A natural wood floor is unrivaled for adding richness and warmth, but if you install it in a high-traffic area, be prepared to deal with scuffs and scratches, and to provide routine maintenance if you want it to retain its handsome appearance.

Taking a comprehensive look at the types of flooring available and their most appropriate applications will make choosing your new floor a piece of cake. As you review these flooring options, remember that some can be mixed and matched for an interesting and creative design variation that combines expensive and inexpensive materials. Wood planks, for example, might be bordered by ceramic tile strips, or top-quality stone edging might provide an unusual border for a relatively inexpensive expanse of carpeting.

CHOICES IN WOOD

In bygone eras, a wood floor was simply one that was created by laying wide wood planks side by side. Later, as the milling of lumber improved, homeowners were able to choose narrower planks that look more refined than rustic. Parquet floors were created by woodcrafters with a flair for the dramatic and an appreciation of the artistic richness of wood grains set in nonlinear patterns.

Today's manufacturers have made it possible to have it all. The wood floor, factory- or custom-stained to suit a particular style or mood in a room, is still a traditional favorite. It's readily available in strips of 1 to $2\frac{1}{4}$ inches wide, or in country-style planks of 3 to 8 inches wide. The formal, sophisticated look of a parquet floor is unparalleled for richness of visual texture. Prefinished hardwood tile blocks are now manufactured in a variety of patterns, making parquet possible at a reasonable price.

Right: Wood flooring companies provide a variety of finish options, but you can also create your own. Here the designer painted the checkerboard pattern on an existing wood floor. Several coats of polyurethane protect the paint job.

TYPES OF WOOD FLOORING

Wood varieties available as a surface material are vast, and cost varies widely, depending on the type and grade of wood and on the choice of design (strips or parquet).

Softwoods, like pine and fir, are often used to make simple tongue-and-groove floorboards. These floors are less expensive than hardwoods but also less durable. Softwoods are not suitable for high-traffic areas, for rooms with heavy furniture (which can "dig" into the wood), or for kitchens or dining rooms, where chairs or other furniture will often be moved around. The hardwoods—maple, birch, oak, ash—are far less likely to mar with normal use. A hardwood floor is not indestructible; however, it will stand up to demanding use.

Both hardwoods and softwoods are graded according to their color, grain, and imperfections. The top of the line is known as clear, followed by select, No. 1 common, and No. 2 common. In addition to budget considerations, the decision whether to pay top dollar for clear wood or to economize with a lesser grade depends on use factors and on the design objectives. For example, if you plan to install a wood floor in a small room and then cover most of it with an area rug, the No. 2 common grade may be a good choice; lesser grades are also fine for informal rooms where a few defects just enhance a lived-in look. If your design calls for larger areas of rich wood grain that will be exposed, with scatter rugs used for color accents, a clear or select grade will make an attractive choice. Another factor to use in determining what grade to choose is the stain; imperfections are less noticeable with darker stains.

Above: You can either stain a wood floor yourself or purchase a prefinished material. Dark, rich stain colors work well when a formal feeling is desired, such as in this grand foyer. Lighter colors are more casual and create a feeling of openness.

FINISHING OPTIONS

Color stains—reds, blues, and greens—may work in settings where a casual or rustic feeling is desired. This, however, is a departure from the traditional use of wood. Wood is not typically used to deliver color impact; instead it blends with and subtly enhances its surroundings. Natural wood stains range from light ash tones to deep, coffee-like colors. Generally, lighter stains make a room feel less formal, and darker, richer stains suggest a stately atmosphere. As with lighter colors, lighter stains create a feeling of openness and make a small room look larger; darker stains foster a more intimate feeling and can reduce the visual vastness of a large space.

Creative patterning of a wood floor can enrich a design. For example, create an Old World look by laying strips in a herringbone pattern. Decorative inlay with strips or parquet patterns can enhance richness and visual interest. Use inlays to "frame out" activity areas in large spaces that have multiple uses, such as living and dining areas.

INSTALLATION

Unless you're particularly adept at measuring and cutting wood and have the time and skill necessary to finish the flooring surface, the installation, staining, and finishing of strip or plank floors can be a formidable project. Therefore, if the design plan calls for the laying of unfinished wood strips, factor the cost of hiring a skilled professional into your budget. Many manufacturers offer products with installation kits that make wood flooring a do-it-yourself option for those whose skills are good but don't necessarily approach a professional carpenter's level. Some make strips or planks already finished and sealed so that once the last nail is tapped into the flooring the project is complete. Most parquet tiles come finished and sealed as well.

MAINTENANCE

If a wood floor is appropriately installed and properly sealed with polyurethane, maintenance consists of vacuum cleaning or dust-mopping as needed. It's important to promptly vacuum up any gritty material that may be tracked in from outdoors, because sand and gravel can scratch or even gouge the surface of a wood floor. Waxing isn't necessary, although some who live with wood floors like the patina that results from periodic applications of wax.

Right: **Is it real, or is it laminate? In this case it is a laminate floor made to look like wood. You can also find laminate products that look like ceramic tile or natural stone.**

LAMINATE FLOORING

Laminate flooring is the great pretender among flooring materials. When your creative side tells you to install wood but your practical side knows it just won't hold up in the traffic-heavy location you're considering it for, a wood floor look-alike might be just the thing. Faux wood and faux stone laminate floors provide you with the look you want tempered with physical wear and care properties that you and your family can live with. Laminate is particularly suited to rooms where floors are likely to see heavy duty—kitchens,

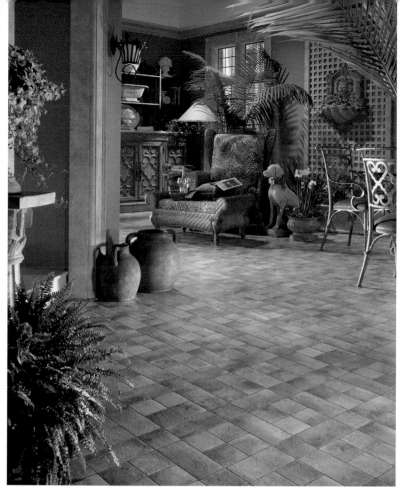

Left: Vinyl sheet flooring is a good choice for high-traffic areas, such as kitchens, family rooms, and playrooms. Most products have a no-wax finish that is easy to maintain.

Laminate is available in sheets that are ideal when your design calls for a uniform look, such as monotone stone, or a linear design that mimics strip or plank wood flooring. Laminate planks, squares, and blocks offer added design flexibility: with them, you can design your own tile patterns, lay strips of wood-look planks with alternating "stain" finishes, or border your floor with a contrasting color.

Proper care for this type of material includes routine vacuuming and an occasional damp-mopping. Add a cup of vinegar or ammonia to a gallon of water for an inexpensive but effective cleaning solution.

VINYL SHEET AND TILE FLOORING

Like laminate, resilient flooring is also available in design-friendly sheet or tile form. Resilient floors can be made from a variety of materials, including linoleum, asphalt, cork, or rubber. However, the most commonly used material in manufacturing today's resilient floors for homes is vinyl plastic.

Price, durability, and easy maintenance make resilient flooring an attractive and popular choice. Do-it-yourself installation, an option even for those who are not particularly skilled or experienced, can mean further savings.

SHEET VERSUS TILES

Resilient flooring comes in an enormous array of colors and patterns, plus many of the flooring styles have a textured surface. With the tiles, you can combine color and pattern in limitless ways. Even the sheet form of resilient flooring can be customized with inlay strips.

Cushioned sheet vinyl offers the most resilience. It provides excellent stain resistance; it's comfortable and quiet underfoot

family rooms, hallways, and children's bedrooms and playrooms—anywhere stain and scratch resistance and easy clean-up count. Prolonged exposure to moisture will damage some laminate products, but many can now be used in wet areas. Manufacturers of laminate offer warranties against staining, scratching, cracking, and peeling for up to 25 years.

Laminate is made from paper impregnated with melamine, an organic resin, and bonded to a core of particleboard, fiberboard, or other wood byproducts. It can be laid over virtually any subflooring surface, including wood and concrete. It can also be applied on top of an existing wood, ceramic, or vinyl tile, as well as vinyl or other sheet flooring. You can even install it over certain types of carpeting, but check the manufacturer's guidelines before doing so.

INSTALLATION AND CARE

The installation of laminate flooring is a reasonably quick and relatively easy do-it-yourself project. It requires sheets of a special foam underlayment followed by the careful placement, cutting, and gluing of the laminate.

and easy to maintain, with no-wax and never-wax finishes often available. These features make the floor especially attractive for areas with lots of kid traffic. Beware though: only the more expensive grades show an acceptable degree of resistance to nicking and denting. In rooms where furniture is often moved around, this could be a problem. Although the range of colors, patterns, and surface textures is wide, sheet flooring is not as flexible as vinyl tile when it comes to customizing your look.

Regular sheet vinyl is less expensive than the cushioned types, but it carries the same disadvantages and is slightly less resilient. Except for the availability of no-wax finishes, a vinyl tile floor is as stain resistant and as easy to maintain as the sheet-vinyl products. Increased design possibilities are the trade-off.

Here, as with other flooring materials, one possible way out of the choice maze is to take the unconventional step of mixing flooring materials. For example, use a durable cushioned sheet vinyl in more trafficked areas, but frame it with a pretty vinyl tile or laminate border.

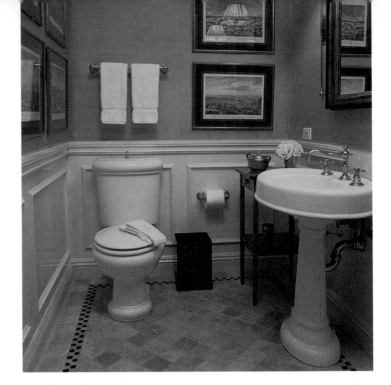

Above: Selecting ceramic tiles for floors allows you to to mix field tiles with borders to create a unique design. Tile suppliers carry colored grouts to enhance your design further.

Below: Ceramic tile provides a tough floor that can stand up to a number of conditions. Here large tiles with white accent tiles are used on a sunroom floor.

CERAMIC CHOICES

Ceramic tile—actually fired clay—is an excellent choice for areas subject to a lot of traffic and in rooms where resistance to moisture and stains is needed. These features, combined with easy cleanup, have made ceramic tile a centuries-old tradition for flooring, walls, and ceilings in bathrooms and kitchens. Color, texture, and pattern choices available today make ceramic tile the most versatile flooring option in terms of design possibilities.

TILE OPTIONS

Some handcrafted ceramic tiles are very costly, but today's manufacturers have created a market full of design, style, and price

Right: Stone floors provide unsurpassed beauty, but they come with a hefty price tag. One popular way to obtain the natural-stone look is through the use of natural-stone tiles, such as those in this foyer.

options. It's possible to create an elegant ceramic floor design even on a relatively tight budget. You can control costs further with do-it-yourself installation. Tiling tools are not very expensive, and many tile retailers will rent them—some will even make the trickier cuts for you. The adhesives, mortars, and grouts available today are easier to use than ever before.

Tiles come in a variety of sizes, beginning with 1-inch-square mosaic tiles up to large 16 × 16-inch squares. Other shapes, such as triangles, diamonds, and rectangles, are also available. Tile textures range from shiny to matte-finished and from glass-smooth to ripple-surfaced. Tiles are available either *glazed* or *unglazed*. Glazed tiles have a hard, often colored, surface that is applied during the firing process; the resulting finish can range from glossy to matte. Unglazed tiles, such as terracotta or quarry tiles, have a matte finish, are porous, and need to be sealed to prevent staining.

In creating a flooring design, consider whether the other elements in the room allow for an intricate pattern or work better with one light color as the dominant feature. Once you make that basic determination, create the design directly on a copy of your floor plan.

Consider using accent borders to create unique designs, such as a faux area rug, that visually separate sections of a room or separate one room from another. When added in a random pattern, embossed accent tiles add interest, variety, and elegance to an expanse of single-colored tiles.

Alas, no surfacing material is perfect. To assess whether ceramic tile is the right surface for your floor, take into con-

sideration both the positive and negative points. Ceramic tile offers long-lasting beauty, design versatility, and simplicity of maintenance, but it also has some hard-to-live-with features. Tile is cold underfoot, noisy when someone walks across it in hard-soled shoes, and not at all resilient—always expect the worst when something breakable falls on a tile floor. If you have infants and toddlers around, it may be best to wait a few years for your tiled floor.

NATURAL STONE

Like ceramic tile, stone and marble are classified as "nonresilients." Like tile, these materials offer richness of color, durability, moisture and stain resistance, and ease of maintenance. They also share with tile the drawbacks of being cold to the touch, noisy to walk on, and unforgivingly hard. Stone and marble floors are clearly, unmistakably natural. As remarkably good as some faux surfaces look, no product manufactured today actually matches the rustic irregularity and random color variation of natural stone or the richness and depth of color in veined marble.

DECISION-MAKING FACTORS

With the kind of beauty and singularity you find in stone inevitably comes a high price tag. Whether it's polished marble, random-cut fieldstone, slate, brick, terrazzo, or limestone, the materials are expensive and the installation requires professional-level skills. Also, you may have to go through an interior designer for the flooring because some suppliers of stone and marble won't take small residential projects. Stone may pose a safety hazard on the floor, too, because it gets slick when wet. A fall on a stone floor can cause serious injury. Older persons and children are at particular risk. If you choose one of these materials, use slip-resistant rugs over it.

Above: Wall-to-wall carpeting adds warmth and richness to a space. Use this type of floor covering in formal areas, such as living rooms, dining rooms, and bedrooms.

CARPETING AND RUGS

The terms carpet and rug are often used interchangeably, but they're not the same, in terms of both manufacture and design application. Carpeting is manufactured in rolls ranging from just over 2 feet wide to broadlooms that measure as much as 18 feet wide. Carpeting is usually laid wall-to-wall and can be installed over raw subflooring. Rugs are soft floor coverings that don't extend wall-to-wall and are used over another finished flooring surface. A mat is a small rug.

Differences in fiber composition, construction, color, texture, and cost make choosing a carpet or rug a complex job. Carpeting can be made of natural wool, synthetic fibers, or blends of wool and synthetics. Other natural fibers commonly used in area rugs, scatter rugs, and mats are cotton or plant materials known as cellulosics—hemp, jute, sisal, or grasses. Synthetic fibers are acrylics, nylon, olefin, and polyester.

HOW IT'S MADE

Carpet construction refers to the manner in which the yarn fiber meets the carpet backing, and carpeting may be manufactured by several construction techniques. *Weaving*, once the industry standard, is done on a loom. Weaving has given way to today's most commonly used technique, *tufting*, in which yarn is pushed through the backing from the underside, forming loops on the surface. Some tufted carpeting has a latex backing to prevent the tufts from pulling loose. Carpeting may also be *needlepunched* or needlebonded, techniques that involve the insertion of yarn into backing with hooked needles. A knitted carpet is created when needles are used to knit pile and backing together; a latex backing is usually added in this type of construction. Finally, carpeting may be flocked. *Flocking* employs static electricity to stand short fibers on end and uses an adhesive to bond the fibers to backing.

Left: **Left:** Area rugs provide a chance to inject a spark of color into a room. Use area rugs over finished flooring or even over wall-to-wall carpeting.

of a uniformly cut, deep-pile carpet. The relatively informal look of a sculptured surface is created with multilevel loops.

ADVANTAGES

Wall-to-wall carpeting adds softness and warmth to a room, both visually and physically. Carpeting also muffles room noise and, when installed on upper floors, reduces the amount of sound that is transmitted to rooms on lower floors of the house or adjacent ones.

In general, woven carpet is the most durable; flocking, the least. The durability of the other carpet types fall somewhere in between. Type of fiber used, the density and height of the pile, and the thickness and quality of the yarn all contribute to a carpet's durability.

The texture of a carpet or rug is determined by a number of factors, including the height and type of pile. The term "pile" refers to the carpeting surface, created when the yarn is connected to the backing. When carpet construction creates yarn loops on the surface, the loops may be left intact (*loop pile*) or may be cut (*cut pile*); in some cases, a carpet may be a combination of cut and uncut loops (*tip-sheared*). To further complicate the picture, loops, cut pile, or both may be of uniform height or may be of varied heights. The resulting possibilities range from the informal, uniformly short-loop-pile carpeting, such as Berber, to the soft velvet

With most types of carpeting, a padding underlayment enhances softness underfoot and increases the life of the carpet. Several types of padding—from rubber to a variety of natural fibers—exist, and some are coated with adhesive. The padding choice will depend on the type of carpet you buy; follow manufacturers' recommendations on what type to use. Cushion-backed carpet, made with the padding, is another option.

MAKING YOUR SELECTION

Carpeting offers a huge variety of material, style, color, pattern, texture, and cost options. The simplest way to narrow down your choices is to decide on a cost and examine the options within your price range. That is not to endorse making a purchase strictly on price. Quality does matter when it comes to carpeting. The most durable carpeting (in terms of construction and fiber) is usually the most expensive. The converse is also true—the less expensive the carpet, the shorter its useful life. Ask yourself this question: "Do I really intend to stick with this carpet for the next 30 years?" Sure you need a durable carpet, but just how long is long enough? Think about it before you buy. Wool carpeting is the most durable and the most expensive; it also has the advantage of being naturally fire resistant. Carpeting made from synthetic fibers offers the greatest variety in terms of color, pattern, and texture, and in the short run is certainly more affordable. A good compromise choice would be a wool-synthetic blend, offering a reasonably wide variety of design options plus some enhanced durability without a pure-wool price tag.

Area rugs are an excellent device for creating small areas within a larger space, such as marking off an intimate conversation area in a living room. They are also a relatively inexpensive way to add accent colors and to help tie room designs together.

Some area rugs are inexpensive, manufactured floor coverings that come in a variety of sizes, colors, and patterns. Others are specialty items, such as the handmade *dhurrie* rugs from India, *rya* rugs from Scandinavia, and hooked, braided, and rag rugs made in a number of places throughout the world. Perhaps the most versatile in terms of decorating are the Orientals, which can blend extremely well with a variety of styles, from traditional to modern. Authentic, handmade Oriental rugs from the Near and Far East can be extremely expensive—essentially you're purchasing a work of art for your floor. A number of manufacturers make excellent reproductions, printing traditional Oriental rug patterns on factory-made rugs. Area rugs can also be made from smaller-than-room-sized pieces of carpeting; the section of carpeting must be bound at the edges to prevent unraveling and to create a finished look.

SPACE CONSIDERATIONS

In decorating with area rugs, the general rule is to allow at least a foot of floor space on all four sides, creating a three-dimensional art piece consisting of the rug, furniture, and accessories, all set within that foot-wide frame. This rule, however, need not apply if your goal is to create special-use

Above: Designers often use area rugs to divide up large spaces. Here a colorful rug sets off a dining area from the rest of a large sunroom.

Opposite: Big rooms can often seem cold and inhospitable. Warm them up by using area rugs as the foundation for furniture groupings, as shown in this large living room.

sections within a larger space. For example, a round hooked rug can be the perfect device for pulling together two comfortable wing chairs and a small coffee table, creating a conversation area within a large living room. In a large kitchen, an area rug slightly larger than your table and chairs can offset this eating space, separating it from the work space. A round or oval rug in a small rectangular or square space can allow you to "float" furniture away from the walls, visually enlarging an otherwise crowded-looking room.

Finally, carpet tiles, manufactured in squares of one or two feet, are an option if your decorating plans call for a softer tile pattern. Some types of carpet tiles must be glued to the subflooring, but loose-laid styles are also now available.

CARE

Carpeting and area rugs are easy to maintain—vacuum cleaning is all that is required for regular maintenance. Many small area rugs are machine-washable; others can be dry-cleaned. For both area rugs and carpeting, a wide range of spot-cleaning products are available for taking care of the occasional soiling problem. A periodic cleaning with a professional steam or shampoo machine will keep most good-quality carpets looking and smelling fresh throughout years of use.

PICKING A FLOORING MATERIAL

Now that you've got the facts about each floor surface option, picking the right one for your design will be much less confusing. The following Smart Steps can make it downright simple.

ONE: Make a "use/ abuse" analysis. Begin by asking yourself the most important question: How is this room used? Your answer should tell you just what kind of traffic the future floor surface will endure. With a relatively expensive investment like a floor, it's best not to guess. Instead, use this system to arrive at an accurate use/abuse analysis:

Imagine yourself in the room on a weekday morning through the entire day and determine who is likely to come through the room at those various times. Then do the same thing with a typical weekend. On a piece of paper, make columns headed "Who" and "Activities," and then list who in the family uses the room and what activities occur there. Do the kids play with toys on the floor? Do they do arts and crafts projects with paint, glue, and glitter? Does the family gather on Saturday afternoons and snack while watching a football game on television? Is it a formal living room where you entertain your friends and business clients? Is it a busy kitchen? Does the hallway extend from your front entrance or from a busier back door where the kids drop off their hockey skates?

The answers to these questions will help you to determine how durable and resilient a flooring surface needs to be, whether warmth and softness are requirements, and how much maintenance will be necessary to keep the surface clean and in good repair.

Above: Wood floors are good choices for a variety of different rooms. You can enhance the design with area rugs or with a decorative border inlay as shown above.

TWO: Determine your design objectives. Are you replacing just the flooring in the room? If so, your choices are limited by the style already established by other elements in the room. Your color choices can enhance the existing palette. If your project is a complete room makeover—including walls, furniture, and accessories— you have more flexibility, although your job is a bit more complex and involves more decisions.

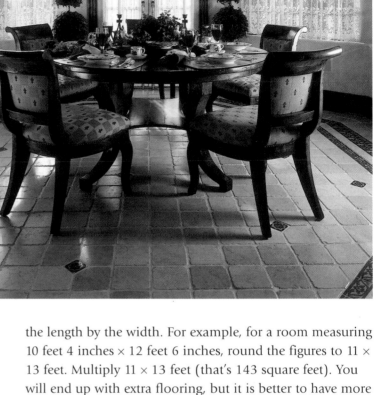

Right: Ask yourself how the floor will be used when selecting a material. Here, ceramic tiles with a rustic look combine a tough finish with an attractive appearance.

Once you've determined your design objectives, compare your use/abuse analysis to the types of flooring that meet both your style and use needs. From the list of options that are left, you can narrow down your choices even more in terms of your budget.

THREE: Draw and use a floor plan. After the use/abuse analysis and the list of design objectives have been completed, draw up a floor plan—a separate one for experimenting with your flooring ideas. Follow these guidelines: measure the length and width of the room, and plot it on graph paper, using a scale of 1 inch to 1 foot. If your room is larger than 8 × 10 feet, you can tape two pieces of 8½- × 11-inch graph paper together. Measure and mark the locations of entryways and any permanent features in the room, such as cabinets, fixtures, or appliances.

Make several photocopies of your floor plan. Reserve one copy as a template. Use the other copies for previewing pattern ideas for flooring that comes in tiles (ceramic, vinyl, or carpeting tiles). Buy multicolored pencils, and fill in your grid. You'll be able to determine not only how the pattern will look but also how many tiles of various colors you'll need to buy to complete the project.

FOUR: Convert your overall budget to cost per square foot. Chances are you have a budget in mind already, with an upper limit established. After you've completed the use/abuse analysis, determined your design objectives, and created a floor plan, the next step is figuring out how much of what kind of flooring material you can afford.

Most flooring is priced in terms of square feet. To determine how many square feet are in your room, round the measurements off to the next foot. Then simply mulitply

the length by the width. For example, for a room measuring 10 feet 4 inches × 12 feet 6 inches, round the figures to 11 × 13 feet. Multiply 11 × 13 feet (that's 143 square feet). You will end up with extra flooring, but it is better to have more than less.

Some flooring—like carpeting—is priced in terms of square yards. To determine the number of square yards in your room, divide the number of square feet by nine. In our example, there are just under 16 square yards in 143 square feet.

Let's say you have a budget of $850 to purchase tile for your 10-foot 4-inch × 12-foot 6-inch room. For the sake of the illustration, let's assume your subflooring is adequate, you have the tools, and the cost of adhesive and grout for your room is about $75. That leaves you with $775. To determine how much you can spend per tile, divide the remainder by the number of square feet in the room. In our example, $775 divided by 143 square feet equals about $5.40 per square foot of tile. Now that your flooring has been decided, it's time to consider treatments for walls and windows.

a gallery of...

1 Pavers installed inside an entry extend the patio and the rest of the outdoors into the house.

2 Vinyl sheet flooring comes in a variety of colors and patterns and can mimic the look of ceramic tile or natural stone.

3 Carpeting provides a luxurious look, but the quality of the padding underneath helps determine its longevity.

4 Vinyl provides comfort and the ability to stand up to high-traffic areas like kitchens.

5 Wood flooring comes in a variety of widths and lengths. Light colors, such as the floor shown here, open up a space. Dark colors have the opposite effect on a room.

6 Mix flooring to create personal designs, such as the one shown in this short hallway.

...smart ideas

1 Flooring materials provide color, and they contribute unique textures to the room.

2 Laminate flooring can mimic any flooring material. Here a wood look enhances a home office. The material is also available in stone designs and solid colors.

3 Wood floors provide a warmth and richness not found in other flooring materials. Many products come prefinished for easy installation.

4 A natural wood floor at the bottom of a curving staircase contributes to this formal design.

5 An area rug defines a sitting area in this large room without completely hiding the beauty of the stone floor.

3

4

5

WALL AND WINDOW TREATMENTS

ASSESSING YOUR WALLS ■ DECORATIVE PAINT TECHNIQUES ■ PAINTING WALLS AND TRIM ■ SELECTING WALLCOVERINGS AND BORDERS ■ WINDOW TREATMENTS

Although they play such an important role in interior design, changing wall and window treatments are relatively inexpensive ways to update a room. New wall finishes allow you to set the tone for the room's design scheme, and they give you the opportunity to introduce color and texture to the room. Window treatments not only contribute to the design, they allow you to control natural light and seal off drafts and unwanted heat gain from outside.

When designing, it's important to consider these two architectural elements together. For a cohesive look, think of a window as part of a wall, and a wall as an extension of a window, then apply the basic principles of scale, proportion, line, balance, harmony, and rhythm to your plans.

Today's choices for decorating walls and windows are probably more varied than ever before. For windows, they run the gamut from neoclassical looks in swags and draperies to contemporary coverings such as pleated shades and Venetian blinds. For walls, there are infinite options, including painted effects as well as wallcoverings in simple stripes and plaids or detailed florals and textures. Your ultimate decision will affect not only the finished appearance of the room in terms of its style but also the way it is perceived

Above: This traditional wall treatment includes a bold-patterned wallcovering sandwiched between wainscotting and crown molding that are both painted white.

ASSESSING YOUR WALLS

The very size of the wall makes it an important element in your decor. A wall can stand as a dramatic statement on its own or serve unobtrusively as a backdrop, letting the furnishings take center stage. Paint and wallcovering are your two basic choices for finishing them, but the myriad options and versatility within these two categories are bountiful.

Generally, walls in contemporary interiors should be kept simple. Fussy wallpaper patterns won't work. Wallpaper designs that represent natural materials (especially texturous ones) look best, as do walls painted in neutral hues or in faux renditions of stone.

However, feel free to dress up the walls of traditional and country-style interiors with lots of color, pattern, and pattern-on-pattern designs executed in wallcoverings or with paint. Florals, stripes, or heraldic patterns work well with traditional interiors; plaids, checks, and mini-prints look particularly appropriate in country-style settings. Stenciled borders and other unpretentious painted effects look equally at home. (See page 98.) Use these Smart Steps to help make your decision.

with regard to size and shape. (Refer to the first two chapters, "The Basics of Design," on page 12 and "Adding Color and Texture," on page 32, for more information.)

In this chapter, you'll learn how to narrow down all of the available options and make the right choices for your project. Plus, you'll find some easy instructions for applying popular painted techniques to walls, as well as designer tips to give your window treatments expert flair. If you don't want to do the work yourself, there are professionals who can turn your plans into reality, whether it's a faux-painted wall or custom window dressings.

SMART steps

ONE: Assess the condition of the walls and the existing treatment. Before deciding whether to paint or use wallcovering, examine the condition of the surface. No matter which treatment you choose, make sure that the walls are smooth for the best result. What's the point of investing time and money in a new wall treatment if there are bumps or dents that will mar the new surface? Small holes can be fixed with joint compound and a light sanding. Large holes in wallboard or cracks in plaster will need more attention, perhaps from a professional. Minor imperfections can be ignored. Wallpaper will hide them, and some painted effects, such as faux stone or aged plaster, may actually look more authentic thanks to them.

If the existing treatment is wallpaper, remove it before painting or applying new wallpaper. Paneling presents other problems. If you take it down, you risk damaging the wallboard underneath it. However, you can paint over paneling as long as you lightly sand the surface first. You can also hang wallpaper over paneling, but you will have to install a special liner paper over the paneling to give it a smooth surface for the new application.

TWO: **Narrow down your choices.** Sometimes it's easy to know what you want immediately. But at other times, the freedom and variety of a multitude of options can quickly become a case of too much of a good thing. How often have you decided to just paint the walls white or beige until you're ready to decide what to do with them? How often have you left them that way? There's nothing wrong with painting walls white or beige, as long as it isn't done as a cop-out. So for the sake of cohesiveness, choose a wall treatment at the same time that you're making decisions about the rest of the room's furnishings. For inspiration, look at the pictures in this book, visit decorator showhouses, and read home-decorating magazines. If you're putting together a period-style room, go to the library and do some research about the colors and patterns that were popular during that era. Numerous well-known paint companies and wallpaper manufacturers offer products that have been inspired by or authentically reproduce historical colors or patterns. Ask your retailer about them. If he or she doesn't have samples, ask about the company's 800 number or Web site address so you can order a brochure.

To narrow down the field even further, try out different options on your sample board. (Review Step One, "Create a Sample Board," on page 42.) Get paint chips or swatches of wallpaper, and compare them with the fabrics and carpet you've selected for the room. Live with them for a few days before making a final choice.

Left: Wallcoverings and window treatments serve as a background for the room. Consider them at the same time you are picking furniture and floor coverings.

DECORATIVE PAINT TECHNIQUES

Solid-color painted walls will never go out of fashion, but these days the decision to paint can extend far beyond simply picking a hue. In addition to providing color, painted effects, such as sponging, stenciling, and *trompe l'oeil*, can add texture and dimension to an interior. These and other time-honored techniques are enjoying a renaissance of popularity because they offer an easy and inexpensive way to add uniqueness and personality to a room, whether contemporary or traditional. Some of them are simple to do even if you're not particularly artistic. Others require an experienced hand. To give you an idea of what you can expect and whether you'll need to call in a professional, here is an overview of the most popular painted effects.

SPONGING, RAGGING, AND COMBING

Sponging, which involves using a sponge to apply or remove wet paint, is probably the easiest and most versatile of all the decorative paint techniques. It produces a highly textured surface that has great visual depth, which helps to disguise imperfections in walls and hide fingerprints and soil in heavily trafficked areas such as hallways and children's rooms. First, select your paint colors or shades of the same hue—one for the wall background and one or more for sponging. The background color, often a light neutral shade, can be applied to the wall straight from the can, whether it's a latex or oil-based product, but the paint that you choose for the sponging has to be thinned first. Latex paints can be thinned with water to create a wash. Use paint thinner with an oil-based paint to make it a glaze. (The latex wash is often referred to as a glaze, too.) Commercial glazes are available and can be tinted to create the desired color. Sponges for sponge painting are available from paint stores and home-decorating centers. Wear rubber gloves when working the paint on or off the wall.

Left: Sponging on a glaze gives a wall a textured look. You can sponge on one or more colors. This technique hides minor imperfections in the wall.

Sponging technique: Paint the wall with a base coat. Dip a natural sea sponge into a colored glaze, and then dab the glaze onto the wall. Try to avoid applying the glaze in a set pattern.

Sponging on entails dipping a moistened sponge into the wash or glaze, wringing it out, then dabbing it against the wall repeatedly until it runs out of color. This process is carried out over the entire surface. To sponge off, apply paint to a section of the wall (not too much, because the paint must remain wet to sponge off), and blot it with a sponge. Rinse the sponge in an appropriate solvent (water or paint thinner) when it becomes saturated with paint.

Ragging on and *ragging off* are similar processes to sponging on and sponging off, except the sponge is replaced with a clean, lint-free cloth. For this effect, it's a good idea to have a lot of extra cloth on hand because the fabric is easily saturated and more difficult to rinse than a sponge.

With *combing* or *dragging*, the background color is revealed as a comb, brush, or other tool is dragged over a freshly applied layer of wash or glaze. (Appropriate tools are available at home-decorating centers.) For this technique, as with sponging off and ragging off, it is important to maintain a brisk work pace because the paint must be wet for the combed texture to take successfully.

Ragging techniques (from top): Apply the glaze by dipping cheesecloth into the glaze and then pouncing the cloth up and down over the surface. To rag-roll a color off of the wall, bottom, paint the wall with a glaze and then remove it with a bunched cloth.

Below: Ragging creates a smooth texture on the wall. Here the designer created the illusion of clouds.

STENCILING AND STAMPING

Stenciling is simple, stylized, and charming. It has an honorable history going back as far as Pompeiian villas and Early American homes in this country, and it is enjoying a widespread revival today. Stencils are frequently used as wall borders and accents in country-style interiors, as well as friezes in traditional decorating schemes such as Victorian. Craft and home-decorating stores have pre-cut stencils in nearly every imaginable motif, plus brushes and appropriate paints. Pre-cut stencils come with instructions for use. If commercial designs don't suit you, there are materials available for cutting your own.

The success of a stenciled design depends largely on your ability to keep the stencil straight. Pre-cut stencils should have registration marks, but you will have to make them on any hand-cut stencils. Keeping the stencil flat against the surface is also key. You will need a separate brush for each color you're using. Also be careful not to overload the brush with paint. After blotting the brush on a paper towel, work the stencil in a light dabbing motion.

Above: Stencils are used to create decorative borders on walls and ceilings. They have been popular since colonial times.

Left: Stencils are not confined to walls. They can be used to decorate furniture, as well as floors, doors, and woodwork.

Technique: Place the stencil, which you buy or make on your own, on the wall and apply the paint.

Technique: To glaze or color wash a wall, paint a base coat on first. Apply the glaze in vertical strokes, then horizontal strokes, and then vertical strokes again. Go over the still-wet glaze with a damp sponge to add texture. Finally, go over the wall with a dry staining brush, shown above, in a series of alternating figure-eight strokes.

Left: Color washing adds a look of depth to walls, giving them a worn, rustic quality. Most painters use base coats and glazes of similar colors.

Another quick and easy technique is *stamping*, which uses raised patterns for block-print painting. Random stamping is easy: just dip the stamp into a small amount of paint, and then press it onto the surface. Formal designs require plotting your motif on the surface beforehand.

GLAZING AND WASHING

A *glaze* is a paint or colorant mixed with a transparent glazing medium and diluted with thinner. A glaze produces a luminous translucent finish. A *wash* is a thinned-out latex or acrylic paint. It creates a flat, gauzy film of color. Both add a sense of added dimension to walls. Remember, with thinned paint, the color or shade of the wall beneath the glaze or wash will show through. Choose colors for the wall, and wash or glaze with this effect in mind. It is a good idea,

with quicker-drying latex especially, to do an entire wall at one time so that paint dries evenly. To apply, use a paint roller, finishing the corners and edges with a brush.

MARBLING

Applied with a steady, practiced hand, an oil glaze or latex wash can also yield a beautiful faux marble effect. *Marbling* is fabulous for adding classical details to a room, but it can also work well in contemporary kitchens and baths where natural materials abound. The technique for marbling is more advanced than the others discussed so far, however. The background and the effect are applied at the same time, and paint must be worked while the surface is still wet but not too wet. After adding the colors, blot them off gingerly with a clean rag. You can do the veining freehand using a feather and artist's oils or acrylics, depending on whether you're applying a glaze or a wash. You'll have to blot the veins, too. Make sure they are subtly blended before brushing a final glaze on top of the design. A bit of advice: if you don't have the patience to practice this technique until you've mastered it, hire a professional artist for the job.

GRAINING

Wood graining, a technique suitable for wall panels, doors, and moldings, simulates a specific grain, such as mahogany or oak. It involves dragging with special graining brushes and detailing with rubber combs to make grains, knots, and whorls. The basic way to create the look of wood is to drag a dark brown wash or glaze over a yellow-painted background. Once the dragging is complete and before the paint dries, another tool called an overgrainer (available at home decorating and craft stores) can be used to further manipulate the paint to look like wood grain. After the paint dries completely, it is sealed with a transparent surface coat that gives the "wood" its luster. Recreating the grain of a specific wood species is much more complicated and generally requires professional know-how. However, as with marbling, practice helps.

TROMPE L'OEIL

Increasingly popular with designers and homeowners alike is *trompe l'oeil* painting, used to make living spaces sophisticated or fun. *Trompe l'oeil,* or effects that "fool the eye," can be full-wall murals or simply small details. They can give the illusion of depth in a small space, for example, or create scenes such as a landscape or a sky that are so realistic that they appear to be what they depict. Unless you're a skilled artist, hire a professional for this job. The box above right explains how to find one.

Right: When executed properly, a *trompe l'oeil* can truly fool you into thinking you are seeing the real thing rather than a painting. This is a technique best left to professionals.

SMARTtip Finding a Special-Effects Artist

To find an artist who can give his or her clients a one-of-a-kind look that completes a decorating scheme, designers simply turn to their directories and pick up the phone. You may have to look a little harder, but not much. You can get a referral from a designer yourself, or check the source list at the back of any decorating magazine that features someone's work you may have admired. Designers who work at home centers or the staff at your favorite paint and wallpaper store may also have leads to recommend. And certainly, if you have admired a painted effect in someone else's house, ask how to contact the artist. Be sure to look at as many examples as possible of an artist's work before hiring him or her for your job. Any professional will be happy to show you a portfolio and supply references.

PAINT PRODUCTS—INSTANT EFFECTS

Homeowners who don't have artistic aspirations but do have the desire to add something special to painted surfaces can do so with paint products that yield special effects and easily applied textured surfaces. With all of these products come specific instructions that must be followed carefully. Some require spray applicators; others can be sprayed or rolled on directly from the can. If you're investing in one of these premium finishes, spend the extra money for high-quality tools, which can make a big difference in the final result. Because these paints cost more than standard products, you may want to use them sparingly or limit them to trimwork. Wherever you're applying an instant-effect paint, it's always a good idea to test the application on poster board before painting it on your walls. Help is available wherever these paints are sold. Instructional videos can make it easier to follow directions. A few of the looks you can create with a direct application product include stone, metal, pearl, suede, denim, and a crazed or crackled finish.

Top right: Mimicking the look of stone blocks provides a rustic look.

Techniques (left to right): Paint the wall with a flat paint and then draw the grid on the wall. Mask off each stone with painter's tape. Apply the paint between the tape in the stone color that you want. Use a flat knife and an artist's brush to draw shadow lines.

Faux stone; finishes that simulate the shadowy, brushable nap of suede; and satiny pearl effects should be applied with a high volume, low-pressure sprayer. A professional painter might be able to get the desired look from this kind of paint by using a good, short-nap roller, but it is not the application method recommended by the manufacturer, especially for an inexperienced do-it-yourselfer. Another faux-stone product comes as a two-process spray kit. First you apply the base coat, and after allowing it to dry, you finish it with a topcoat. When working with a sprayer, be sure to cover nearby areas to protect them from overspray. With a little practice, you can use a hand-held paint shield.

The aged effect called crackle, which resembles the dried, crazed quality of paint in old houses, can also be applied using a two-part method of paint and crackle medium. This is a popular technique to use on furniture. When working with paint, always keep the room well ventilated.

Above: Decorative finishes add a dimension to walls that you cannot duplicate with standard painting techniques.

KID PLEASERS

Formulated and marketed for children's rooms, glow-in-the-dark paints and glittery topcoats are easy to apply. The glow paint is designed for highlighting designs such as stars, for example, that have been painted, stamped, or stenciled onto sections rather than for an entire wall application. To produce a really dramatic effect, you'll have to apply multiple coats of the paint. The glitter goes on over the base coat or the painted design with a roller. Even-handed rolling is important when using a glitter product. If you have to redo some spots with a second coat, the glitter will clump, and those areas will look uneven. As with any textured treatment, you'll have to lightly sand glitter-treated walls if you want a smooth surface when you repaint them later. Think about this before going ahead with this project.

PAINTING WALLS AND TRIM

Even if you prefer to give your walls just a standard coat of paint (always a dependable decorating strategy), you've got a wide range of colors from which to choose; even neutral hues come in a variety of shades and tones. Professional designers typically bring samples of the fabric and carpet to the paint store to have a custom color mixed to match. These paints are more expensive but are worth it. Even two shades of white can clash. (See Chapter Two, "Adding Color and Texture," on page 32, for more advice.) You can also bring home sample color chips. Look at them with your furnishings in all types of light and at various times of the day. To pull your interior together, select a color that you can pick up from the upholstery or drapery fabric, in either a matching or contrasting tone.

Generally, flat paints are best for walls and ceilings. They tend to mar easily, so you may not want to use flat paints for a surface that is prone to abuse or hand marks, such as a wall next to a staircase. For trim, a semigloss finish is the

SMARTtip — Paint Basics

Most interior paints are either alkyd-resin (oil-based) products or latex (water-based) varieties. Oil and water don't mix, and generally neither do the paints based on them. For multilayered effects, stick to one type or the other.

Alkyd paints are somewhat lustrous, translucent, and hard-wearing. But alkyds, and the solvents needed for cleaning up, are toxic and combustible, requiring good work-site ventilation and special disposal methods. Professional decorative painters often prefer slower-drying alkyds, which allow more time to achieve complex special effects. Alkyd paints are better suited to techniques such as combing and ragging, where glaze is brushed on in sections and then manipulated.

Latex paints, which now approach alkyd's durability and textural range, are nontoxic and quick-drying, and they clean up easily with soap and water. Most nonprofessionals find latex paint easier to deal with and capable of creating many popular decorative finishes. In general, latex paints are best suited to effects that are dabbed on over the base coat, as in sponging or stenciling. The short drying time can be an advantage, because mistakes can be painted over and redone.

Latex paint is usually the best choice for covering an entire wall, too, because the job can be completed from start to finish in just a few hours.

typical choice, although you may prefer a high-gloss enamel. Usually glossy paints are reserved for the kitchen and bathroom because they can stand up to the moisture and grime that accumulates in these rooms.

In addition to a variety of colors and shades from which to choose, top-of-the-line paints usually go on easier and require fewer coats. They also clean easier and will remain looking fresh longer. The money you spend on a better-quality paint saves the expense of more frequent repainting.

Left: Test colors you select for walls and woodwork by painting a small portion of the area and seeing how it reacts to light at different times of the day.

SELECTING WALLCOVERINGS AND BORDERS

Wallpaper, fabric, tile, paneling, and mirrors are your choices in decorative wallcovering. *Mirrored glass* installed from floor to ceiling is a nifty device for creating the illusion of space in small quarters, but it is one that should be used sparingly. Solid *wood paneling* can look rich or rustic depending on the finish and trimwork. It also has insulating and sound-deadening properties. *Ceramic tile* is typically used in kitchens and bathrooms, but the vast number of decorative designs on today's market offer creative possibilities for wall decor, including murals, in any room in the house. *Fabric* such as silk, linen, brocade, wool, and suede are delicate, elegant, and expensive. *Wallpaper*, on the other hand, can be affordable, stylish, and durable depending on what it's made of—paper, vinyl, or other natural or synthetic materials—and its finish. Myriad motifs, textures, and patterns add to its appeal.

DECORATING WITH WALLPAPER

There's no getting around it: wallpaper is versatile, with an almost infinite number of styles, colors, patterns, and textures from which to choose. It's also a great mimic of fabric, natural materials such as stone, wood, grass, or bamboo, and even painted effects. These lookalikes are cheaper to install than the real thing and are more durable and easier to care for. But what we call "wallpaper" may not be made of paper at all. (In fact, it rarely is, with the exception of some custom-made specialty designs.) Here's a rundown of more common types.

Vinyl Coverings. Vinyl is the most popular wallcovering because it can take a beating. Finger marks, grease, moisture, and water pose no threat to its long-lasting good looks and wear. There are three types for your consideration.

■ **Fabric-backed vinyl** has a vinyl top layer over fiberglass or cloth. It's tough, so you can scrub it when necessary. The material is heavy, and it usually doesn't come prepasted. Because it's porous, manufacturers recommend using a vinyl adhesive that contains a mildewcide, especially if you plan to use it in a room where there's a lot of moisture—a bathroom or kitchen, for example.

■ **Paper-backed vinyl** is lighter and typically prepasted, peelable, and washable. There are thousands of colors and patterns in its repertoire. Raised or expanded vinyls come with increased surface texture. These wallpaper products can simulate other materials, such as grass cloth, granite, textured painted effects, and decorative plaster work; their texture does a good job of concealing problems with irregular and cracked walls.

■ **Vinyl-coated paper** is inexpensive, but it doesn't have the durability of fabric- or paper-backed vinyl. Its thin protective coating tears easily and doesn't hold up to dirt and stains. Even natural oils from your hands can permanently mar it.

Left to right: You can find wallcoverings that fit with the design of a formal living room, such as the room to the far left, or a casual child's room. Manufacturers make it easy to coordinate print wallcoverings with complementary borders.

Left: One way to mix patterns is to duplicate a wallcovering pattern on furniture. Note how pattern on the chair matches the wall pattern.

Natural Coverings. Grass cloth, hemp, and other natural weaves bring texture to a room. They are particularly suited to contemporary interiors. Some are very delicate and require application over liner paper. They can also fray and are not washable. These coverings should be professionally installed.

Embossed Coverings. *Lincrusta,* which is made of oils, resins, and wood pulp over canvas, is a heavy linoleum-like covering. Its embossed surface features stylized designs that simulate raised moldings made of

Foil Coverings. Like mirrors, foil wallpapers can make a room seem larger. But for these delicate coverings, the surface of the wall must be as smooth as glass because foil will magnify any of its imperfections. Installing liner paper before applying the foil can help. A painted effect over a plain foil can look dramatic. You might consider this as one idea for creating a focal point in a bland room. Avoid using foils in sunny rooms—their reflective surfaces can result in too much glare—but do consider them to bring cheer to a room that's dark. Foils are available with or without a prepasted backing. Because they are delicate and difficult to handle, professional installation is recommended.

Flocked Coverings. Popularized in the eighteenth century, flocked coverings feature a raised, fuzzy pattern that resembles expensive cut velvet. They look at home with traditional or period interiors, but use them sparingly; they can be too ornate at times for contemporary tastes. Some flocked wallpapers are prepasted, and most are strippable. Their washability depends on the design. Certain patterns may camouflage slight wall imperfections.

wood, plaster, tile, or leather. *Anaglypta,* which is cheaper and lighter, is made of cotton-fiber pulp. Both types were first manufactured in the late nineteenth century and are once again popular. These rich-looking, durable coverings can be painted and repainted several times over the years. They also camouflage imperfect walls. You can use them for an entire wall application or halfway up the wall, chair-rail style. Anaglypta also comes as a border for friezes. You can find these papers in home centers today, but follow the installation directions carefully. Because of its weight, leave Lincrusta to a professional installer.

Fiberglass Weaves. Mainly commercial-grade products, fiberglass weaves are yet another option. Made of thickly woven strands of the material used for insulation, they are quite heavy. You can even apply them over concrete-block walls. What's even better, they won't rot, burn, or support mold or mildew, so they are excellent for use in areas exposed to moisture. The look of fiberglass weaves is varied and ranges from gauze-like patterns to designs that resemble vinyl wallcoverings. If you don't see them in your retail store, inquire about contacting a manufacturer directly.

Now that you've got the lowdown on the types of wall-coverings that are on today's market, here's what you need to do to select the right one for your project.

ONE: Apply the principles of good design. When you're shopping for wallpaper, consider the scale and proportion of the pattern in terms of the room you're decorating. Although a particular design in a sample book may attract your eye, think of how it will affect the perception of the size and shape of the room. There is no rule that says you can't use a large print in a small space; however, oversize designs can overpower tiny rooms. Of course, they can dramatize them as well. If your project is a formal dining room or an entry hall, go for boldness. But if it's the family room, you might want to be more conservative in your choice because you spend more time in this space and a large print may tire you. In terms of line, choose a pattern that can add the illusion of height in a room with a low ceiling. Vertical stripes would be excellent in this case. Install wallpaper halfway up the wall with a border paper at chair-rail height to visually lower tall ceilings. Think about balance. If all of the other features in the room tend to be oversize, a mini-print might look out of place. And don't forget harmony. Coordinate all patterns and colors with the other hues and fabrics in the room, as well as those in adjoining areas.

TWO: Try it out for size. Don't ever guess about wallpaper. You may think it matches everything else, but as with paint, once you get it home and hold it up to the sofa or the curtains, you may realize you've made a mistake. Bring home wallpaper samples and try them out on your sample board. Sometimes a retailer will let you take home the book for a few days. When you think you've

Top right: When selecting wallcoverings, consider how the scale and proportion of any design will fit with the other prints and fabrics in the room.

Right: A bold stripe provides the perfect background for furniture painted in fun colors. Decorating a child's room gives you the chance to experiment with color.

found the right pattern, buy just one roll at first. Cut a few wall-length strips that you can tape to the wall and live with for a week. This will allow you to get a more realistic feeling for the effect the wallpaper will make on the overall room and at different times of the day in varying levels of light. It's worth the small investment in a single roll of wallpaper to make sure it's right for your project. If you don't like it, you really haven't lost much.

Right: One sure way to bring a room together is to use the same material for window treatments that you choose for the furniture, as with this window seat.

Below: Bedroom window treatments need to blend with the decor, and they must provide privacy. The designer selected formal drapes for the large window and a balloon shade for the smaller opening.

WINDOW TREATMENTS

You can accomplish a number of things with a window treatment: control the amount of natural light permitted into the room; limit summer heat gain and winter heat loss; enhance a good view or conceal a bad one; provide privacy where necessary; camouflage architectural blunders, such as ill-proportioned or oddly placed windows, or (conversely) dress the window without obscuring its handsome features; or create a focal point for a room or underscore its decorating scheme. Typically interior designers will make recommendations about window decor during the planning stages of a project. For the sake of cohesiveness, it's not a good idea to wait until everything else is done. That isn't to say that you can't change a window treatment unless you make major alterations in the room. Of course you can; in fact, it's a good way to give a tired scheme a face lift. But if you are doing a major makeover, don't leave the windows as an afterthought. Here's how to get started.

 SMART steps

ONE: Assess the window's style. Window style is the first thing to look at: compare it with the window treatment you're considering. What kind of architectural details does the window have or lack that you can modify or enhance? (See Chapter Six, "Distinctive Touches," page 120, for information on window styles and ornamental trim.) Always remember that decorating and architectural styles are linked; not necessarily in the strictest sense, but there should be a relationship between the two. Heavy velvet panels paired with formal swags will appear out of place in a country parlor. In the same way, ruffled calico curtains strike the wrong note in a room that's streamlined and contemporary.

TWO: Remember the function of the room. A bedroom needs to feel cozy, so you'll want a window treatment that will keep out drafts at night but let in air and light in the morning. A bathroom requires something that can

stand up to moisture and is easily washed. The same can be said for a kitchen, which in addition to moisture must suffer the assaults of the cooking grease and the grime that sticks to it.

THREE: Note the room's orientation. Review the section on natural light in Chapter Three, "The Right Light," and consider the time of day that you use the room and its orientation in terms of the sun. This will tell whether you need to control natural light at the time of day you're most likely to use the room. It will also help you decide whether or not the window treatment should play a role in insulating the space—particularly if the window faces north, which means it receives no direct sunlight.

Left: Here the designer extended the look of the ready-made valance by creating a shower curtain cover of the same material.

Below: The floor-length drapes and the pleated-and-gathered valance add a touch of formality to this living room.

FOUR: Consider the size of the window.
Particularly in older homes, windows are often too small, even for modest-sized rooms. Sometimes that's just because the technologically advanced glazings we have today weren't available when the house was built, so the architect or builder kept the window small to avoid problems with heat loss. But you can create a more harmonious balance between window size and the room with the right treatment and installation. For a short window, install the rod above the trim or just below the ceiling line. Hang extra-long panels, and let them puddle on the floor just enough to make the windows appear grand. For a window that isn't wide enough for the wall, extend the window treatment beyond the frame on each side.

Some windows have the opposite problem—they're so large that they overwhelm everything else. In this case, you can tone down the scale by keeping the look simple. If a window is too tall, don't use long panels. Break the length up by dressing the top of the window with a valance or swag that's different from the rest of the design. When windows in a room are different sizes, deemphasize the difference with curtains that are all the same length. Don't pile on several layers, and avoid heavily patterned fabrics.

FIVE: Look in, look out. What do you see through your windows—both from the inside and out? Whatever is seen through the windows becomes part of the decor. Likewise, remember that whatever you leave exposed to the world outside is on public view. In this crowded society, few people have the privilege of a great view with no neighbors. For most windows, you'll need something that you can open and close easily. A combination of heavy panels and sheers or shades, blinds, or shutters can be one solution to the problem.

Above right: Colorful shades not only strike the right chord in this room, they also block out the afternoon sun.

Right: Handy tiebacks allow the full-height French doors to be opened without interference.

SIX: Estimate your budget. How much or how little you have to spend will determine whether you will order custom window treatments, buy ready-made versions, or make them yourself (something that requires skill and patience). The first option typically includes professional installation. Complex designs often require special skills because the window treatments are actually constructed on the window itself. This also means that the installer will have to remove them for cleaning and reinstall them. Ready-made window treatments are offered in several standard sizes to fit standard-size windows. See the box, "Smart Tip: Adding Professional Flair," below, which will help you put designer touches to any window treatment no matter how much or how little you have to spend.

SEVEN: Think about maintenance. It's expensive to have window treatments cleaned professionally and then reinstalled by an expert, so take these factors into account when making your plans. If you can't afford to spend a few hundred dollars on this periodically, rethink your choice.

Right: A sheer curtain provides needed privacy, but it does not completely hide the top of the window.

Below: Cellular shades block out unwanted heat gain, when necessary, while the colorful fabric enlivens the room.

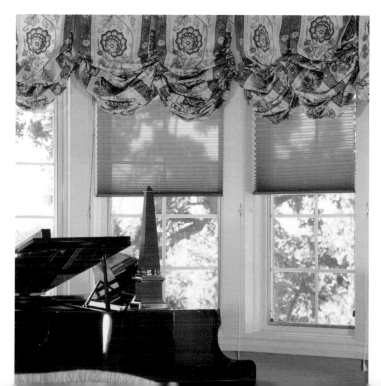

SMARTtip   Adding Professional Flair

You can give your window treatment designs a professional look by using decorator tricks to customize ready-mades or dress your own home-sewn designs. These could include contrast linings, tassels, cording, ribbons, or couture trimmings such as buttons, coins, or bows applied to edges. Another trick is to sew a fine wire into the hem of curtains or valances to create a pliable edge that you can shape yourself. Small weights that you can sew into the hem of drapery panels or jabots will make them hang better. For more inspiration look at fashion magazines and visit showrooms.

FULL FORMAL WINDOW TREATMENTS

A full formal treatment often involves two or three layers. One layer, called the *casement curtain*, is installed inside the window trim area. Typically it's a sheer, solid, or lace panel that lays straight or is gathered at the top. *Over-draperies*, often referred to simply as draperies, make up the second layer. Generally, they cover the window and the trim and, space permitting, extend beyond it either to the sides or above the window.

The words "draperies" and "curtains" can mean the same thing, but some people make a distinction between the two. Generally, draperies are pleated and hang from hooks that attach to tracks in a traverse rod, which allows them to be drawn (closed) with a cord. Curtains hang on rods from rings, tabs, or ties; they're drawn by hand. Formal draperies and curtains should be lined to give them body. An insulated interlining that reduces cold penetration and muffles sound is also a good idea. When installed, they should brush the floor. Draperies that can be drawn may eliminate the need for a shade or blinds because well-lined draperies reduce sun glare efficiently.

The third, and optional, layer of a full formal window treatment is a *valance*, sometimes called a *pelmet*, which runs horizontally across the top of the window and covers the drapery or curtain heading. To some eyes, the window treatment is unfinished without this last element, but this is strictly a matter of taste.

A simple or soft valance made of fabric may hang on a separate rod, or it may be attached to the drapery or curtain. It may be composed of the same fabric as the drapery or a coordinating one. There are various styles including a swag or cascade, a pinch-pleated version, a tab-top, or a free-form valance that can be created

Clockwise (from left): This wrought-iron holdback not only fulfills its function, it also looks good doing it. These simple curtains with the tabbed heading work well with the casual design of the room. For this casement window, the designer added a colorful swag to complete the look. Matching treatments for a window and French doors add a touch of symmetry to this formal living room.

by draping scarves or fabrics over a rod. The fabric can be the same as the drapery fabric or one that coordinates with it. Ornate soft valances often feature vertical gathers that make horizontal pleats for *ruched*, *ballooned*, or *festooned* effects. Many valances are trimmed or shaped into points or scallops at the bottom. Ruffles, fringe, tassels, and piping all add dressy details to the edges.

A hard valance, also called a *cornice* or a *lambrequin*, is usually made of wood and covered with fabric or upholstery. It is permanently fastened to the wall with screws. Box shapes and scalloped edges are the most common. Because they can't be removed easily for cleaning, the fabric covering valances should lay flat against the board backing or upholstery filler for easy vacuuming.

Fabrics that lend themselves to formal window treatments include luminous silks and damasks, velvet, wool, tapestry, and brocade. (See Chapter Two, "Adding Color and Texture," on page 32 for more information.)

INFORMAL WINDOW TREATMENTS

Casual window treatments may consist of one or two layers or nothing at all. If location and privacy considerations permit, a beautiful window looks attractive without the dressing—especially when there's also something pleasant to see outside. Sometimes simple casement curtains installed on handsome decorative rods or just a valance looks attractive in informal rooms. If only the lower half of the window needs covering, café-style curtains offer privacy without blocking light.

Swag-and-tail arrangements can look refined yet informal. Swags are often confused with valances because, like valances, they cross the window horizontally at the top. Unlike valances, however, the tails (or *jabots*) cascade down the sides of the window. Swags may sit over draperies in lieu of a valance, or they may be used alone. Decorative details like *rosettes* (clusters of fabric that have been gathered or pleated to look like a rose) can be used to attach swags to the window frame instead of the traditional rod. This is a good way to create a no-sew swag with just a bit of fabric gathered and fastened at each corner and left to swoop across the top of the window in the center. You can do this with inexpensive fabric remnants, sheers, or even sheeting to create an informal window dress-up for pennies. Special hardware is available that makes creating rosettes easy, too.

Fabrics that lend themselves to an informal look include anything cotton, such as chintz, ticking, toile, linen, gingham, and muslin. Unlike the fabric of formal draperies and curtains, most of these are washable. Just be sure to preshrink fabric if you are making the curtains yourself.

If minimal treatments pose a problem with light control or privacy, you can easily pair them with shades, blinds, or louvered shutters that roll out of sight when not needed.

Clockwise (from above): Bamboo shades have the right texture for this home office. Operable shutters provide privacy for a window seat. When privacy isn't a factor, a colorful swag may be all that is needed. The same fabric used in these Roman shades was used on the throw pillow. A lightweight window shade in a checked pattern is perfect for this country kitchen.

SHADES, BLINDS, AND LOUVERED SHUTTERS

Shades. Generally considered soft window treatments, shades are made of a single piece of fabric or vinyl attached to a roller and operated with a cord or via a spring mechanism. Ones made of fabric can be flat, pleated, or gathered. Shades are versatile, too; they can block out the light entirely or simply filter it. Use them alone on a window for a casual look, or pair them with curtains for something formal. Popular variations include:

■ **Roman shades.** When pulled up, roman shades feature sleek, flat, horizontal pleats. They are well-suited to contemporary-style interiors.

■ **Balloon shades.** When pulled up, the gathered fabric forms billowing festoons or fans. An eighteenth-century design, balloon shades suit period and traditional-style rooms.

■ **Pleated fabric shades.** Lightweight pleated shades stack so tightly when rolled up, they almost disappear under a curtain. They come in a variety of colors and fabrics.

■ **Cellular shades.** The pleated-fabric construction of cellular shades resembles a honeycomb. They are available in a wide range of styles, colors, and faux finishes.

Blinds. Whether made of metal or vinyl, blinds effectively block the sun and the outdoors in general when they are closed. Today's many styles include myriad colors, textured fabric finishes, and wood, and the choice of vertical slats or horizontal slats in standard, mini, or micro widths. Contrasting tapes are available to create interesting decorative details. Verticals are strictly suited for contemporary rooms, but the others look at home anywhere. Pair blinds with another treatment or let them stand alone.

Louvered shutters. Wooden shutters always lend a tony appearance to any interior. Open them for air; close them for privacy. Stained wood finishes complement country or traditional-style rooms. Some types come with a fabric panel that can be coordinated with other furnishings. "Plantation" shutters, which feature wide louvers, painted white or off-white, complement contemporary settings.

1

2

a gallery of...

3

4

1 You can buy decorative hardware, or you can choose to make your own.

2 A bold red-striped wall is anchored by classic white chair-rail molding and wainscotting.

3 Decorative wallcovering borders are most often used near the ceiling, but for a different look try installing them at chair-rail height.

4 A truly confident homeowner agreed to this distinctive wall treatment. Note the window box installed on the inside.

5 The right wallcoverings, borders, and insets can help you create a design for a themed room.

6 Coordinated curtains, light fixture shade, and table covering pull this room together.

...smart ideas

1

1 The bright print on these simple fabric shades is echoed in the colors of the sofa, ottoman, and area rug.

2 The design on the vase, chests, and other containers resembles the print on the wallcovering, making the grouping work.

3 Plain, operable shutters installed on a window next to the table let in light and air while providing privacy as needed.

4 French doors become a focal point when gathered sheers over the glass are framed with a graceful swag and jabot.

5 Although strong, the colors of the wallcoverings are at the warm end of the color spectrum and tend to promote a feeling of rest and well being.

CHAPTER 6

DISTINCTIVE TOUCHES

ELEMENTS OF DESIGN ■
SPECIAL DETAILS

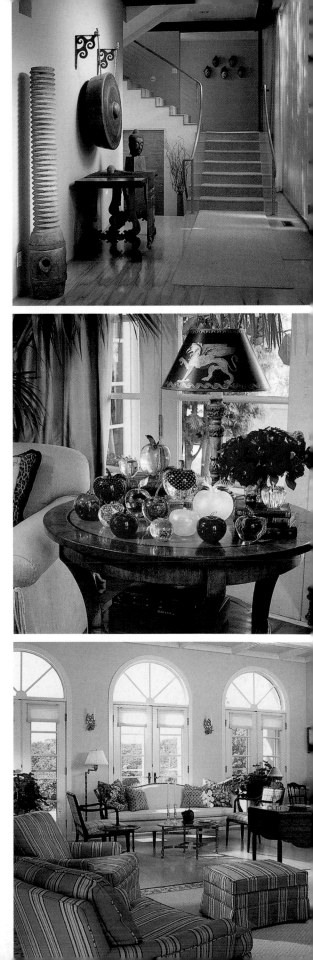

Unfortunately, many recently built houses lack such architectural elements as moldings, handsome door and window styles, and interesting fireplace mantels that add character. If this sounds like your home, there are a number of things you can do to improve its look.

For interiors, character is created with the addition of architectural elements and decorative accessories. Architectural elements enhance the structural bare bones of a room. By exchanging a pair of flush, windowless doors for French doors, a dark dining room can be changed into a sunny, well-lit space; by adding an ornamental ceiling medallion and a cornice, a plain ceiling can become a showpiece. Decorative accessories pull a design scheme together and reflect individuality. A display of majolica turns built-in shelving into a noteworthy feature; a staggered arrangement of black-and-white photography adds interest to a stairway.

In the course of planning your room design, you have two perfect opportunities to give character to the space on which you're working. The first occurs early on as you assess the basic room. Does it lack moldings? Do you want a fireplace? This is the time to decide what architectural features you want to change or incorporate. The second chance arrives once you've settled on the major design elements and turn your thoughts toward your accessories. Is there a collection that you want to highlight? Is there a tabletop or a niche that looks too empty? Then take stock of what items you have, and keep an eye out for accessories that appeal to you. This chapter will show you how to bring all of these elements together in an attractive—and very personal—decorating scheme.

ELEMENTS OF DESIGN

At the initial planning stage described in Chapter One, when you analyze structural features, the room under scrutiny may not have any architectural or decorative details. Unless it's been altered over time, a period house, such as a Colonial or Victorian, may be rich with ornamentation. Today, however, many houses replicate the facades of those period buildings but eliminate the architectural elements inside. If you are faced with a nondescript room, you can introduce those features with store-bought trim or architectural salvage. The result can be an elegant foundation upon which to layer your carefully chosen design.

You can create a sense of style and history by changing door or window styles; replacing stair rails, balusters, and newel posts; or adding fireplace mantels. A window or fireplace can easily become the new focal point of a room. Other, more subtle touches, such as molding, ceiling medallions, and hardware, give a room a well-heeled resonance.

DOORS

If an uninteresting interior door does nothing for a traditional or period room's design, you might consider replacing it with a door style that provides greater visual interest.

Most doors are made of either wood, metal, glass, or a combination of these three. The two most common types of

Top left: The glass panels on the door to the room adjoining this bedroom echo those of the window over the bed.

Left: A wall of windows and French doors opens this bedroom up to the views outside. The square window helps define the shape of the gable wall.

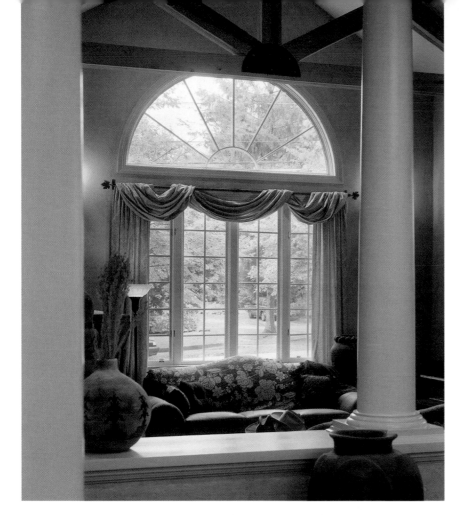

Left: Fanlight windows not only let in an abundance of natural light, they also serve as a focal point for any room.

Bottom left: The styles of these windows and doors not only complement the decor but also make the view a part of the room.

wood doors are flush and panel. *Flush* wood doors have a smooth surface; these doors may have solid or hollow-core construction and are preferred for contemporary settings. *Panel* doors consist of stiles (vertical members) and rails (horizontal members) with panels inserted between them; this type is favored for traditional interiors. An older and less common type is a *plank* door. It is composed of vertical boards (usually four or more) anchored together by two horizontal members and one diagonal member, which form a "Z" on the back of the door. Plank doors are suitable for country or rustic designs. In terms of styles for wood doors, there is quite a range, including double, pocket, Dutch (divided), louvered, and folding (accordion) types.

Metal doors, constructed of hollow steel with a solid-fiber infill, are rarely used for interiors in private homes, unless there is a need for protection from fire. Aside from flush-metal doors, some styles come with glass panels or louvers that may work for contemporary rooms.

Although frameless styles exist, glass doors are usually framed in wood or metal, such as French doors or siding glass doors. The glass itself offers a variety of decorative options: it can be etched, beveled, curved (slumped), and cut, as well as composed of stained or leaded glass or iridescent art glass.

WINDOWS
Replacing ordinary windows with decorative bow, bay, arch-top, or even casement windows is another change that pays off big in terms of

style. Before you choose a replacement window, consider how it will look from the exterior as well as the interior of your house; the new windows should be compatible with the architecture.

Residential windows come in wood, vinyl, or aluminum. *Wood* is the old standard; it can be painted or stained to match any decor, but it requires constant upkeep because weather exposure can cause deterioration. *Aluminum-* and *vinyl-clad wood* windows are two other choices; both are rot-proof and provide good insulation. A *vinyl* window is a sensible, low-maintenance option because it does not require painting or protective coatings, it resists corrosion and denting, and it offers excellent insulation. The color selection—white, gray, beige, and brown—is limited, however. Vinyl windows are available with wood cladding on the interior. *Aluminum* windows are easy to install but offer poor insulation qualities. They can be left unfinished (a metallic color) or coated with paint, enamel, or lacquer; wood cladding is also available.

Next, consider the basic types of windows and how they function. *Fixed* windows cannot be opened and are often used in combination with *operable* windows. *Double-hung* windows are the most common of the operable types; they have two sash that move up and down, which means that only half of the window can be open at any one time. *Casement* windows are hinged vertically to swing in or out in a doorlike manner; they are operated by a crank. *Awning* windows are hinged horizontally to swing in or out. *Jalousie* windows have horizontally placed, narrow strips of glass that are opened louverlike by a crank. *Sliding* windows have top and bottom tracks on which the sash move sideways.

These practical considerations are important for your comfort, but you should also explore the various architectural styles of windows to match one with your decor. A group of three windows with an arch over the center unit is the classical makeup of a *Palladian* window. Some variations have three arches (one large, two small) or one fanlight-style

Above: Arranging windows in unusual ways can produce interesting decorating effects. Note how the colored glass in the small window catches your eye.

Opposite: Walls made of windows turn any room into a sunroom or solarium. If you like this look, be sure the glazing you select is appropriate for the climate of your area.

arch over the three windows. This window tends to visually dominate a room, so it is good as a focal point.

A *picture* window is made up of one large fixed window flanked by two casements or double-hung units. As the name describes, picture windows are for framing dramatic views.

Like Palladian and picture windows, *bay* windows are also composed of three parts. The difference is that the windows are set at an angle to each other, creating an alcove. A curved version of this window is called either a *bow* window or a *circular bay*. A large bay window adds about 4 feet of extra space to a room, where you can situate a chair or a small dining table.

Clerestory windows are made of a strip of small, horizontal panes set high on a wall, near the ceiling. These windows are a good solution in spaces where you want natural light but need privacy.

There is also a variety of special small window shapes that are almost strictly decorative. These windows can be used independently or in combination with the standard types. An *elliptical* or *arched* window is often placed above double-hung or fixed windows, but it is also used alone in situations where a larger unit won't fit, such as in a dormer or a small bathroom. An *oval* (or *cameo)* window and a *circular* window are used in much the same way; both are sometimes located on narrow staircase landings to add light. For a more modern shape, a *triangular* window or a *trapezoidal* window is often paired with a large fixed window.

STAIRS

A staircase is also a good opportunity for embellishment, particularly because it is often the focal point of a space. Decorative newels, balusters, and railings are common stock millwork items. They're available in a variety of turned profiles, as well as standard sizes. With them, a staircase that was once only functional can become an attractive part of the room.

Other specialized brackets, with carved flourishes and fretwork-like designs, can further enhance a staircase. If you view a staircase from the side, the long leg of these L-shaped pieces fits beneath the edge of a tread, with the shorter leg extending the length of the riser. The bracket is simply nailed to the carriage the same way that you attach ordinary trim.

Clockwise (from left): Fireplaces are generally the focal point of any room. The fireplace mantle at left is a simple shelf that works well with this casual family room. Compare it with the more formal mantel below it. Mantel surrounds can consist of brick, fieldstone, or as shown here, marble or granite. Stairs also make a distinctive design statement. Decorative newel posts and turned balusters are easy-to-find stock items.

Another way to dress up an open stair is to paint it in contrasting hues. The newel post, railing, and treads can be painted in a dark color, while the balusters, trim, and carriage echo the color of the walls in the room. Installing ceramic tiles on the risers can also add color and pattern to stairs.

MANTELS

A fireplace is invariably the focal point of any room in which it's located. There is good reason why it's one of the most desirable features in any home, new or old. It adds warmth—visually or literally—and it's striking in looks.

You may have an existing fireplace that needs to be dressed up because of a missing mantel, or you may want to add a new fireplace to your home. Either way, learn before you go shopping for a mantel and other fireplace parts so that you get exactly what you want. Here's a quick review of the basics:

■ A *mantel* can be just a horizontal shelf above the fireplace opening or ornamental framing around the top and sides of the opening.

■ An *overmantel* is a decorative treatment above the mantel that often incorporates a picture, mirror, or some shelving. Many Victorian mantels had overmantels with mirrors flanked by shelves that displayed knickknacks, for example.

■ A *lintel* is a wood or stone beam that supports the top of the fireplace.

■ The *jambs* are vertical supports along the sides of the fireplace, holding up the mantel.

■ A *chimneypiece* is made up of the fireplace opening, mantel, and the overmantel.

■ A *hearth* is the floor that extends from the fireplace into the room. It is usually covered in a fire-resistant material, such as tile or brick.

■ A *flue* is the pipe or opening through which smoke from the fireplace is released.

■ Because the *chimney breast* contains the flue, it projects into the room. It is usually made of a fire-resistant material, such as stone, brick, or concrete.

Next, consider what type of fireplace will suit your decor best. The pared-down simplicity of a contemporary interior may call for a mantel-less (flush) fireplace, such as a stucco-finished wall around the opening, or an unadorned mantel. For traditional rooms, there is an unlimited choice of reproduction and salvaged mantels in period styles, including Colonial, Federal, Gothic, and Victorian. Mantels are usually made of marble, stone, wood, cast iron, or copper. A brick mantel is constructed as part of the entire fireplace; a wood mantel shelf is used for cobblestone and adobe fireplaces.

When choosing a mantel, keep certain clearances in mind. Make sure that woodwork, trim, and other combustible materials are at least 6 inches away from the fireplace opening. (This is the reason you'll often notice decorative tiles between the fireplace opening and a wooden mantel.) If a wooden mantel projects 1 1/2 inches, it should be at least 12 inches from the fireplace opening.

When buying a mantel from an architectural salvage source, have your measurements ready before you go. You don't want to guess whether this expensive—not to mention heavy—item will fit. Plus, salvaged mantels are one-of-a-kind pieces; the one you want may no longer be there if you have to leave and return on another day.

If you buy a salvaged wood mantel, you may want to strip off the paint. Proceed carefully, particularly if it is ornamented. Much of the detailing on period mantels (and some current types, too) is made not from wood but from composition ornament (called "compo" for short), a pliable material that is molded into intricate designs, such as

urns, swags, and rosettes, and that is painted or stained. Paint strippers may dissolve compo, so it is a good idea to work around these ornamented areas.

MOLDING AND TRIM

Decorative trim gives a room a finished appearance. Installation is fairly easy, and materials are reasonably priced. An enormous variety of stock and specialty trim exists in a wide range of materials, such as wood, plaster, and fiberglass.

From the ceiling to the floor, shaped trim called molding is used on most parts of the wall. The cornice is placed at the top, where the wall meets the ceiling. Moldings for cornices come in two main types: dramatic *crown molding* that is frequently combined with other molding styles for an opulent look or the simpler *cove molding* that eliminates the ceiling line but doesn't stand out. The *frieze* is a wide band, sometimes ornamented with swags, that runs under the cornice but above the picture rail. As the name suggests, the *picture rail* is used to hang artwork. A *chair rail* (or *dado cap*) is placed on a wall, around the room, 30 to 35 inches from the floor and is often used in conjunction with a *wainscot* or *dado* (waist-high paneling) on the lower portion of the wall. *Base moldings* give the floor line a higher profile and can be as elaborate or simple as you like. Window and door trim, called *casing*, is necessary to seal the gap between the jambs and wall. But again, it can be quite plain or more decorative, depending on taste.

Most of the molding profiles in use today have been around for centuries. Although the classical names for molding profiles may be off-putting, be assured that their forms are as familiar to most of us as is a panel door. Some of the common

profiles are *cavetto* or *cove*, a concave quarter-circle; *ovolo*, a convex quarter-round; *scotia*, a concave semicircle; *torus*, a convex semicircle; *ogee* (also called *cyma recta* and *cyma reversa*), an S-shaped form; *beaded*, a smaller, convex rounded form; and *fillet*, a flat, narrow strip separating other moldings. These profiles can be used to frame walls and openings without being intrusive on the design; they add a three-dimensional quality that most rooms need.

More-ornate moldings command more attention when incorporated into a design and should suit the overall decor. Some of the classic motifs that adorn moldings are: *acanthus*, a lobed leaf ornament; *anthemion,* the stylized flower and leaf of the honeysuckle; *dentil,* a series of ornamental notches; *egg-and-dart*, an oval-shaped detail that alternates with an arrow or tongue form; *guilloche*, a series of circular interlaced bands; and *paterae*, a cup-shaped ornament.

Left to right: **Adding crown molding to this relatively simple room provides a certain character that the room would not have otherwise. Many complex looking molding profiles, such as the one on this fireplace mantle, consist of a series of simple moldings installed together to achieve the finished appearance. A number of different molding and trim techniques come together in this formal foyer.**

HARDWARE AND GRILLES

Another place to look when scouting areas for embellishment is to the doors, large and small, that may provide a backdrop for decorative hardware. Door levers, knobs, and cabinetry pulls can be highly ornamental and a cost-effective way to deliver style. Metalwork such as heat registers, grilles, and grates are all available in decorative designs as well.

SPECIAL DETAILS

Once the basic room and all of its elements are in place, that's your cue to make the space truly your own. The decorative objects you choose to accent your rooms reflect your personality and can give your design an individuality as unique as your own.

Basically, decorative objects fall into two categories: art and accessories. Art can be paintings, framed prints or photos, sculpture, pieces of architectural salvage that are used as *objets d'art*, and even textiles. Accessories tend to be small

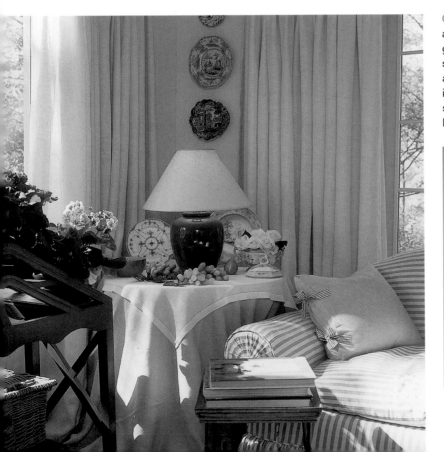

Clockwise (from above): The use of decorative objects adds a personal touch to your home. Try to create a theme for your groupings. For example, the rare books and personal items shown above bring warmth to a corner of this study. A casual area near the back door is a good location for the garden-inspired setting above right. Groupings are also a chance to show off personal collections as with the birdhouses shown below and the decorative plates at left.

color. Now imagine the same sofa table, but with porcelain figurines that are the same size, shape, and color but different images. The arrangement would still look balanced. *Asymmetry* is the opposite of symmetry. Using visual weight as a guide, unlike elements are grouped together to achieve an informal balance. An intricate wire birdcage can be placed with a small display plate on a stand and adjacent to three topiaries in various sizes, for instance. Each element in the arrangement is a counterpoint to the other: the wide birdcage plays against the tall topiaries and the round plate. (For more guidance on symmetry and asymmetry, see Chapter One, "The Basics of Design," on page 12.)

objects that are introduced into a room for either a practical reason or an aesthetic one (or for a combination of these purposes). A delicately patterned soup tureen flanked by silver candlesticks makes a functional and beautiful centerpiece on a dining room table, for example.

Art and accessories shouldn't always be treated as an afterthought in the design scheme. A large piece of art can influence your room's decor, as may collections. Consider these elements as you are designing the room. Accessories may play a background role, however, and can be worked in during the last phase of the design process.

Whether you are hanging a group of prints or displaying a pottery collection, the configurations are either symmetrical or asymmetrical. *Symmetry* is an arrangement that is a mirror image on either side of a central (unseen) line. Picture a sofa table with a pair of brass lamps and matching porcelain figurines flanking a flower-filled vase, for example. You can achieve *visual* symmetry with objects that don't match perfectly but are approximately the same size, height, or

ART

Historically, every inch of wall space was filled with art, creating visual chaos. Today the thinking is different. Art is shown to its greatest effect in uncluttered surroundings. A large modern painting has more impact if left alone on a wall, for instance. Small- or medium-size artworks or drawings are more impressive when placed together on a wall.

If you are displaying drawings or photography, make sure that the frame is large enough to accommodate a mat. The frame should be 1 to 3 inches larger in dimension than the picture. For an up-to-date look, the trend is to make the mat at least 6 inches larger than a photograph or an illustration; this can be an effective way to draw attention to a small piece of art or photography.

When choosing matting, try picking up accent colors from your decor. If you feel your accents don't work with the art, look at your room's main hues. If all else fails, pick a neutral color that you like from the work itself to serve as the mat's color.

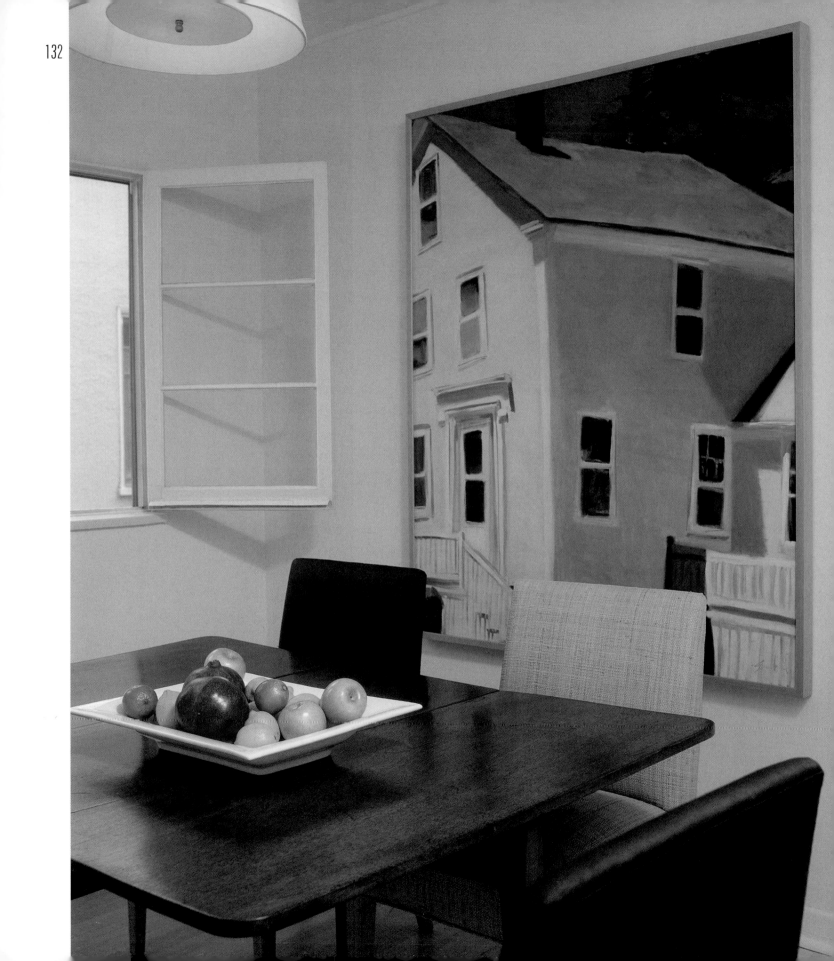

Frames should coordinate with but not necessarily duplicate any other frames used in the room. Unless you're making a statement with the juxtaposition, the frame style should also reflect the overall look of the room.

When buying a frame, examine the quality of the material from which it is constructed. Does it feel flimsy? Make sure that there aren't any gaps at the joints (the mitered corners of the frame). What is the condition of the finish? There shouldn't be any flaking or discoloration of metal frames; the finish on wood should be smooth and blemish free.

It takes some trial and error to create a pleasing wall arrangement. Here's how to do it.

SMART steps

ONE: Experiment with the elements. Before you hammer a nail into the wall, place all of the art on the floor, and try out different arrangements. A vertical grouping will make a room seem higher; a horizontal one will make the room seem wider. Don't get stuck in a rut: you don't have to arrange everything in a row. A triangular shape might work for an end wall in a room with a cathedral ceiling; a rectangle or oval in an area above a mantel or sofa. Check out the other geometric placement possibilities for art on page 134.

TWO: Find the right location on the wall. Art should sit 6 to 9 inches above a sofa or at eye level when you are seated. Too high, and it will look like it's floating; too low, and it will interfere with headroom. When working with more than one picture, start by marking and measuring the spot for the center print. Then hang the middle row vertically, and follow with the rest.

THREE: Check the proportions. A framed piece that is too small will look insignificant over a large piece of furniture. The frame should be approximately two-thirds the size of the piece over which it hangs. If you still want to use the small piece, pair it with another that is approximately the same size.

FOUR: Balance out the arrangement. In groupings where frames vary in size, try to keep the weightier pieces on the bottom, or place two smaller elements next to it. A large piece will anchor the grouping and keep the arrangement from seeming top-heavy or from trailing off.

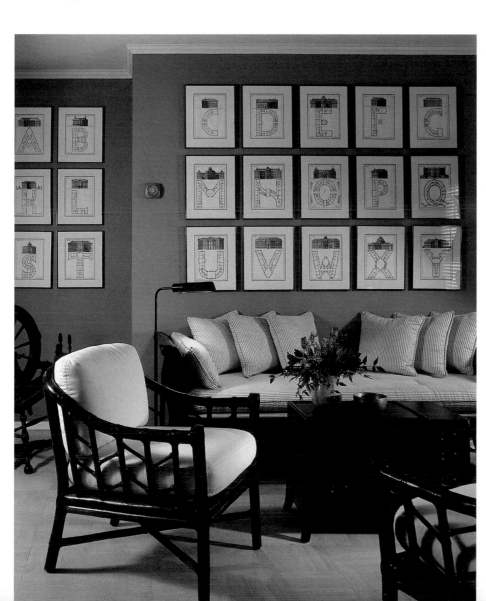

Opposite and left: The sparse furnishings in this room provide balance without softening the impact of the painting. Framed architectural "alphabet" drawings arranged in a symmetrical pattern help bring order to the room at left.

Art Arrangements

Don't get locked into arranging framed pieces in rows. Try imagining a circle for prints hung in an entry. Or let the shape of your walls influence the arrangement, such as a triangle for a gable wall. Even if you stay within the framework of a rectangle, pictures and objects in various sizes will keep the grouping from looking too rigid. Just make sure to balance the visual weight of the arrangement (below and top right). A grid pattern works when you have different size mats; the orderly rows unify the pieces (bottom right).

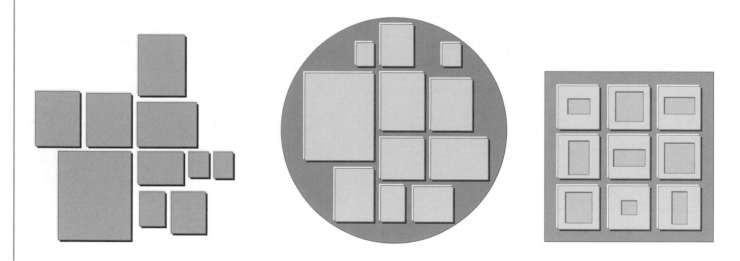

FIVE: Create unity. A mixture of art that doesn't have a common theme or color can be unified by using matching frames or mats. Conversely, art with a common theme or color, such as black-and-white photography, will work well as an arrangement even if the frames don't match.

TEXTILES AS ART

Don't overlook the beauty and versatility of textiles when choosing your decorating accessories. Quilts, tapestries, appliqués, and printed cloths such as batik can stand alone on a wall, adding texture and color to the room. Textiles can be mounted on a wall in a number of ways. Smaller cloths can be conventionally framed and sandwiched between glass. Because it is difficult to keep fabric straight and balanced within the frame, you might consider turning the job over to a professional framer.

Larger cloths or rugs can be tacked directly to a wood furring strip, or 1×2, that has been nailed into the wall studs. As an alternative, you can attach the fabric to a wooden or cast-iron dowel with decorative finials (the type used for draperies). To attach the fabric to the dowel without damaging it, create a pocket by looping the top piece over the dowel and stitching it together.

ACCESSORIES

With decorative accessories, there is no right or wrong in the pieces you choose. Use favorite found objects, collectibles, and tabletop items such as candlesticks, vases, and pottery. While there are no hard and fast rules about what will and won't work, there are certain guidelines that can help you determine where and how to display the items you select. Familiarizing yourself with them will make it easy to create attractive tabletop arrangements.

ONE: Group objects by similarities. Choose items that share the same color, material, shape, or motif. For instance, even if the pieces aren't the same height and shape, a collection of blue-and-white delft pottery can make an impressive arrangement because the color ties the group together. Likewise, a row of Fiestaware pitchers, each in different color, will work visually because of the repeating shape.

TWO: Vary the elevation. Any grouping benefits from including elements of different sizes. Pairs of objects that are all the same height can be monotonous. Instead of placing two topiaries with two candlesticks, try putting the topiaries with two picture frames. Small items, such as figurines or a decorative plate, can get lost in an arrangement. Try raising them up with a small pedestal or a stand.

Right: Group together similar items to make an interesting decorative display. Sometimes the location is as interesting as the items themselves.

THREE: Add depth. Don't always place items in a straight line, which can look static. Instead, stagger the pieces from back to front. For example, if you have three objects, place them in a triangle. With a larger number of objects, experiment with overlapping triangles.

FOUR: Choose a focal point. If the grouping is not coming together, arrange everything around one major object, such as a sculpture or a framed print.

FIVE: Don't overdo it. A display of too many items looks like clutter. Choose accessories judiciously. Store extra items away, and freshen up your arrangements periodically with these pieces.

a gallery of...

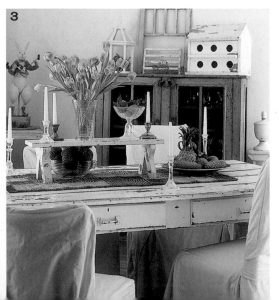

1 A stone fireplace with a cut-stone mantel is the focal point of this room.

2 A collection of personal items adds visual interest to this stairway and makes use of what would otherwise be wasted space.

3 A short bench makes an unusual centerpiece for this dining table.

4 A random-pattern wall treatment provides background for these groupings of decorative objects.

...smart **ideas**

1 A fanlight window and exposed trusses add interest to the high end wall of this room.

2 A window provides a setting for showing off
prints. Place the art at eye level for best results.

3 French doors often add more architectural interest
to a room than doors with a single pane of glass.

4 Sheer full-length curtains filter the natural light
without hiding the door.

5 Distinctive molding around an interior doorway
enriches the entire room.

THE FACTS ON FURNITURE

FURNITURE FOR YOUR HOME ■
MAKING CHOICES ■ **FURNITURE STYLES** ■
JUDGING QUALITY ■
RECYCLING YOUR FURNITURE

Furniture plays a major part in your home's design. Fortunately, there is much from which to choose—everything from just-created designs to reproductions of classic pieces. Your choices will depend on your personal tastes, of course, but there are other considerations as well.

As with all aspects of design, you'll want to examine the function of both the room and the furniture. Does the furniture have to be versatile and comply with a multitude of needs? How much wear and tear do you expect it to handle? Are you planning to use it in a room intended for occasional entertaining or everyday use? Should it be casual or formal, built-in or movable?

Next, you'll have to decide on a style. Taking cues from your preferences and the other elements that you've chosen for your decorating scheme as well as the architectural style of your house will help you narrow down your choices.

You'll also have to think about cost. Nearly all furniture styles are available in low-end to high-priced versions. Paying top dollar doesn't mean you're buying the best—only durable materials and reliable construction can ensure that. But if an item is very cheap, something probably has been skimped on in the manufacturing or finishing process to bring down the cost.

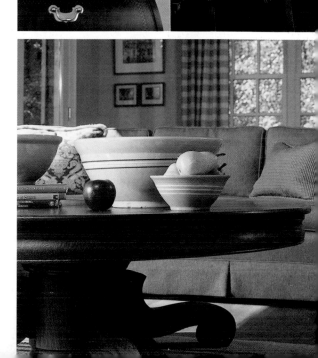

Working with existing furniture is always an option. Although the cost of reupholstering or refinishing may be comparable with buying something new, older pieces (those manufactured before the 1950s) may be better constructed or more valuable for sentimental reasons.

In this chapter you'll become acquainted with all of the issues that deserve your consideration in order to make sound decisions about furniture.

FURNITURE FOR YOUR HOME

Furniture has three basic functions: for seating, sleeping, and storage. Furniture can also efficiently divide space. Within a large room, you might want to create a cozy sitting area in front of a fireplace while storing entertainment equipment at the other end of the room. Or you may need to define living and dining areas within one room. A low-backed sofa can act as a room divider, as can a shelving unit or a sofa table. The key is not to block sources of natural light when dividing space with furniture.

SEATING

Furniture that functions as seating comes with a variety of options. It can roll, swivel, tilt or recline, stack, fold, or convert to another use such as a bed. Seating can also take numerous forms. Sofas, for instance, come in all shapes and sizes. There are three-seaters and two-seaters (sometimes called love seats). Other sofa terms are Chesterfield (overstuffed, tuffted upholstery with padded arms), Lawson (arms lower than the back), and tuxedo (arms the same height as the back). Backs of sofas can be termed camel back, channel back, or tufted back, all of which are firm, spring-supported styles. Pillow backs are available as either attached or loose. Multi-pillow backs, or scatter backs, have more back pillows than seat cushions. Base treatments include skirts (with various pleating designs), upholstered legs, plinth (block) bases, and bun feet.

Chairs are categorized as upholstered or occasional. Popular upholstered chairs are termed club or wing. A barrel chair has a rounded back that extends in a smooth line with the

Above: In addition to storing items, casegoods can serve as room dividers and window seats as shown above. This arrangement would work in a bedroom or a family room.

arms. A club chair is square with arms lower than its back, and a wing chair has a high back with winglike extensions at head level. Occasional chairs are usually smaller than upholstered chairs. Characterized by wooden arms and legs that are combined with seats and backs that are sometimes upholstered, occasional chairs are often traditional in design.

Modular seating comes in any number of armless units, single-arm end modules, and corner pieces that can be arranged in various configurations to suit different spaces and needs. This type of seating is differerent from a sectional sofa, which consists of simply one corner unit and two end pieces.

SLEEPING

Furniture for sleeping ranges from futon frames to platform beds and bedsteads with head- and foot-boards. Some bedsteads also include bedside stands, lamps, and built-in storage compartments. Convertible sofa beds offer extra sleeping accommodations for small spaces. Other options are the loft bed, which is on a raised platform and frees the space beneath for other uses; bunk beds; and trundle beds, which slide under another bed when not in use.

STORAGE

Storage furniture is available to suit a wide range of needs. In the furniture industry, it is referred to as *casegoods* because of its boxlike structure (although tables also come under this category). It may include bookcases or any other type of open shelves, cabinets with hinged or sliding doors, cabinets that house audio or video equipment, breakfronts, chests, armoires, or desks. Casegoods come in many shapes and sizes and offer a place to display or protect collectibles and other valuables. Modular pieces can be used to create storage walls or room dividers. Storage walls are connected units that fit from floor to ceiling. They divide space while providing access to storage from both sides. Room dividers serve a similar purpose but do not extend to the ceiling or from wall to wall. They are most commonly used to divide living and dining areas.

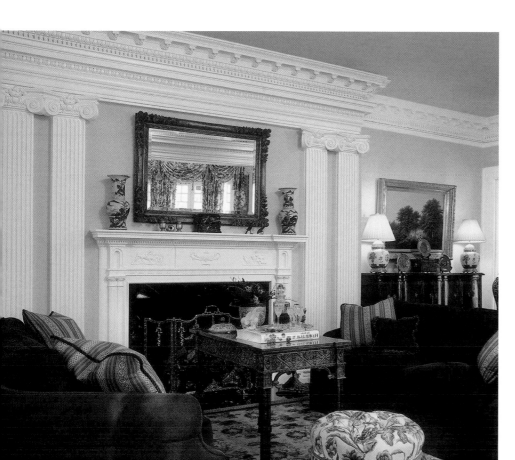

Storage furniture for the bedroom consists of dressers, vanities, and chests. These pieces are categorized by the size of their contents. The smallest is a lingerie chest, followed by the drawer chest. The door chest is larger still, with drawers at the bottom and two doors at the top. The armoire, or wardrobe, is the largest chest available. A clothes rod inside defines it as a wardrobe.

Sometimes these pieces can serve multipurpose needs, so think about which ones you can get the most from, particularly if you are short on space. An armoire is an excellent example. It can be used in any room in the house. In the kitchen, it becomes a pantry; in the family room, it's an entertainment center; in the bedroom, it's a clothes closet; and in a spacious bath or in a hallway, it's a handy place to store linens and toiletries.

Left: Furniture styles dictate the style of the room. These traditional pieces work well with the fireplace and woodwork.

Above: Buy the furniture you like, but also consider the way in which the room will be used before making a purchase.

MAKING CHOICES

Once you've considered how you want to use the furniture in a room, you'll have to decide on a style that will coordinate with your decor. This is a matter of personal taste and your lifestyle. Even if you have a particular look in mind, you may want to take your time before making a final decision. Following these Smart Steps will help.

ONE: Look around you. What are your favorite pieces of furniture? What do you like about them? List the colors that most appeal to you. Do you have special items, such as artwork or family heirlooms, that you'd like to blend with new furnishings? List the things that you would like to keep

and what you think you may want to replace, either now or in the future. If you're on a tight budget, plan for things for which you might be able to save in the meantime.

TWO: Consider your family's lifestyle. Do you have young children or pets? Do you spend a lot of time at home, or are you always coming and going? Do you entertain frequently? How do you entertain, with a backyard barbecue or a formal sit-down dinner? Be smart: don't buy delicate upholstered pieces for the kids to flop on with the dog. Sometimes it makes sense to put your hankering for such things on the back burner and shop for something durable. Similarly, if you're an expert chef and love to serve meals on fine china by candlelight, splurge on your formal dining room's furniture.

THREE: Play up the architectural style of your house. Find out when your house or apartment building was built. Research its architectural style using books on architectural history from the library, if necessary. Consider a period decorating style like Victorian or Colonial if it works well with the house style. Be sure to design around architectural details such as built-in cabinets or bookcases, which add character to your home. If you have hardwood floors laid with an interesting or contrasting pattern around the perimeter of the room, don't obscure them completely with the furnishings you choose. Detailing around your door and window frames and at the tops and bottoms of your walls can help you decide whether a room would look best as a formal or informal setting. Think about how some types of furnishings complement these details.

FOUR: Narrow down your choices. If you're still at a loss, look at magazine pictures of room settings. Clip out your favorites. After you've collected a few, look at them all together. If they all have things in common, *voilà*: you may have just found your favorite style. If you've clipped examples of different styles, group the similar rooms together, and pin up each grouping in separate areas on the wall. Keep them pinned up for several days, and look at them as you walk by. At the end of the week, can you say which group of pictures is your favorite?

Right: Although recently manufactured, traditional-style furniture, such as this four-poster bed and drawer chest, is based on designs that were popular before 1900.

FURNITURE STYLES

Three general furniture styles to consider are traditional, contemporary, and country. Within each of these categories are several different styles of furniture that work together.

Traditional. Traditional-style furniture takes its design cues from furniture made before 1900. Here you will find familiar period pieces, such as a Queen Anne chair or a Chippendale table. The original designs take their names from influential people of the times as well as from architectural styles, such as Baroque, Gothic, and Victorian. Traditional sofas and chairs are often upholstered with heavy, luxurious fabrics and elaborate trim. Most furniture of this style is tailored with kick-pleat skirting and rolled arms. You'll find button-tufting and nailhead trim as well as fringe, braid, and cord trim and other fine upholstery details on the cushions and frame.

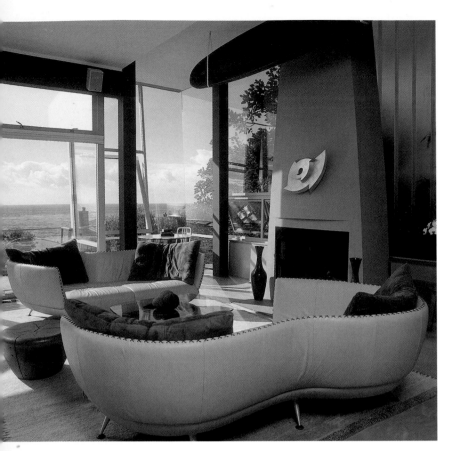

Contemporary. Furniture styles from 1900 to the present are termed contemporary. These styles also reflect the Modern movement, including Arts & Crafts, Art Deco, and Art Nouveau. Contemporary furniture designs are streamlined and incorporate natural materials such as wood and stone with metal and glass. Upholstered sofas and chairs tend to be larger than traditional styles—you won't find buttons or skirts on these pieces.

Country. Like its European counterparts, American country-style furniture is casual and unpretentious. It often has a period flavor, but one that is rustic rather than genteel. Upholstered pieces might include ruffled skirts, pillows, and other homespun details. Tables and storage pieces are usually made of pine or oak, sometimes painted rather than stained.

You may choose to stay true to these design themes or create an eclectic mix of styles in your home. Think about softening the hard lines of contemporary furniture with a few country-style accents, such as handcrafted pillows or rugs. A few pieces of antique furniture can complement the architectural style of your home no matter which general decor you've chosen.

JUDGING QUALITY

Even if you have a good idea of what types of furniture you're looking for as well as the general style that appeals to you, there is a maze of purchase options you'll have to negotiate. How do you know what you're getting for your money? What's the difference between the $800 sofa and the $1,200 one? How do you judge the quality of a table? These are important questions. To answer them, it will help to understand what's beneath the upholstery of a sofa and how a wood chair or table is put together.

Above left: Contemporary furniture relies on designs made popular during the 20th Century.

Left: A wood cabinet and rustic wood island display the casual feeling of country-style furniture.

Clockwise (from left): **How do you tell quality furniture from so-so furniture? First, check the frame; it should be made of kiln-dried hardwood, such as maple, poplar, or ash. Look for eight-way hand-tied springs that move up and down easily. A layer of cotton prevents the upholstery fabric from touching the springs or frame.**

ANATOMY OF A SOFA

Quality furniture is comfortable and durable. Four elements determine the integrity of upholstered furniture: the frame, the springs, the cushions, and the upholstery fabric.

Frames. High-quality frames are made of seasoned hardwood, kiln-dried to resist warping. The frame is joined using dowels and corner blocks that are screwed and glued together. Legs should be extensions of the frame and not attached with screws. Center legs add additional support.

Springs. The spring systems in upholstered furniture are either hand-tied coils or sagless (sinuous) constructions. Eight-way hand-tied springs are of the highest quality. These funnel-like coils are tied with twine to each of the eight adjacent coils and attached to a heavy-duty webbing underneath with steel clips. This type of construction gives even comfort and prevents "bottoming out" of the seat no

matter how heavy the sitter. Four- or six-way tied springs are not nearly as supportive. Good-quality webbing is tightly woven and may be reinforced by steel straps under each row of springs.

Sagless, or sinuous, springs are S-shaped, flat wavy bands of steel that are fastened to the front rail and run front to back a few inches apart. Sagless springs have a firmer feel than coil springs and are often used in contemporary pieces that are lower to the floor.

Right: Modular furniture allows for a number of different configurations. As with other materials, leather is available in a number of different grades.

Cushions. The frame and springs are the foundation for the cushions. A good frame is padded with cotton or poly-dacron so that the upholstery fabric never touches the wood. Quality seat cushions and loose back cushions consist of a combination of down and other feathers wrapped around a polyurethane foam core—or loose down or feathers for back cushions. Test the quality of a cushion by lifting it. If it feels light, it may be made of poor materials. A 2- × 2-foot cushion should not weigh less than 2 pounds.

Back cushions are supported by springs or webbing. If back cushions are loose as opposed to attached, there are

SMARTtip — Terms of the Trade

Collection: A grouping of related furniture pieces from the same manufacturer. Furniture is usually displayed in collections.

Reproductions: Copies of fine antiques made with materials and details similar to those of the originals.

Adaptations: Furniture designs that are loosely based on originals. Tags may say "based on," "adapted from," or "in the style of."

Sectionals: Upholstered seating pieces that are made in three or more sections that fit together in a particular configuration.

Modulars: An unlimited number of pieces that are upholstered and may be used in many configurations.

COM: Custom-ordered material; means the furniture is made to your specifications. For instance, manufacturers may offer you a choice of COM fabrics or let you supply your own.

Apartment-size furniture: Furniture that has been scaled down to fit in smaller spaces.

RTA: Ready-to-assemble furniture; comes in pieces. Because you put it together, it costs less.

no springs. Webbing will supply the only support. This type of construction is less expensive than attached cushions and will feel less resilient than spring support. Pocketed springs are best for comfortable back cushions. You may also find some pieces with sinuous spring backs for less money.

Upholstery. You can often choose from a range of price levels, called *grades,* of fabric or coverings. These grades are assigned a letter from A to D, with A at the high end. Grading is determined by the quality of the materials, the amount of fabric needed for a good match of the pattern, and the source of the pattern design (with famous designers' patterns costing more). An important factor to consider when selecting upholstery fabric is durability. In general, tightly woven fabrics wear best. Fabrics with woven-in patterns wear better than printed fabrics. Various natural and synthetic fibers offer different looks and textures as well as cleanability and wearability performance.

Natural fibers include cotton, linen, wool, and silk. Cotton is soft to the touch and durable. However, its fibers will disintegrate under prolonged exposure to direct sunlight.

Right: Both natural fibers, such as cotton, linen, and wool, as well as man-made fibers, such as polyester and nylon, are available for upholstery. Make your decision based on the look, feel, and durability of the fabric.

Cotton is also less stain resistant than synthetic fibers. Linen has a tailored, crisp feel and is one of the most durable fibers available. It is most often found in natural colors because it does not dye well. It, too, can be damaged by sunlight. Wool is extremely hardy, as well as abrasion and stain resistant, but should be mothproofed before use. Silk is a beautiful but fragile fabric. Soft and luxurious, it is difficult to clean and discolors when it is exposed to strong light.

Synthetic fibers have been developed as alternatives to natural fibers and are often blended with them. Polyester is strong and easy to clean. It withstands direct sunlight and is flame- and abrasion-resistant. Rough in texture, it is often blended with natural fibers to soften its touch. Olefin is used to create heavy, textured fabrics. It is a coarse and bulky fiber that is strong and stain resistant. However, it does not wear well under direct sunlight. Nylon is the strongest and most soil-resistant fiber. Recent developments in nylon give it the look and feel of wool. It, too, is sensitive to sunlight.

As an informed shopper, you will be able to make your purchase with confidence. Never judge the quality of an upholstered piece solely by the fabric you see on it. The fabric can be easily replaced, but the frame and support system cannot. Always go to a reputable furniture retailer when purchasing upholstered pieces. Because you can't see what's underneath the fabric, you'll have to ask questions

SMARTtip — Price Points

Keep the following in mind if you want to trim off some of the cost of your purchases:

Frame design: Curves, such as rounded arms, are more expensive to cover than straight lines.

Pattern design: Large, complex patterns are harder to match than small, overall designs.

Details: Trimmings, such as pleats, welts, braids, buttons, and fringe, all add to the final cost.

about the construction. So it's important that the salesperson be knowledgeable and trustworthy. If you're still not satisfied, contact the manufacturer.

THE SIGNS OF GOOD CONSTRUCTION

Furniture can be constructed of hardwood or softwood. Hardwoods come from deciduous trees, such as cherry, maple, oak, ash, pecan, teak, walnut, mahogany, and poplar. Hardwoods are often used in high-quality furniture because they are stronger than softwoods. Softwoods come from conifer trees, such as fir, pine, redwood, cedar, and cypress. Softwoods have to be well-seasoned and kiln-dried before use, or they will split and splinter easily.

Veneers are thin sheets of hardwood that are glued to a core of less expensive wood. They were once associated with poor-quality furniture, but today's wood veneers may sometimes be stronger than solid wood: wide boards of solid wood will warp and crack with changes in temperature and humidity, while veneer is much more stable in these conditions.

A "solid wood" label allows use of composition boards, such as plywood and particleboard, in areas of the furniture that will remain unseen. You will find these materials applied this way in medium-priced furniture. In budget-priced furniture, they may be used more extensively.

Joining Methods. Wood can be joined together with staples, nails, screws, joints, and glue. Several of these methods may be used in one piece of furniture. To evaluate quality, look for strong construction at the joints. Joints are where one part of a piece of furniture matches up with another. They are usually glued together or fastened with screws. Staples are used only on the cheapest furniture and should not be used to join any piece that bears weight.

Furniture joints can be made using one of the following joining methods.

■ *Butt joints* simply join the flat sides of two pieces where they meet. They are weak joints and should be used only in places that are not subject to stress or weight, such as where a bureau top meets the frame.

■ *Miter joints* are often used to join pieces at right angles. The ends of the two pieces are angled to fit together perfectly. These joints may be reinforced with dowels, nails, or screws.

■ *Tongue and-groove joints* are used to join two boards together side-by-side, as in a tabletop. A groove is cut into one side of a board and a tongue on the other. When placed side-by-side, the tongue of one board fits into the groove of the next and so on.

■ *Dovetail joints* are used to join drawer sides. Notches cut into the ends of each piece should fit together tightly.

■ *Double-dowel joints* use two dowels to peg joints together. These are sturdy joints used in casegood framing and to attach legs to side rails of chairs.

■ *Mortise-and-tenon joinery* is the strongest method of joining pieces of wood at right angles. The end of one piece of wood is shaped to fit into a hole in the other.

■ *Corner blocks* provide extra support for dowel joints. They can be held in place with either glue or wood screws. However, screws should not be used on everything just because they hold the joints rigidly. A good example is a chest of drawers. Glue blocks should be used to attach the top of the frame because wood panels can expand and contract, which causes the wood to split.

Left to right: The classic wing chair, with its distinctive design, has been a mainstay of traditional living rooms for years. An updated rocking chair would complement a number of home designs. Improved manufacturing processes allow for mass production of distinctive chair designs. The metal frame of the chair above is offset by the stitched leather arms and upholstered seat.

Identifying Your Furniture

Poke your nose into almost anyone's basement, attic, or garage, and you'll likely find a hodgepodge of old furniture. Style clues to look for include the shapes of the arms, legs, and back, as well as any ornamentation and finish. Mixing similar styles is perfectly acceptable and may even add interest to a boring room. Just keep in mind that some combinations work; others don't. Here's a quick reference that can help you decide whether to take a particular piece of furniture out of storage and incorporate it into your home's decor.

◄ Ball-and-Claw Leg
A cabriole—a furniture leg that curves and narrows down into an ornamental foot—distinguishes this style. It mixes well with other formal, eighteenth-century-inspired designs.

▼ Spindle Leg
In a highly polished rich wood, spindle-legged furniture is at home with other traditional styles. Made from pine or oak and sometimes with a painted finish, it takes on a country-style personality.

► Chippendale Leg
The later, less ornate version of Chippendale style pairs well with any eighteenth-century look, especially formal English-inspired furniture such as Queen Anne or Windsor.

► Contemporary Leg
Streamlined contemporary pieces crafted in natural or man-made materials defy fads. Other styles that coordinate well with the look are simple Shaker and geometric Art Deco pieces.

◄ French Provincial Leg
The French version of country style has graceful, curvaceous legs that make it a good match with almost any furniture that has European flair.

◄ Tuxedo Sofa
A rectilinear frame and cushions look contemporary, but you can mix this plain sofa with practically any other style.

► Chesterfield Sofa
Rounded arms and tufted upholstery are its hallmarks. Pair it with any eighteenth-century-style pieces.

◄ Camelback Sofa
The undulating shape of its back inspired its name. Depending on the uphostery, it works well with country, traditional, or period pieces.

► Lawson Sofa
Both traditional and country-style furniture coordinates with this sofa, which has rounded arms that are lower than its back.

Finishes. The final touch on a piece of wood furniture is its finish. Finishes can add color and protection through the use of stains, paints, or lacquers. A clear finish will allow the natural grain of the wood to show through. Wood stains will change the color of the wood. Finishes can make a piece of furniture look refined or rustic.

Distressing is a popular means of making new wood look old. The wood is literally battered before the finish is applied, aging it and enhancing its rustic charm. These finishes tend to hide any scratches or fingerprints the furniture may be exposed to, so they make good choices for use in active areas such as family rooms and for rustic, country-style decors.

Painted finishes are also popular for a nostalgic look. Unlike a distressed finish, however, paint tends to highlight flaws in the wood. This makes painted pieces more expensive than those with natural finishes because extra care must be taken at the factory to remove imperfections from the wood.

Finishes should always be strong enough to resist moisture. Inexpensive pieces may be simply coated with a layer of polyurethane. The finishing of high-quality furniture includes sanding, applying multiple coats of a clear finish with sanding between coats, waxing, and hand buffing. Compare the look and feel between inexpensive and expensive pieces. Always check that the surface is hard, smooth, and even. Watch for uneven colorations, bubbles, or cracks in the surface. If you're debating about whether or not to retain your existing furniture, examine the integrity of its structure and the condition of its finish. If you own genuine antiques that need repair, contact the American Institute for Conservation of Historic and Artistic Works, in Washington, D.C., to find a qualified restorer. Antiques are loosely defined as pieces more than 100 years old.

SMARTtip — Casegoods

Casegoods refers to any piece of furniture that is used for storage, such as a chest of drawers; tables are also part of this category. The furniture industry uses a variety of labels to denote the construction materials. The meanings of these labeling terms are regulated by the Federal Trade Commission.

■ *Solid wood* (i.e., "solid oak" or "solid pine") means that the exposed surfaces are made of solid wood without any veneer or plywood. Other woods may be used on unexposed surfaces such as drawer sides and backs.

■ *Genuine wood* means that all exposed parts of the furniture are constructed of a veneer of a type of wood over hardwood plywood.

■ *Wood* means all of the parts of the furniture are made of some type of wood.

■ *Man-made materials* refers to plastic laminate panels. The furniture may also include molded plastic that mimics wood panels, carving, or trim.

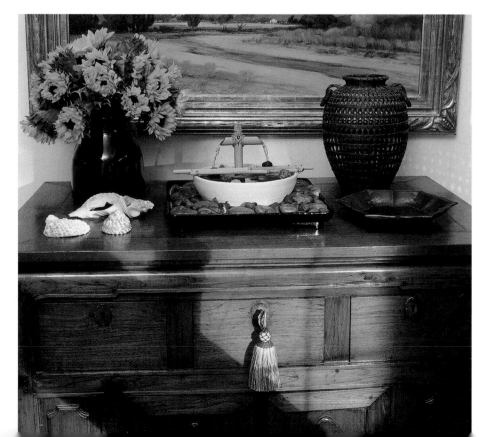

SMART tip   Quality Checks

When shopping for wood furniture you'll find varying levels of quality and pricing. Use this checklist to judge what you're getting for your money.

Frames

- ◼ Veneers and laminates should be securely joined to the base material.

- ◼ Joints bearing weight should be reinforced with corner blocks.

- ◼ Back panels should be screwed into the frame.

- ◼ Long shelves should have center supports.

Drawers

- ◼ Drawers should fit well, glide easily, and have stops.

- ◼ Drawer bottoms should be held by grooves, not staples or nails.

- ◼ Drawer interiors should be smooth and sealed.

- ◼ Drawer corners should have dovetail joints.

Doors

- ◼ Cabinet doors should open and close smoothly.

- ◼ Hinges and other hardware should be strong and secure.

Finishes

- ◼ All finishes should feel smooth unless they are intentionally distressed or crackled.

Opposite: Furniture tags can tell you much about the piece. "Solid wood" means all exposed parts are made of the named species. "Genuine wood" means exposed sections are made of plywood or hardwood covered by a veneer.

Above right: The traditional method of staining wood and then protecting it with a clear finish is still among the most popular furniture treatments, especially for traditional furniture. Look for smooth finishes with even color throughout.

Right: Painted finishes are good choices for less expensive woods. They allow you to express your individuality, and they help the piece fit with the decor of the rest of the room. Factory painted finishes are often more expensive than clear finishes.

RECYCLING YOUR FURNITURE

Do you have a favorite old chair, or is there a wonderful piece you found at a flea market last month that you'd love to include in your new room? If so, slipcovering, refinishing, or reupholstering may be an alternative to shopping for brand-new furniture. Although re-covering won't necessarily save you money, it will save those family heirlooms and antique shop rarities. As long as the wood frame is well-constructed and in good condition with no dry rot, worm holes, or loose or broken joints, those pieces can be brought back to life using new fabric.

ONE: Assess the level of skill needed. You can choose to do the work yourself or hire a professional. Depending on the shape it's in, wood furniture requires various levels of skill to restore or refinish it. Fitted slipcovers require careful measuring, good sewing skills, and many hours of labor. Reupholstering is a fine art that uses special techniques. You may be able to find classes in your area if you'd like to learn these skills.

Finding a professional upholsterer or furniture restorer is best done by word of mouth. Ask your coworkers and neighbors for references. Fabric stores that carry upholstery material might be able to refer you to someone, or look in the Yellow Pages of your local phone book under "Furniture" or "Furniture makers." Make an appointment to visit the person's shop. Ask to see examples of their work.

TWO: Know what to expect. Make sure that the refinisher or upholsterer shows you what he or she plans to do with your piece beforehand and gives you an estimate for the work. First, the frame should be stripped and checked for any weaknesses. Repairs should be made to weak joints by redoweling, regluing, and rescrewing (never nailing) joints together. All hardware should be removed and the frame cleaned. If the seat platform of an upholstered piece is weak, the upholsterer should replace it and cover it with burlap. This should be hand-sewn to the springs in a diamond pattern to prevent it from slipping. A layer of horsehair gives resiliency to the seat and should be covered with cotton to prevent the horsehair from poking through. A fine upholsterer will then cover the cotton padding with muslin.

The vertical surfaces of the frame should always be covered with webbing, never cardboard, and then layered with bonded Dacron. Depending on the desired plumpness of the filling, an upholsterer may use polyester wrapped in either Dacron or down. Down is the most expensive option.

Two, "Adding Color and Texture," for more information.) It's always a sensible idea to buy fabric that has been treated at the mill for stain resistance if it will get a lot of use, but it's not worth the extra money for a sprayed-on treatment that you can apply yourself.

Also, keep in mind that a talented reupholsterer can change the look of your furniture in subtle ways with fabric. For instance, a contemporary piece can be made more traditional by adding a skirt along the bottom. Neat pleats in the skirting will give the piece a tailored appearance, while ruffles will complement a country-style decor. When ordering fabric, think about extra material for coordinating window dressings and throw pillows.

FOUR: Calculate yardage. Some upholsterers will work with fabric you supply; others will sell it to you. Whether working with a professional or on your own, make sure you calculate the needed yardage carefully before buying the fabric. Here are some general guidelines for how much you will need for reupholstery; slipcovers require slightly more.

Opposite: Use found furniture, or pieces that have outlived their original usefulness, in different ways to achieve a unique look. Here an old cupboard holds bed linens.

Above: Slipcovers offer new life to furniture that is worn but still structurally sound.

THREE: Select the fabric. Fabric considerations for reupholstering are comparable to selecting a new piece of furniture. For a formal look, consider a brocade, damask, or velvet. If your style is casual, a linen or chintz may be more suitable. (See "Upholstery," on page 148 of this chapter, and the box "Design Materials," on page 43 of Chapter

■ **Three-cushion sofa:** No skirt, 10 yards; tailored skirt, 12 yards; pleated or gathered skirt, 14 yards

■ **Wing chair:** No skirt, 5 yards; loose seat cushion, $5^1/2$ yards; skirted, $6^1/2$ yards

■ **Club chair:** No skirt, 5 yards; skirted, $6^1/2$ yards

Lastly, avoid trendy looks. Buy classic, quality pieces that will last a lifetime. Remember, the new furniture that you buy today may have heirloom value tomorrow and may possibly become a treasure for the next generation to enjoy.

a gallery of...

1 A chest contains elements of traditional and modern designs.

2   Polished wood furniture with upholstered seats enhances a formal dining room.

3 Casegoods include entertainment centers for large televisions, DVD players, and the like.

4 Simple, functional designs, such as this pine table and cabinet, are often part of country-style homes.

5 Black breuer-style chairs add a spark of interest to the neutral colors in this room.

6 Furniture should complement the decor of the room without overpowering it.

7 Window seats often provide extra storage and seating.

...smart ideas

1 Some modern furniture has the ability to blend into the room, allowing something else to be the focal point.

2 The designer of this bedroom used the furniture as a background and created a theme with accessories.

3 Bedrooms are the most private rooms in the home and a good place to express individual personality.

4 An old barrel with a coat of paint and a glass top form a new table.

5 Furniture should support and finish off a room's design; it should also be comfortable and functional.

3

4

5

THE ROOMS IN YOUR HOME

FOYERS AND HALLWAYS ▪ LIVING ROOM ▪ FAMILY ROOM ▪ DINING ROOM ▪ KITCHEN ▪ BEDROOMS ▪ CHILDREN'S ROOMS ▪ BATHROOMS ▪ WORKING WITH PROFESSIONALS

Now it is time to get down to business. The preceding chapters have all dealt with some aspect of decorating from a general point of view. The information applied to all rooms and all spaces in your home. It is important, and it provides a solid foundation for what comes next: decorating individual rooms. In this chapter, we will go room to room and with the help of professional designers show how general decorating principles apply to specific spaces. Not every issue we raise will be relevant to your home, but certainly some will prompt you to consider aspects of design that you may not have thought about before.

It is important to recognize that, for many homeowners, the houses they live in are far from ideal. Sometimes you have to adjust a room's design to accommodate a lack of space elsewhere in the house. For example, much as it may inconvenience you, you may occasionally have overnight visitors sleeping in your living room if there is no separate guest room. You should plan for this in your living room's design. The room can still look lovely and accommodate practical, multifunctional needs. Many of the circumstances addressed in this chapter pertain to multipurpose room planning; others cover the specific needs and functions of certain rooms.

The whole-house tour in this chapter begins in the foyer and proceeds through the hallway into the living room, family room, dining room, kitchen, bedrooms, children's rooms, and bathrooms. For many of the problematic issues presented within each section, there are possible solutions offered. Decorating tips from professional designers abound.

FOYERS AND HALLWAYS

First impressions count. Your foyer should be a reflection of your style and an introduction to the rest of your house. Although many people treat the foyer as a solely utilitarian space, filling it with umbrella stands, hall trees, and the like, it can also be an ideal spot to display cherished family photographs or interesting artwork. Touches like these make your entry warmer and more inviting.

Hallways should tie into the rooms they connect. "Do not forget to treat the walls," says Barbara Schlattman, ASID, of Barbara Schlattman Interiors in Houston, Texas. "That area 5 feet above the ground is especially important because that's what your eye sees." Faux paint finishes, art, and mirrors all add visual appeal.

FURNISHINGS

Pick up a color or pattern from an adjoining room, and use it on the walls of your foyer or hallway. If you decide to use the same wallcoverings in the foyer and living room, change the molding or floor treatment to differentiate the two spaces. Ceramic tile is a popular choice for entryway floors because it stands up to harsh weather conditions and dirt that's tracked in. Large foyers might have a hardwood floor with a colorful area rug in the middle. If the space is long, break it up visually with two area rugs. Always consider safety when choosing a flooring material for your foyer. The surface shouldn't be slick, and rugs must lie securely, so use a rubber pad.

If space permits, designers often add a console table and an interesting wall mirror in a foyer for both aesthetic and practical reasons. This arrangement is also fitting on stair landings where space permits. The table provides the ideal spot to drop off the mail or the keys, leave a note, or quickly write a check. A mirror helps to visually expand what is often a small or narrow space. Most designers draw the line at mirrored walls, though. The foyer is a well-trafficked spot and mirrored walls will make it look too busy.

Left: **A colorful area rug over a wood floor is a traditional foyer design treatment. When possible, provide a table in the foyer for both decorative and functional purposes.**

LIGHTING

Hallways have to be well lit. Use one ceiling fixture in a small hallway or wall-mounted sconces in a larger one. Halls 75 to 150 square feet in size need only a single fixture, which should be at least 12 inches in diameter. A chandelier should be at least 18 inches in diameter. A small space (20 to 75 square feet) requires a fixture that is 8 inches or more in diameter. If you install a pendant lamp or chandelier, make sure it clears the top of any door that opens into the space. Recessed lamps in foyers or halls

SMARTtip   Foyers

Pale paint colors may brighten a narrow hallway or entry, but keep in mind that constant traffic will take its toll on the walls. Consider using warmer colors that are less likely to show marks. A gloss-finish paint will wipe clean easier than a matte-finish product, too. If you prefer wallpaper to paint, use a simple pattern that will provide a spark of color but will not overwhelm the space.

should be on dimmers. "Although having enough lighting is important, you don't want a foyer to be glaringly bright, especially when coming in from a dark night," notes Melinda Sechrist, of Sechrist Designs in Washington, D.C.

LIVING ROOM

The living room is actually a multipurpose space in many instances, acting as an everyday gathering spot for family, a place to entertain guests, as well as the media room where the computer, television, and stereo system all find a home. The living room might also double as the kids' play area or a guest room in a crunch. So unless your living room is off-limits except for company or it's covered in plastic (remember those slipcovers?), it must be able to withstand plenty of wear and tear.

STYLE AND COLOR

The style of the living room should complement adjacent spaces. But often it's the style and palette chosen for the living room that sets the tone for the rest of the house. Go with a look that appeals to you and complements your lifestyle. For example, if your living room

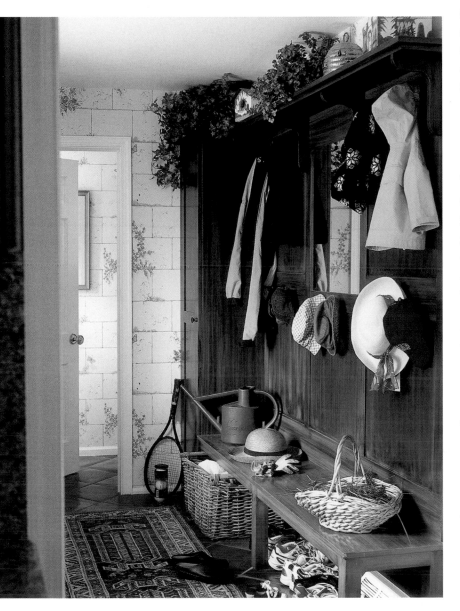

Left: A bench for putting on and taking off boots and pegs for coats and hats turn an area near a back door into a much-needed mudroom.

functions essentially as the family room, with kids, toys, pets, and typical everyday clutter, it will be difficult to maintain the "less is more" philosophy of the minimalist contemporary style. You can try it, but it will never look the way you want. On the other hand, an informal country room will allow you to add rustic trunks and ruffled baskets that can contain the clutter and are in keeping with the popular homespun style.

In houses with a family room, the living room may take on a full-time formal look. Keep in mind that formal doesn't mean stuffy and uncomfortable. You might go with richer woods and colors or more delicate patterns, such as small roses or stripes, but the upholstered seating should be inviting and the other furnishings usable. You want to create an enjoyable space for conversation that makes guests and family members feel relaxed.

When making your mind up about colors for your living room, choose hues that you wear and in which you look best. Stay away from trendy hues. Copy a trick designers like to use: repeat colors. For example, you might use a wonderful fabric on the sofa, then pick up one of the colors in its pattern for the window treatments or chair cushions. Accent solid-color sofas and love seats with vibrant throw pillows. If you're choosing white for the

SMARTtip   Living Rooms

You may not need new furniture for your living room—just a fresh perspective. Try rearranging the pieces. For instance, pull furniture away from the walls; create two or more conversation groups; or arrange some pieces, including sofas, on a diagonal to make a room seem wider. Also try paring down the amount of furnishings in the room. For example, two wing chairs can make a cozy setting, but three can be overkill.

walls, select the paint shade carefully. Avoid stark white in traditional settings. Warm yellow-tinted versions lend a soft tranquil feeling to rooms. Cool whites, those with blue tints, work better in contemporary settings.

Think twice about using light solid colors on the furniture in busy living rooms. An all-white sofa will look great the day that it arrives, but not for long if kids, guests, and you use it everyday.

Left: Here's a recycling idea: this designer used an old painted bench as a coffee table.

Right: When selecting colors for your living room, stay away from trendy color schemes.

Far right: Every room has a focal point. Here it is the fireplace, but it could be a window or furniture.

FOCAL POINT

"Every room benefits from a focal point. When you walk into a room, your eye bounces from place to place until it finds somewhere to rest—if nothing stands out, it keeps bouncing," says Dale Bruss, director of training and education for Decorating Den Interiors. "If you find that you feel a little uncomfortable in a room and you don't know why, the lack of a focal point might well be the reason. Accenting or creating one is the designer's job."

The focal point in many living rooms is the fireplace. If there is no fireplace, a large picture window can assume the role. However, a main area of focus can also be created with a dramatic piece of furniture, such as a bookcase or wall unit, a large coffee table, an eye-catching painting, or a sculpture.

FURNISHINGS

Give careful consideration to the furniture you choose for seating and storage. Always be practical. Choose pieces that can be easily moved around on special occasions when you may have to add chairs to accommodate guests or make room for the Christmas tree, for example. Seating should be comfortable and durable, especially when it takes daily use. Buy the best pieces you can afford. If you avoid trendy styles, good furniture will remain serviceable for many years. To judge the quality and construction of a piece, see Chapter Seven, "The Facts on Furniture," on page 140. If you have a family room, you will probably reserve the living room for company or special occasions, so you may be able to get away with less expensive seating covered in fabric that is beautiful as well as durable.

Avoid furniture suites. Just because a sofa, love seat, chair, and coffee table are grouped together in a showroom does not mean that you have to buy them as a set. Furniture retailers create these groupings to sell products from the same line together, especially if you're unsure of your own design skills. But this kind of buying robs you of the fun and satisfaction of choosing furniture piece by piece. There's no reason a cherished antique or a family heirloom can't fit into your design, for example. Items like these add comfort and reflect your personality more than static sets. "Things that are too matching become very boring," says Sechrist. "Often, putting in an old piece makes the room much more interesting." You might reupholster an old chair in a floral fabric that coordinates with the new solid-color sofa or select a reproduction table in a similar style as the antiques in the room.

However, some old pieces may have to go when you're redecorating because they no longer suit the new design scheme you've created. "If it's a piece you're not crazy about or one that clashes with your new design, even if it cost you a bundle at one time, out it goes. Try moving it to another room," suggests designer Cheryl Casey Ross, of Cross Interiors in Van Nuys, California.

When choosing furniture, keep an eye out for scale. Don't choose oversized furniture for a small living room, no matter how comfortable it is. Once you cram it into the space, in the only location it can possibly fit, you're stuck with it—in the same spot—for the duration. It's nice to rearrange a room occasionally and this will preclude that pleasure.

In living rooms that function also as family rooms, storage is a must for eliminating clutter. Select an entertainment center for the TV, VCR, and stereo. Try to find one that puts these devices behind closed doors when not in use. Add shelves to hold decorative accessories and books.

If your living room will double as a guest room, buy double-duty furnishings, such as a sofa bed or a love seat

Below: The fun of decorating comes in choosing each piece of furniture rather than relying on showroom groupings.

Above: Keep scale and proportion in mind when selecting living room furniture. It looks better than furniture that is too big or small, and it is easier to rearrange later.

Right: Furniture groupings can define spaces within a large room. The chairs and sofa at right form a conversation area with the fireplace as the focal point.

with a pullout bed. Some extra-large chairs also feature this option and are handy in smaller rooms. Another practical idea is to use an attractive trunk as a coffee or end table. That way, you can tuck sheets, blankets, and an alarm clock in the chest. Other options include storage ottomans or even a bench with a hinged top. Stay away from the large toy box you'll have to empty out every time your little one can't find the tiny figurine hidden at the bottom.

DEFINING SPACE

"Furniture should be arranged conducive to how it will be used," says Barbara Schlattman. "So if an area is going to be used for conversation, create a U-shape or box shape with the seating." This way people can face each other when they speak.

Designers also keep furniture away from the walls whenever possible. Float some pieces and create a cluster. In a large

living room, create several groupings: one in a square configuration for conversation, another around the TV area, and a quiet corner for one or two people to enjoy a book. For easy passage around or through furniture clusters, leave a minimum of 28 inches clearance. For help with your furniture plan refer to Chapter One, "The Basics of Design," on page 12, and the furniture templates in the Appendix, on page 268.

When the living room plays more than one role, decorative screens can help divide separate areas and close off what you don't want to be seen, such as paperwork or clutter in a home office. Also, look for furniture that can house an entire office-worth of computer equipment or a media center behind doors. Use a different area rug to define separate spaces or wall-to-wall carpeting with contrasting carpet borders. Wallcoverings and wall colors can change throughout the space, but keep the change subtle to avoid creating visual chaos.

LIGHTING

Concentrate on general lighting in addition to task and mood lighting. Ceiling fixtures or recessed canisters with dimmers are good for providing ambient light. The dimmers allow you to adjust light levels to create mood. If you will read, watch TV, do paperwork, or perform some other activity, you'll have to provide specific task lighting. In general, floor lamps that are 40 to 49 inches from the floor to the bottom of the shade provide generous light spread. Table lamps with shades are ideal because they direct light upward and downward with little glare. For reading, the bottom of the shade should be just below eye level. Each smaller area within the living room must have its own lighting dictated by activity. Lights might be dimmed when entertaining on a winter night as the fireplace is roaring. (See Chapter Three, "The Right Light," on page 52, for more information.)

Above: **In addition to being attractive, family-room furniture should also be easy to clean and durable.**

FAMILY ROOM

The family room is often the home's real *living* room and perhaps the busiest room in the house. This space often has to pack in a lot—from TV viewing to play. Many considerations for living rooms and family rooms are the same, so see the section on "Living Rooms," above, for more information.

STYLE AND COLOR

Because this room is going to get a workout, select patterns, colors, and materials that are durable and will still look good over time. The family room is the place to be a little more personal, so display family photos or collections. There's no need to be formal. Some designers refer to the sought-after family room look as "casual elegance."

Special consideration should be given to great rooms— family rooms and kitchens contained in one open space. Coordinate them, but create visual separation, too. This

can be achieved by arranging the family-room furniture to face away from the kitchen or by alternating materials. Use ceramic tile on the kitchen floor and hardwood in the family room, or use hardwood throughout the space, and cluster family-room furniture around area rugs.

When planning the two spaces, remember that the color and style of the kitchen cabinets should be similar or identical to cabinetry in the family room. High-gloss lacquer cabinets in the kitchen will look out of place with a colonial pine entertainment center nearby. Some custom cabinetmakers will design bookshelves, computer desks, and entertainment centers to match kitchen cabinets for a fully coordinated look, and even some semi-custom or standard cabinet lines feature coordinated pieces. (See Chapter Nine, "Creating a Kitchen Design," on page 190.)

The family room is the place to let your personality shine, though. Showcase a doll collection or a series of your favorite artist's prints. Frame some of your kids' artwork, or display your own handiwork by hanging a quilt on the wall.

FOCAL POINT

The focal point of a family room might be a fireplace, an entertainment center, or a large view of the great outdoors. With all of the different activities that take place here and all of the furnishings that are required, it's important to have a focal point to anchor the room.

FURNISHINGS

Your shopping list might include a love seat, sofa, entertainment center, desk for computer, file cabinet, toy chest, game table, and so forth. Today's family rooms often include a snack center with a mini-refrigerator and sink. The furnishings in your family room depend on how you're going to be using the space.

Designers often advise their clients to select the best quality furnishings they can afford. Don't go for the least expensive sofa because you think, "the kids will ruin it anyway." Sturdy construction can always be reupholstered. Stay away from solid light colors that will show every bit of dirt. Use patterns which hide the wear. "If you want to have a relaxed room, you need to create a comfortable place, where you won't be

SMARTtip   Family Rooms

Probably the most common activity that takes place in your family room is TV viewing. To make your "home theater" experience ideal, select window treatments that open and close easily and can block out glare-causing sunlight. Leave a distance that is three times the size of the TV screen between the screen and opposite seating for optimal viewing.

uptight about having the kids use it," says Melinda Sechrist. Select some lightweight pieces of furniture that can be easily moved—when suddenly more seating is needed around the television or you want to create mingling room when entertaining.

If the family room doubles as a playroom for kids, storage is essential. Select smaller bins that kids can handle rather than one large toy box that swallows up small items. Children are more likely to help pick up if it doesn't seem like an overwhelming task. A small bookshelf with clear bins to hold toys, baskets for stuffed animals, and shelves for games is a good idea.

LIGHTING

Every activity that takes place in the family room has special lighting requirements, so start by making a list of those activities. A reading chair requires intense task lighting. Plan moderate task lighting over a game table. For the TV and computer, use low general lighting that doesn't create glare. Include bright supplementary lights for extra-fine detail tasks, such as crocheting, needlework, or other crafting pastimes. Follow the advice offered for living rooms, and consult Chapter Three, "The Right Light," on page 52.

Left: Family rooms usually contain an entertainment center and space to play games. There is often a connection to the outdoors.

DINING ROOM

Although today's fast-paced lifestyles often mean quick and easy meals, the dining room should be a place where people can sit down, relax, and enjoy a leisurely meal. If you use your dining room on a daily basis, you'll have to be practical and play it safe. But if you serve meals there only a handful of times during the year, you can be a little more daring.

STYLE AND COLOR
The dining room often opens to the living room, kitchen, or foyer, so the style and colors should coordinate with those spaces. The room can take on a more formal look if the family eats primarily in the kitchen. In fact, most interior designers and homeowners like to create a show-stopping dining room for entertaining and special occasions.

Dining rooms look great with a wonderful wallpaper that includes a color found on the adjoining room's walls. Stay away from overbearing patterns. Soft florals and stripes are good choices in traditional dining rooms, while faux finishes and textured looks can perfectly complement contemporary or transitional decors. Wallpaper borders, used with an all-over wallcovering or alone, are also an option that you can use to introduce another pattern into the room.

Keep walls all the same color or wallpaper pattern for continuity. On the ceiling, use a bright white paint. If you're painting the walls a light neutral hue, however, why not add color to the ceiling? Pick up the burgundy or colonial blue on the upholstered chairs as an accent and for a formal touch, for instance. Or for drama, paint the walls a deep color and accent them with trimwork.

THE FOCAL POINT
The focal point of a dining room is often the table itself or an interesting hutch, depending on the placement of the furniture and the orientation of the doorway. Add a centerpiece to the table for visual appeal. Anything from a vase of flowers to a seasonal display or dramatic sculpture will do it. A large window, painting, or mirror can also become a focal point. If a hutch is too large for your room, replace it

with a buffet topped with a colorful painting or enlarged photograph from your last vacation. This, too, becomes a focal point.

FURNISHINGS

"How many will be in the room? How will it be used? If it's small, do you really need anything in the room other than table and chairs?" asks designer Barbara Schlattman. Space can be tight in a dining room, so select as big a table as you can comfortably fit. Leave a minimum of 32 to 36 inches between the table and the wall so that you can move easily out of the chair. The floor covering is especially important in a dining room where chairs are moved in and out and the table might be expanded to accommodate more people. Choose a floor covering that will allow you and your guests to move the chairs easily. If you use an area rug, a popular choice in dining rooms, make sure it will fit under the table when it's expanded to maximum size.

Most dining-room furniture is sold in sets. A set immediately gives you a coordinated look, but it isn't your only

SMARTtip   Dining Rooms

Change the look of your dining room by slipcovering chairs. Short-skirted slipcovers give a more informal appearance; fabrics in graphic patterns, such as checks or floral prints, complement this style of slipcover best. Long-skirted covers are elegant additions to a formal dining room, particularly in solid color or tone-on-tone fabrics. Ties, buttons, or trim can add personality.

option. "It's much more interesting to buy the pieces separately. The chairs don't have to match the table, and the hutch doesn't have to match the table, either," says Barbara Schlattman. "Styles can mix—a traditional chair with a sleek table—or work with different woods."

A china closet is practical and aesthetically appealing. But rather than displaying your crystal and dinnerware, showcase objects that reveal a little of your personality. Or select a buffet, and use the wall space to group a collection of plates.

Left to right: Seldom-used dining rooms are good spots for formal or period furnishings. Most dining room furniture is sold in sets, making it easy to coordinate pieces, but you can create a personal look by selecting individual pieces. The chandelier over the table is the classic lighting option for dining rooms.

LIGHTING

A chandelier or hanging fixture should hang above the center of the table. This may not be the center of the room, though, after arranging a hutch or other furniture. In a dining room with an 8-foot ceiling, install the fixture so that its bottom is 27 to 36 inches above the table. Raise the fixture 3 inches for every additional foot of ceiling height. A crystal chandelier looks great in a formal, elegant dining room, while a ceiling light and fan combination can add charm to a well-dressed transitional space. Display cases should have interior lighting. Wall sconces add decorative appeal and can draw attention to a buffet or painting. Make sure that lighting is sufficient for instances when the dining-room table doubles as workspace. (See Chapter Three, "The Right Light," on page 52.)

KITCHEN

The kitchen represents a real design challenge. Large appliances, plenty of storage, work space, and possibly a casual eating area must come together in harmony. And in the kitchen, efficient function is crucial. "If it doesn't function, it doesn't matter how good it looks," notes Lori Jo Krengel, CKD, CBD, of Kitchens By Krengel in St. Paul, Minnesota. (See Chapter Nine, "Creating a Kitchen Design," on page 190.)

STYLE AND COLOR

You want the kitchen to coordinate with the rest of your rooms, but since it's essentially a work space, you've got some leeway here. If the kitchen is self-contained, meaning that it's not open to another room such as the family room, then it can comfortably depart from the main style of the house. There's nothing wrong with a

Above right: Even if you elect to have white cabinets, you can bring color to the kitchen through accents, such as the tile on the backsplash and the seat cushions.

Right: This simple country kitchen is enhanced visually by the collection of delftware hanging on the walls and in the wall-hung cabinet.

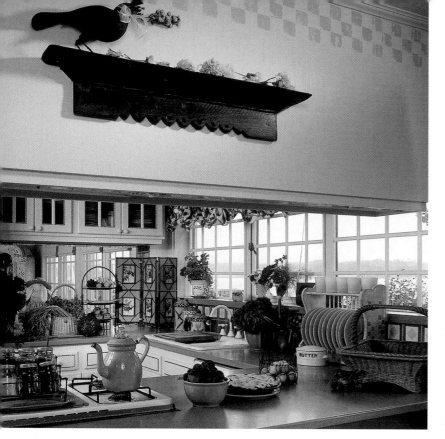

relatively high-tech kitchen in a traditional-style home, as long as it doesn't clash outright with the integrity of the house. You might, for example, use white cabinetry here and another type elsewhere. But the door style might closely resemble that of the hutch in the dining room. Your accessories can also bring a taste of your main decor into the kitchen. For instance, if you are displaying a blue-and-white china collection in the family room, bring some pieces into the kitchen.

Cabinets are the dominant design element in the kitchen. If you're not sure what you want, play it safe with a traditional raised-panel door. That type of door style can take on a variety of looks, from contemporary to country, depending on the surroundings.

Light cabinet colors are best in small kitchens. If your heart is set on a dark wood stain, brighten up the space with a light countertop and backsplash, white or almond appliances, and ample lighting.

If you want a colorful kitchen, approach it as you would any other room: Get swatches and material samples from the manufacturers. Some terrific spots to add decorative color in the kitchen are a tiled backsplash or a ceramic tile floor, a solid-surfacing countertop inlaid with a stripe or custom pattern, or even a laminate floor that features a border. Mix countertop colors and materials. For example, use butcher block or granite on the work island and solid-surfacing material elsewhere. Cabinetry can be stained in colors, such as shades of red or blue. A cast-iron sink in a vibrant blue or green always looks dramatic or, if you're more daring, there are even ranges available in bright colors, such as royal blue and red. But you may want to play it safe with neutral colors on permanent fixtures in general.

Above left: Kitchens that are open to other rooms should have some connection to those rooms through cabinetry selection, color scheme, and the like.

Left: Appliances are becoming an increasingly important component in kitchen decor. Note the sleek lines and curved profile of this undercounter oven.

FOCAL POINT

Cabinetry is the backdrop of a kitchen, but the focal point is often the window or the area around the range. Many designers like to dress the latter space up with a hand-painted mural or other interesting ceramic tiles. Sleek, shiny metal range hoods also help to emphasize this area.

In a great-room setup, where kitchen and family room become one, a fireplace might become the focal point. That's fine, but you'll also want to create some sort of separation between the spaces. An island or peninsula often doubles as a buffer.

FURNISHINGS

More and more kitchen designers are specifying freestanding furniture for their clients' kitchens. A hutch will provide sought-after storage space for dinnerware, glasses, or even pantry items. Glass-fronted cabinetry looks great, but the storage space inside needs to be neat and orderly.

Granite- and marble-top tables can act as a movable center island ideal for working with dough. Select a table and chairs that fit the style of the kitchen. Find interesting stools for an island that offers a casual eating area.

LIGHTING

Professional designers always try to include as much natural light in a kitchen plan as possible. Task lighting, often under wall cabinets or above the island, is a must—although it's often tempting to eliminate the added expense. There also must be a light over the sink and some type of general lighting. Some designers and home-owners prefer the look of decorative hanging fixtures to

all recessed lighting. You might also want to consider lighting inside cabinetry. Because of all the different tasks performed in a kitchen, devising a light plan for this room can become complex, so consult Chapter Three, "The Right Light," on page 52, for specific guidance.

BEDROOMS

The master bedroom is your getaway space, so design it to please only yourself. Invest in a luxury touch here and there—beautiful bed linens or a four-poster bed, for example. In a busy world, everyone needs a pleasant day's-end retreat.

STYLE AND COLOR

The master bedroom generally conforms to the style chosen for the main rooms of the house. If possible, try not to allow the bedroom to become a multipurpose room. Don't give in to the idea that one corner could house a mini-office space perfectly—taking "work" into the bedroom is not a restful concept. If the master bedroom is

SMARTtip   Kitchens

Don't choose trendy cabinetry for the kitchen—it can quickly look dated. Instead, add bold decorative touches with those things that are easy to change—novelty hardware, for instance. Backsplashes, countertops, sinks, and wallcoverings are also good choices. Replacing these items may require a little more effort, but the job can definitely be done without tremendous fuss.

shared, decide together whether or not to include a TV or stereo. To maintain a restful look in the room, choose cabinetry that conceals this equipment.

You can draw your color scheme from the palette you've chosen for one of the other spaces in the house, or you can pick favorite colors or those that look good on one or both of you. If you're a morning person and have the time to luxuriate in the bedroom until later, consider warm, invigorating colors. If you want your evening retreat to soothe away the cares of the day, pick from the cooler hues.

FOCAL POINT

The bed is usually the focal point of a bedroom, so dress it up with attractive bedding, including comfortable throw pillows. Often the headboard or space above it catches the eye as well. An ornate headboard will serve as a focal point, as will a canopy suspended from the ceiling and arranged with coordinating fabrics. A nicely framed painting or print—or perhaps a coordinating pair or groupings—over the bed can also look attractive.

Clockwise (from below): **A decorative headboard and a bright pillow enliven a guest bedroom. If your bedroom is a personal retreat, include furniture that will make you comfortable. The light colors in this attic bedroom make the space appear larger and more open. Master bedrooms usually reflect the decorating style of the main rooms in the house.**

A low dresser leaves the space above it as a possible focal point. Consider an ornately framed mirror, a series of interestingly shaped mirrors, or a mirror flanked by framed prints or a collection of items such as straw hats.

FURNISHINGS

There are some practical aspects to be addressed in a master bedroom, in which two people are often waking up and getting dressed at the same time. If space permits, separate storage for each one should be included: dresser and bureau, two closets, and twin night stands. A decorative screen can provide an interesting backdrop that will also create a small dressing area. A full-length mirror, whether freestanding or mounted on closet doors, is another important element.

If there's room, also include a comfortable chair along with a small table and a lamp. This quiet spot is great for read-

SMARTtip   Bedrooms

Whites, neutrals, or pale colors—blues, greens, or pinks—create a restful ambiance in the bedroom, making sleeping easier. Cheery colors, such as yellow, work for those who like rising with the sun (or those who need help waking up). All-over wallpaper patterns, particularly large-scale ones, can sometimes make a bedroom feel too enclosed, so use bold patterns sparingly.

ing, relaxing, or enjoying evening tea or morning coffee in the privacy of your retreat. Designers seldom purchase bedroom furniture in complete sets. Buy interesting individual pieces instead. Matched suites are passé.

Window treatments should be room-darkening to ensure that you're not awakened at first light: if you install lightweight curtains, use shades or blinds underneath for controlling light. For privacy, install two-way shades or half-curtains.

LIGHTING

On each nightstand or above the bed there should be separate reading lamps for each party. For ambient lighting, an overhead light fixture is more decorative than recessed lamps. It should hang centrally. Consider an overhead ceiling fan/light combination, an asset on warm nights. Be sure to include proper task lights for applying makeup or other grooming habits. (See Chapter Three, "The Right Light," on page 52, for more guidance.)

Left: Inadequate lighting is a common problem in many bedrooms. This room uses a combination of table lamps and recessed ceiling fixtures to provide illumination.

CHILDREN'S ROOMS

A good designer will interview both the child and the parents when designing a kid's room. From the child the designer will get personal preferences, and from the parents, he or she will hope to get an idea of how the room must function. "Too often, people focus on the look of the room, and function is an afterthought," says Michele Rohrer, Allied ASID, of Michelle's Interiors, in Grayslake, Illinois. "In a child's room, it's crucial to write down all of the functions of the room."

An older child uses it for doing homework, playing games, entertaining, and reading, in addition to sleeping. The room becomes the spot where friends come over to play. A baby's room will probably be the spot for diaper changing, lullaby singing, playing, and sleeping.

Above right: Bright, fun colors are usually the norm in a child's room. Be sure to get his or her opinion on color during the design process.

Right: Durability is an important consideration when selecting furniture and flooring for a child's room.

SMARTtip — Children's Rooms

Keep safety in mind when planning a child's room. Make sure that there are covers on electrical outlets, guard rails on high windows, sturdy screens in front of radiators, and gates blocking any steps. Other suggestions include safety hinges for chests and nonskid backing for rugs.

STYLE AND COLOR

"When selecting a palette for a child's room, expect it to meet his or her needs for about 5 to 7 years." As children develop, aquire more interests, and make friends, they—along with their tastes in favorite colors and decorating motifs—change. "A 6-year-old girl will not enjoy the same room or color scheme past the age of 12, nor can an infant room last past 6," notes Rohrer.

Themes are suitable for children of any age, although the approach may change. Select more juvenile characters and patterns for a 3-year-old's bedroom than you would a 9-year-old's—but both can still feature a jungle or train motif. As in all rooms, trendy colors and styles date it. Use them sparingly and on elements that are easy to change. "Good design is always good," says Rohrer, "If something is trendy, like daisies from the '60s, we won't do it on a large scale. We'll use daisies on a pillow maybe."

FURNISHINGS

Furnishings should be selected according to how the space will function. A full-size bed is more practical in rooms where friends use the bed for seating. Children need their own space and their things nearby, from toys to a favorite cap. These years will pass by so quickly. Most designers encourage their clients to give in to some of their kids' whims. A child's room should be fun and lively.

Trundle beds and bunk beds are often used in kids' rooms to accommodate sleepovers. Flooring should be durable and comfortable. (See Chapter Four, "Flooring Options," on page 74.) Area rugs are easier to remove for dry-cleaning, but they require using a nonskid mat underneath. School-age children need a desk or study area. Line a bookshelf

Clockwise (from top): Your child's taste will change as they grow older, but as they do change try to keep the design fun and lively. Older children do their homework and hang out with friends in their bedrooms, so consider including desks and tables in the design. As with an adult's room, include extra furniture to make the child comfortable and plenty of storage, including both built-in and portable storage.

with clear bins for easy-to-see storage. Under-bed storage keeps things out of view. Take advantage of closet space in small bedrooms by using built-in closet systems to maximize the space. "If a large closet exists, think about using it for clothing, and forego the dressers," says Rohrer. If the room is small, floor space can be used for other necessities.

LIGHTING

Combine general overhead lighting with task lighting: a reading lamp over the headboard, a desk lamp, and perhaps a night light. Avoid floor lamps, which can be easily knocked over. (See Chapter Three, "The Right Light," on page 52, for more information.)

BATHROOMS

In the bathroom, as in the kitchen, you can safely depart from the style of the rest of your house. It's a room, usually a small one, that does a big job, but there's a place for form as well as function in today's bath. (See Chapter Ten, "Creating a Bathroom Design," on page 220.)

STYLE AND COLOR

The master bath and family bath are going to be used frequently, so it's especially important that you select a style and colors that everyone likes. In a master bath, coordinate the colors with those used in the bedroom, or you might draw the scheme for a bath from the hall. A powder room is the place to be more daring, but keep the basics of color theory in mind. "Look at the balance. You don't want a red, green, and purple bath. You have to follow the elements

and principles of design, otherwise it will look like a hodgepodge," says designer Lori Jo Krengel.

In the bath, a neutral scheme can change with your whim simply by replacing the accessories. Shower curtains, rugs, towels, and even some fixtures are relatively easy and inexpensive to change. Small items, such as soap, can inject color.

SMARTtip   Bathrooms

No matter how big or small the room, details will pull the style together. Some of the best details that you can include are the smallest—drawer pulls from an antique store or shells in a glass jar or just left on the countertop. Add period flavor with crown molding, or dress up contemporary fixtures with polished stone fittings.

FOCAL POINT

"There's not necessarily a focal point in a bathroom," says Krengel. "You want an overall feel." You have to decide what that will be.

You can, however, create a focal point at the vanity or the tub. A clutter-free new countertop adorned with a decorative accent piece (from a basket of bathing goodies to a vase with fresh flowers) and backed with a striking yet practical mirrored medicine cabinet can grab attention. The same is true for a tub set in a custom-designed surround. Effective lighting above the tub or on the sides of the vanity can augment drama as well.

FURNISHINGS

There are certain elements that a full bath must include: toilet, tub or shower, lavatory, and storage. Once you make your basic selections, start thinking about how you want to decorate. Permanent fixtures, except storage, should all be the same color for continuity. Add contrast with tile, paint, or patterned wallcoverings.

Storage is essential in a bathroom. If there is room, a vanity is useful and attractive. If you plan to install a pedestal sink, you'll have to find storage elsewhere. Many designers like to add freestanding pieces of furniture for extra drawer and cabinet space. This option is a practical one because it's easy to change. However, make sure that wooden pieces are protected against moisture with a sealant. Take advantage of wall space behind the toilet by adding a rack or cabinet there.

Left to right: In master baths, choose colors and fabrics that coordinate with those in the bedroom. Note how the shower curtain cover matches the other fabrics in the room. Large bathrooms require a focal point, such as this dramatic whirlpool tub. A marble top turns this piece into a vanity.

LIGHTING

Minimally, in a bathroom that is less than 100 square feet, one fixture is sufficient. Add another fixture for each additional 50 square feet. However, you should also plan task lighting for grooming in the sink area. You might also consider adding a light in the shower ceiling or above the tub, but make sure that it is one specifically designed for a damp location and conforming to local building codes.

WORKING WITH PROFESSIONALS

If you have a design dilemma that you just can't solve yourself, consulting a professional is a good idea. These Smart Steps can help you find the right person and communicate your needs effectively.

ONE: **Narrow down your needs.** To figure out the kind of professional you need, first get a clear picture of the level of help you require. Developing a color scheme, for example, requires less specific expertise than, say, space planning for a busy kitchen. If you don't like the colors a friend suggests, you simply don't have to use them. But you may not realize until it's too late that configuring a kitchen layout is too complicated a task for you. So be honest in your assessment of your skills to avoid problems.

TWO: **Locate free help.** Begin with free sources, and see whether you find answers that way. Home and decorating centers often employ designers to get potential customers through tough design decisions. If the advice you receive will mean large financial expenditures, ask the designer, casually, how much experience he or she has. In a freebie situation, it's usually not appropriate to ask for references, except in cases where the designer is not just giving advice on a single issue but designing an entire room.

THREE: **Search the World Wide Web.** If you have a home computer with internet access, you should know that many professional design organizations have Web sites.

Some offer troubleshooting tips or free design advice via e-mail. Web sites change over time and not all offer the same kind of resources, but there are a few worth looking into:

- **www.interiors.org,** the American Society of Interior Designers
- **www.nkba.org,** the National Kitchen and Bath Association
- **www.nari.org,** the National Association of the Remodeling Industry
- **www.nahb.com,** the National Association of Home Builders
- **www.aia.org,** the American Institute of Architects
- **www.aibd.org,** the American Institute of Building Design

Even if you don't get free advice on-line through these Web sites, you can locate design professionals in your area who may be able to help you.

FOUR: Find a professional interior designer. If your project really can't go forward without sound professional advice and you've figured the cost into your budget, you can easily find someone to hire. If you've admired the work of a designer in someone else's home, simply ask for the reference. Sometimes retail establishments can recommend professionals they've worked with in the past. The good old Yellow Pages is always a source. Plus, if there are designers' showhouses in your area, go visit them. A showhouse is a good way to see the work of any local talent.

FIVE: Look at portfolios; call references; check credentials. Make sure that the person with whom you choose to work is registered with a professional organization, such as the ones listed in Step Three. Interview candidates thoroughly about their business. A remodeling project can take a long time, so it is best to be friendly and comfortable with whomever your hire. Ask to examine the designer's portfolio to get a feeling of whether his or her style will suit you, or whether he or she has a wide enough range to meet your needs. Most importantly, don't neglect the final step of checking references. Pretty pictures of someone's dream project are easy to come by, but the whole story of a redesign or remodeling can be a nightmare. Call references, and if possible, visit sites and ask plenty of questions.

Left: Kitchen cabinets were adapted for this home office. Custom-made work surfaces suit the owner's needs.

Below: A hobby or craft room should include easy-to-clean surfaces and plenty of storage.

a gallery of...

1 Small dining rooms that flow into kitchens often look best with casual-style furniture.

2 This family room makes use of ingenious built-in storage solutions for CDs, DVDs, and tapes.

3 A young girl's room receives a playful paint treatment above a dormer window.

4 Is it an office, craft room, or secret hideaway? No matter what you call it, make it comfortable and inviting.

5 An east- or south-facing sunroom is a good location for a dining room or an informal breakfast nook.

6 Brick pavers can stand up to the traffic that goes through a foyer. Ceramic tiles are also a good choice.

7 This living room contains an inviting color scheme, good furniture, and adequate lighting.

...smart ideas

1

1 This living room uses the fireplace as its focal point. Area rugs and furniture placement define spaces.

2 A canopy and flowing bed curtains add elegance and a romantic feeling to this bedroom.

3 This curving bank of windows and window seat serves as the focal point for an informal dining area.

4 A two-story foyer calls for a dramatic treatment that includes a large mirror and flowing fabrics.

5 This bedroom's connection to the outdoors led the homeowner to a crisp, clean design.

6 Fill an office or study with the things that you cherish most, including books, art, or personal mementos.

CHAPTER 9

CREATING A KITCHEN DESIGN

SET PRIORITIES ■ BASIC KITCHEN LAYOUTS ■ CHOOSING CABINETS ■ COUNTERTOP OPTIONS ■ SELECTING FIXTURES

Of all the rooms in a house, kitchens present unique decorating challenges because so much tends to happen in these spaces. In addition to preparing meals, most families use kitchens as gathering and entertaining areas. Kitchens need to be functional, comfortable, and inviting.

This one room has become so important, in fact, that prospective buyers consider it a primary factor in selecting a home. If you are thinking about remodeling the kitchen for resale purposes, you may get as much back as you invest—maybe more, depending on where you live. If you are like most people, however, your motivations are much more personal.

Wouldn't it be delightful to prepare a meal in a kitchen equipped with the latest appliances and configured to let you move effortlessly from refrigerator to sink to cooktop without tripping over the kids, the cat, or your own feet? Imagine opening a cabinet without having to strain, or empty the entire contents to find one small can. Picture a countertop that isn't a catchall for the mail, dry cleaning receipts, phone books, dog treats, antacids, and all the rest of cabinet and drawer spillover. Think about enjoying breakfast in a cheery nook or eating quiet dinners in a space that isn't dark, dingy, and cramped.

Above: If possible, include an eating area, such as this raised snack bar, in your kitchen remodeling plans.

SET PRIORITIES

Design professionals interview their clients at length at the beginning of a project. If you will be your own designer, do the same thing. Likewise, you may even want to videotape your family (and yourself) in the kitchen during typical meal preparation or any other kitchen-based activities. If your parties often spill into the kitchen, for instance, videotape the next party, and pay attention to how difficult or easy it is to interact with guests while you're cooking or serving. Is there enough room for opening the refrigerator door when someone passes behind you? Is there space on the countertop to set up a small, informal buffet or bar?

Note the different situations that typically interrupt or assist your work flow and traffic patterns. Is the aisle you use to reach the oven the same as the one used to walk from the back door into the house? Observe how many times you have to walk across the room for something.

If you consult with a professional, don't be put off by questions. Any good designer has to get to know the habits, likes, and dislikes of the people who will live with the finished project. He or she wants to understand your basic requirements as well as your wildest dreams for the new kitchen.

The place to start, then, is with how you want the kitchen to work—for you and for every other member of your household. Function is the cornerstone of good kitchen design. A highly functional kitchen will not make you a master chef, but it will improve the quality of the time you spend in the kitchen, which some experts say can be as much as 70 percent of your waking hours. With this in mind, remember: Even the smallest remodeling job requires careful planning and forethought. You can greatly increase the efficiency of your kitchen by paying attention to the tiniest details and the smallest of spaces.

A designer will also sketch the existing space to get an idea of what works and what doesn't. This rough drawing may include any adjacent areas that might be considered for expansion, such as a pantry or part of a hallway.

Once again, if you act as your own designer, do the same thing. Talk to everyone in the household. Ask what they think needs improvement, as well as any aspects of the space as it exists that they'd prefer to retain.

For the best results, approach the project in the same calm, analytical manner as a professional, one who understands design and can be objective about what has to happen. Here's how to begin:

ONE: Create a design notebook. It's important to keep all of your ideas and records in one place. Buy a loose-leaf binder, and use it to organize everything from magazine clippings to photos of the old kitchen (extremely important when you choose to resell the house); wish lists; notes and interviews with design professionals and family members; contracts; business cards; sample plans; shopping lists; color charts; tile, fabric, and wallpaper samples; and anything else related to the project. The file should be comprehensive yet not too clumsy to cart around to showrooms, stores, or home centers.

TWO: Analyze the existing kitchen. Decide what you really want to gain by remodeling. You might begin by asking the most obvious question: What's wrong with the existing kitchen? Maybe you and your partner enjoy cooking together, but the floor plan was designed to work for only one cook. Perhaps storage is inadequate or the appliances are old.

To be specific about your analysis, get out your notebook and record answers to questions such as, Is the size of the family likely to grow or shrink in the near future? If the kids are or will be in college soon, you might not need that large-capacity refrigerator. Likewise, if this is your first house and you expect to move up as your family size increases, it might be wise to refinish high-ticket items such as cabinets and hang onto older appliances that are still working, spending only a modest amount of money, time, and energy on cosmetic changes in the kitchen. Other questions to consider include:

■ How many members of the household really cook? Note other ways each one uses the kitchen.

■ How convenient is it to work in the kitchen? Are people always bumping into each other? When cabinet or appliance doors are open, is the traffic pattern interrupted?

■ Is there enough storage? If you keep kitchen- or cooking-related items in other areas of the house such as the garage, it's time to analyze how to increase the storage capacity in the kitchen.

■ What is the condition of existing materials and appliances? How old are they? Are the appliances energy-efficient? Are the walls, floors, and countertops in good condition?

Left: Kitchen islands increase work surfaces, and they often allow the cook to face family and friends who are in other parts of the room.

THREE: Make a wish list. Besides the basic elements, you may want some special features in your new kitchen—a ceramic glass-top range, modular refrigeration, interchangeable cooktop components, or a warming drawer. Perhaps an elegant slate or granite countertop or a gorgeous custom range hood has caught your eye.

Create a list of all the accoutrements you would like to include, whether or not you think you can afford them. When you have a close-to-perfect plan, that's the time to look for areas to trim if your budget is tight. You might choose a countertop fabricated in an affordable stone look-alike and use the dollars saved for something you can't fake, such as an energy-efficient window over the sink or a tiled backsplash.

FOUR: Sketch the old floor plan. Just like a professional designer, draw an existing floor plan. Do a rough sketch first; then transfer your drawing to graph paper with grids marked at $1/4$-inch intervals. Draw it freehand or with a straightedge, but do it to a scale of $1/2$ inch equal to 1 foot. This base plan, or "base map," as it is called, should record the layout of the space as it exists. Include measurements for everything, from the width of every door to how far the refrigerator protrudes into the room.

Start by taking measurements, beginning with the length and width of the room. Then from one corner, measure the location of windows, doors, and walls. Record the swing of each door. Note each dimension in feet and inches to the nearest $1/4$ inch.

Next draw the cabinetry and appliances, and indicate their height. Measure the position and centerline of the sink (showing how far the center of this fixture is from the wall), but don't forget to list its overall length and width. Also measure the height of the walls.

Above left: Take measurements of your existing kitchen, and record the information on a preliminary sketch.

Left: Transfer the drawing to graph paper—a scale of $1/2$ inch equals 1 foot is good—or computer design software.

Include symbols for light fixtures, outlets, and heat registers on the floor plan as well. Note load-bearing walls, which cannot be moved without compromising structural integrity. If you are thinking about tearing out any wall and you don't know whether it is load-bearing, consult an architect or a structural engineer before you do anything.

It's a good idea to list your gripes about the old kitchen on the sketch. That way you can see at a glance what problem areas need to be changed.

Remember: this floor plan is only a guide. It doesn't have to be professionally drawn, only accurate in its rendition and measurements of the current space.

BASIC KITCHEN LAYOUTS

Whether you are reconfiguring existing space or adding on, the floor plan plays a large role in how well the room will function. And while a kitchen addition to an outside wall of the house offers the best possibilities for unencumbered floor space, it is the costliest option. One way to save money is to restrict your addition to a "bump-out" of 3 feet or less. This doesn't necessarily require a new foundation, and it limits the need for a new roof. Consult an architect or builder, first, to make sure the existing structure is sound and can carry the additional load. Remember to inquire about local zoning ordinances before proceeding with your plans.

However you choose to proceed, any kitchen of any size requires a thoughtful arrangement of all its elements to make it both highly functional and efficient.

THE WORK TRIANGLE

Almost everybody has heard of the kitchen's classic *work triangle*. Essentially, it is an area that puts the three major work centers—the range, refrigerator, and sink—at the three points of a triangle. The spatial relationship among these sites and how they relate to other areas in the kitchen is what makes the room an efficient work space. The National Kitchen & Bath Association (NKBA) recommends that there

be at least one work triangle in a kitchen. In fact, today's busy families—and multipurpose kitchens—often call for two or more work triangles. With traditional roles at home changing, so are attitudes about cooking. Two-cook families are more common than ever, and food preparation and cooking have themselves become excuses for social events where even the guests actively participate.

In the classic work triangle, the distance between any pair of the three task centers is no longer than 9 feet and no less than 4 feet.

To conserve walking distance from point to point without sacrificing adequate counter space, the sum of all three lines of the triangle should be no greater than 27 feet and no less than 12 feet. For a large kitchen, plan two or more work triangles. Although pairs may extend inside one another, sharing one side or "leg" of the triangle for maximum performance, do not overlap the sink and range areas. Another approach is to design smaller triangles set within the larger one.

Above: Designers use the work triangle to connect the primary work centers and define the optimal distances between them. It is a building block of kitchen design.

Because a goal of the work triangle is to keep normal kitchen traffic from interrupting the work flow, during your planning stage pay especially close attention to how everyone in the household comes and goes in the existing kitchen. You might even try this unusual but enlightening homespun experiment: dust the floor with a thin coating of cornmeal; then go about your normal food preparation and cleanup. You'll be able to track your movements from cabinets to appliances to the sink, and the rest of the family's moves around you—or whoever does the cooking. Once you see where the kitchen becomes most crowded, you'll be able to make the necessary changes. (And don't forget to sweep up the cornmeal.) Sometimes that's as simple as relocating an appliance—particularly a small one—to a less busy area.

There is some debate today among professional kitchen designers concerning the traditional work triangle. Although most agree that it is still an important element, many see the triangular space evolving as cooking habits and lifestyles change. These designers feel that the more actual living done in the kitchen, the more expanded the basic triangle will have to become. And as kitchens grow larger—which appears to be the trend—they will embrace an increasing number of activities. This will result in the need for several autonomous triangles within the room. Whichever school of thought you believe, the bottom line still is and always will be: design for your sake, not for the sake of design.

As you consider a new layout, check that traffic moves easily from one place to another in the kitchen and from the kitchen to other rooms in the house, as well as outdoors. It is important that through-traffic doesn't interfere with the work triangle. Otherwise, carrying a hot pot from the range to the sink could put you on a collision course with youngsters heading for the back door.

Often you can correct a faulty traffic pattern simply by moving a door or removing a short section of wall. Another way to improve a kitchen's function is to experiment with basic layouts to see which suits your needs.

BASIC LAYOUTS

There are five basic kitchen layouts: one-wall, galley (corridor), U-shaped, L-shaped, and G-shaped. Each has its challenges and advantages.

One-Wall. This arrangement places all of the equipment, sink, and cabinetry along one wall. Since you cannot create a triangle in a one-wall kitchen, maximize accessibility by placing the sink between the refrigerator and the range. Although a one-wall kitchen is more typical in a small apartment, it may be found in a large, open-plan home. If you want to retain this arrangement but would like to close off the kitchen from other public areas of the house, install sliding doors or screens that can be opened or closed at will.

Below: One-wall kitchens take up the least amount of space, but they are the least flexible of the basic kitchen shapes. To accommodate two cooks, place the sink as shown here.

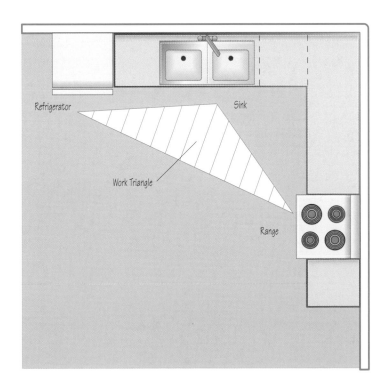

The Galley. Also known as the *corridor style*, this compact layout locates the appliances, sink, and cabinets on two parallel walls in order to create a small pass-through kitchen. It's easy to create an efficient work triangle in this setup, but the layout really caters to one cook. Allow a 48-inch-wide aisle after all fixtures are placed so that cabinets and appliance doors can be opened easily while someone walks through. If space is really tight, you could make the aisle 36 inches wide, but appliance doors may collide with each other if more than one is open at a time. Another tip: avoid installing a doorway at both ends of the galley or corridor. That way, you can keep people from walking through the work triangle while the cook is busy.

To ease as many traffic problems as possible, place the refrigerator near the end of the room—near the entrance into the kitchen. Another option is to install the primary refrigerator in the food-preparation area and a smaller, secondary refrigerator outside of the food-prep area.

The L-shape. This plan places the kitchen on two perpendicular walls. The L-shape usually consists of one long "leg" and a short one, and lends itself to an efficient work triangle without the problem of through traffic. If well designed, it is flexible enough for two cooks to work simultaneously without getting in each other's way.

Another advantage to this layout is the opportunity, if space allows, for incorporating an island into the floor plan. If you do, plan the clearances carefully. Walkways should be at least 36 inches wide. If the walkway is also a work aisle, increase the clearance to 42 inches. A 36-inch clearance is fine for counter seating, unless traffic goes behind it. In that case, clearance should be 65 inches.

Above left: In galley kitchens, try to allow for a 48-inch-wide aisle. If that is impossible, plan for a narrower aisle, but maintain functionality by keeping the width above 36 inches.

Left: L-shaped kitchens provide more flexibility for placing the major work centers than the simpler shapes. If space allows, expand this shape by placing a small island or even a table in the open floor space.

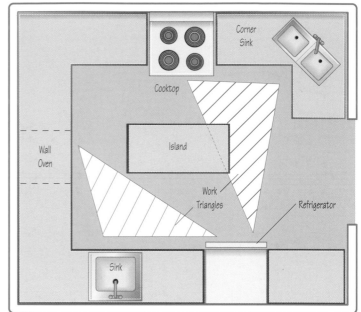

Above: The U-shaped kitchen keeps unnecessary foot traffic out of the work area, and it provides the potential for uninterrupted counter space between the major work centers.

Above: The G-shaped kitchen, which is a variation of the U-shaped layout, can accommodate two work triangles. Note that the refrigerator anchors the triangles shown above.

The U-shape. The U-shaped kitchen is the most efficient design. Cabinets, counters, and appliances are all arranged along three walls. The greatest benefit, perhaps, is the interrupted space for traffic flow.

A U-shaped layout incorporates a logical sequence of work centers with minimum distances between each. The sink is often located at the base of the U, with the refrigerator and range on the side walls opposite each other. The U shape takes a lot of space—at least 8 feet along the length and width of the kitchen. Corners may be a problem because they often create unusable space. However, consider angling cabinets into these otherwise "dead" areas. Upper cabinets with rolltop doors make roomy appliance garages, and bottom units fitted with carousel shelves or a lazy Susan actually make storage more handy than standard units.

Smaller U-shaped kitchens can be dark because of the sheer mass of all that cabinetry. You can counter this with a generous-size window, skylights, or under-cabinet task lighting, or by keeping surfaces a light color.

The G-shape. This is a hybrid of the U-shape with a shorter, fourth leg added in the form of a peninsula. While the G-shaped layout is great for more than one person working in the kitchen, it can feel confining.

This layout may feature a pair of sinks and a separate cooktop, as well as an oven range. One work triangle usually incorporates a sink, the cooktop, and the refrigerator, while the other houses the second sink, the oven, and overlapping the first triangle, the refrigerator. An island is usually placed in the corner of a G-shaped layout, within easy reaching distance to both work triangles.

The G-shaped kitchen often accommodates specialty appliances, such as warming drawers, modular refrigeration, or a built-in grill, to allow as much independence between the two work areas as possible.

ISLANDS AND PENINSULAS

In a roomy layout, you can shorten the distance between the three key work areas by adding an island or peninsula. A peninsula base and ceiling-hung cabinets offer conve-

Above: Adding a peninsula increases both storage and counter space. In the L-shaped layout shown above, the peninsula does not interfere with the work triangle.

Below left: Use kitchen islands to solve a number of layout problems: they can increase counter and storage space; they can hold a sink or cooktop; or they can be the location of an eating counter. They can also divide space and direct traffic away from the cooking area.

Below right: Plan the size and location of tables and chairs. Allow for 12 to 15 square feet per person. To allow for a seated person to push back from the table, allow between 32 and 36 inches between the wall and the edge of the table.

nient storage for tableware and linens. In an L- or U-shaped kitchen, an island can add visual interest by breaking up the space without confining it. It also provides an extra work surface, a spot for snacks or informal meals, as well as a place to set up a buffet.

An island or peninsula can also serve as an excellent location for a cooktop or second sink, if plumbing and ventilation hookups permit. It could also prove the ideal spot for a wine rack or cooler, a wet bar, warming drawers, modular refrigerator units, or additional general storage. For maximum efficiency, be sure the design provides a clearance of 48 inches from the island or peninsula to the wall cabinets.

EATING AREAS

There are specific minimum clearances you'll need to accommodate a table and chairs, which you mustn't forget to include in your design. Plan enough floor space for all of the furniture and for people to sit down, get up, and walk around it comfortably, without interfering with the work traffic.

Seating Allowances. If you feel as if you're a contortionist every time you get into or out of a chair at the table, you haven't done your space-planning homework. When you redesign, follow the guidelines here as you plan the layout, and you won't go wrong.

Even average-size people need a surprising amount of space to make a dining area accessible. Allow 12 to 15 square feet per person. That means a family of four will require at least 48 square feet in an eat-in kitchen. Assume that a 36-inch-diameter round table can seat four adults; a 48-inch-diameter one will accommodate six. Calculate 21 to 24 inches of table space per person for a square or rectangular table.

When planning space for your kitchen table, pay attention to the distance between it and the walls or cabinets. A seated adult occupies a depth of about 20 inches from the edge of the table but will need 12 to 16 additional inches of space to push back the chair and rise. This means you have to plan on 32 to 36 inches of clearance between the wall

and the edge of the table. You can get away with a minimum of 28 inches if chairs are angled to the wall. However, plan on a 44-inch clearance to allow enough room on any serving side of any table, whatever its shape.

If you don't have enough room for a table, a booth (or a table with banquette) or bench seating may be the answer. A kitchen alcove or bay window offers a natural spot for either seating arrangement, or you can back it against an island, peninsula, or wall. Plan 21 inches of table space for each person with at least 15 inches of knee space underneath. This means that a family of four minimally needs a 42-inch-long table that measures 30 inches across. Because you slide in and out of a booth, the table may overhang the

Left: When placing a table in a small room, angle the chairs as shown. This arrangement allows you to place the table only 28 inches from the wall.

Below left: Provide each person with 21 to 24 inches of table or counter space. Allow a 44 inch clearance for serving and table-to-wall clearances discussed above and on page 199.

Below right: Booths can provide seating in small kitchens because a booth that seats four need be only 5 feet across, compared with over 9 feet for a table and chairs.

Above: This counter-height island requires 24-inch-high stools with footrests and 14 inches of knee space for seating comfort.

benches by 3 or 4 inches. Total floor space required for a four-person booth, therefore, measures only 5 feet across, compared with a minimum requirement of about 9 feet for a freestanding table with chairs.

Another popular option for in-kitchen dining is to let the island or peninsula serve double duty as an eating bar. Remember, each adult requires at least 21 inches of table space, so that means a 63-inch-long counter (a typical size) will accommodate three stools at most.

Seating depends on counter height. A 28- to 32-inch-high counter requires 18-inch-high chairs with 20 inches of knee space under the bar. If you make the island or peninsula the same height as the rest of the kitchen countertops (36 inches being the standard), you'll be able to accommodate 24-inch-high stools and 14 inches of knee space. Go up to bar height (42 to 45 inches), and you'll need 30-inch-high stools with footrests, also with 14 inches of knee space.

One more aspect of kitchen design to consider is storage—an element that needs to blend function with style. Once you conclude how you want your new kitchen space to function, you're in a position to tackle the next perplexing yet all-important challenge: selecting the proper cabinetry.

CHOOSING CABINETS

Who can't relate to this scenario: you turn on the oven to preheat it, but wait, did you take out the large roasting pan first? How about the lasagna dish, muffin tins, pizza stone, and cookie sheets that are in there, too? Now where can you put everything that was in the oven while the casserole is baking and the countertop is laden with the rest of tonight's dinner ingredients?

Above: Frameless cabinets do not have a face frame, creating a sleek, contemporary look. This type of cabinet usually lacks moldings and other ornamentation.

Right: Traditional cabinet designs often have raised panel doors and drawer fronts. This type of cabinet is usually of framed design with a frame across the front of the cabinet box.

The oven, it seems, has become the catchall for the big, awkward stuff that you can't fit into kitchen cabinets but is just too darn ugly to leave out. Besides, the countertop is where you keep the toaster oven, food processor, coffeemaker, canisters, hand mixer, portable TV, notepad, coupon file, bills, hand lotion, car keys, and your vitamins! Wouldn't life be grand if there was a place for everything and everything was in its place? Good cabinetry outfitted with an assortment of organizing options can help you there. It can make your kitchen more efficient and a whole lot neater while establishing a style, or "look," for the room. Keep in mind, however, that cabinetry will also consume about 40 percent of your remodeling budget, according to the NKBA. So before making any expensive decisions—or costly mistakes—investigate all of the various cabinetry options that are available to you.

CABINET CONSTRUCTION

Basically, cabinets are constructed in one of two ways: *framed* or *frameless*. Framed cabinets have a traditional look, with a full frame across the face of the cabinet box that may show between closed doors. This secures adjacent cabinets and strengthens wider cabinet boxes with a center rail. Hinges on framed cabinets may or may not be visible around doors when they are closed. The door's face may be ornamented with raised or recessed panels, trimmed or framed panels, or a framed-glass panel with or without muntins (the narrow vertical and horizontal strips of wood that divide panes of glass).

Frameless cabinets—also known as European-style cabinets, although American manufacturers also make them—are built without a face frame and sport a clean, contemporary look. There's no trim or molding with this simple design. Close-fitting doors cover the entire front of the box, no ornamentation appears on the face of the doors, and hinges are typically hidden inside the cabinet box.

Choosing one type over another is generally a matter of taste, although framed units offer slightly less interior space. But the quality of construction is a factor that always should be taken into consideration. How do you judge it? Solid wood is too expensive for most of today's budgets, but it might be used on just the doors and frames. More typical is plywood box construction, which offers good structural support and solid wood on the doors and frames. To save money, cabinetmakers sometimes use strong plywood for support elements, such as the box and frame, and medium-density fiberboard for other parts, such as doors and drawer fronts. In yet another alternative, good-quality laminate cabinets can be made with high-quality, thick particleboard underneath the laminate finish.

There are other things to look for in cabinet construction. They include dovetail or mortise-and-tenon joinery and solidly mortised hinges. Also, make sure that the interior of every cabinet is well finished, with adjustable shelves that are a minimum $5/8$ inch thick to prevent bowing.

Unless you have the time and skill to build the cabinets yourself or can hire someone else to do it, you'll have to purchase them in one of four ways. *Knockdown* cabinetry (also known as RTA, ready to assemble) is shipped flat and, sometimes, unfinished because you put the pieces together. *Stock* cabinetry comes in standard sizes but limited styles and colors; it is often available on the spot or can be delivered quickly. Like stock, *semi-custom* cabinetry comes in standard styles, but it is manufactured to fit a homeowner's specific size and finish needs. *Custom* cabinetry is not limited in terms of style or size because it is built to the designer's specifications.

Below left: Slide-out cutting boards provide an extra work surface without sacrificing storage space.

Below: Lazy Susans turn the wasted area in a corner into valuable storage space.

CABINET ACCESSORIES AND OPTIONS

Most people would agree that no matter how much storage space they have, they need even more. The problem often isn't the amount, it's the inaccessible placement and inefficient configuration of the storage space. One of the greatest benefits today's designers and manufacturers offer is fitted and accessorized interiors that maximize even the smallest nook and cranny inside cabinets and drawers. These accommodations not only expand the use of space but increase convenience and accessibility. Among them are the following:

Appliance Garages. Appliance garages make use of dead space in a corner, but they can be installed anywhere in the vertical space between the wall-mounted cabinet and the countertop. A tambour (rolltop) door hides small appliances like a food processor or anything else you want within reach but hidden from view. This form of minicabinet can be equipped with an electrical outlet and can even be divided into separate sections to store more than one item. Reserve part of the appliance garage for cookbook storage, or outfit it with small drawers for little items or spices. Customize an appliance garage any way you like.

Lazy Susans and Carousel Shelves. These rotating shelves maximize dead corner storage and put items such as dishes or pots and pans within easy reach. A lazy Susan rotates 360 degrees, so just spin it to find what you're looking for. Carousel shelves, which attach to two right-angled doors, rotate 270 degrees; open the doors and the shelves, which are actually attached to the doors, put any item within hand reach. Pivoting shelves are a variation on the carousel design and may or may not be door-mounted. In addition, units may be built into taller cabinets, creating a pantry that can store a lot in a small amount of space.

Right: Manufacturers offer appliance panels that match the cabinets. These help a washer and dryer blend with the rest of the kitchen.

Fold-Down Mixer Shelf. This spring-loaded shelf swings up and out of a base cabinet for use, then folds down and back into the cabinet when the mixer is no longer needed, which reduces clutter by keeping the countertop clear of appliances.

Slide-Outs and Tilt-Outs. Installed in base cabinets, slide-out trays and racks store small appliances, linens, cans, or boxed items, while slide-out bins are good for holding onions, potatoes, grains, pet food, or potting soil—even garbage or recycling containers. A tilt-out tray is located in the often-wasted area just below the lip of the countertop in front of the sink and above base cabinet doors. It looks like a drawer but tilts open to provide a neat nook for sponges and scouring pads that look messy when left on the counter.

Built-in Pantry Units. These fold-out or slide-out units can be fitted into narrow areas that might otherwise remain wasted. Store dry or canned goods here. Fold-out units have door-mounted shelves and an in-cabinet shelf that pivots; slide-out units fit multiple shelves in a cabinet.

In addition to these options, check out everything that a cabinet manufacturer has to offer to make the most of a cabinet's storage capacity. Other items to look for include special racks for trays and cookie sheets, drawer inserts for organizing spices and utensils, watertight recycling bins, wine racks, fold-down recipe book rests, sliding pot racks, built-in canister drawers, and plate racks.

If you decide to make do with your existing cabinets, consider refitting the interiors with cabinet organizers. These plastic, plastic-coated wire, or enameled-steel racks and hangers are widely available at department stores and home centers.

Beware of the temptation to over-specialize your kitchen storage. Sizes and needs for certain items change, so be sure to allot at least 50 percent of your kitchen's storage to standard cabinets with one or more movable shelves.

THE DECORATIVE ROLE OF CABINETS

The look you create in your kitchen will be largely influenced by the cabinetry you select. Finding a style that suits you and how you will use your new kitchen is similar to shopping for furniture. In fact, don't be surprised to see many furniture details dressing up the cabinets on view in showrooms and home centers today.

Besides architectural elements such as fluted pilasters, corbels, moldings, and bull's-eye panels, look for details such as fretwork, rope motifs, gingerbread trim, balusters, composition ornamentation (it looks like carving), even footed cabinets that mimic separate furniture pieces. If your taste runs toward less fussy design, you'll also find handsome door and drawer styles that feature minimal decoration, if any. Woods and finishes are just as varied, and range from informal looks in birch, oak, ash, and maple to rich mahogany and cherry. Laminate finishes, though less popular than they were a decade ago, haven't completely disappeared from the marketplace, but an array of colors has replaced the once-ubiquitous almond and white finishes.

Clockwise (from left): Most cabinet manufacturers include units designed to hold built-in appliances. Don't be afraid to experiment with cabinet placement—note the drawer unit placed on top of a counter and under a wall-hung cabinet. The three small drawers shown far left come in handy for dish towels and cooking utensils. Cabinets offer many storage options, but their principal design function is to set the tone for the entire room.

COLOR

Color is coming on strong on wood cabinetry, too. Accents in one, two, or more hues are pairing with natural wood tones. White-painted cabinets take on a warmer glow with tinted shades of this always popular neutral. Special "vintage" finishes, such as translucent color glazes, continue to grow in popularity, as do distressed finishing techniques such as wire brushing and rubbed-through color that add both another dimension and the appeal of handcraftmanship, even on mass-produced items. Contemporary kitchens, which historically favor an all-white palette, are warming up with earthier neutral shades or less sterile off-whites.

If you're shy about using color on such a high-ticket item as cabinetry, try it as an accent on molding, door trim, or island cabinetry. Just as matched furniture suites have become passé in other rooms of the house, the same is true for the kitchen, where mixing several looks can add sophistication and visual interest.

HARDWARE

Another way to emphasize your kitchen's decorative style is with hardware. From exquisite reproductions in brass, pewter, wrought iron, or ceramic to handsome bronze, chrome, nickel, glass, steel, plastic, rubber, wood, or stone creations, a smorgasbord of shapes and designs is available.

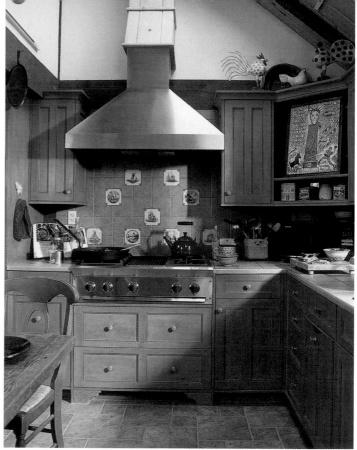

Some pieces are highly polished; others are matte-finished, smooth, or hammered. Some are abstract or geometrical; others are simple, elegant shapes. Whimsical designs take on the forms of animals or teapots, vegetables or flowers. Even just one or two great-looking door or drawer pulls can be showstoppers in a kitchen that may otherwise be devoid of much personality. Like mixing cabinet finishes, a combination of two hardware styles—perhaps picked up from other materials in the room—makes a big design statement. As the famed architect Mies Van der Rohe once stated, "God is in the details," and the most perfect detail in your new kitchen may be the artistic hardware that you select.

Besides looks, consider the function of a pull or knob. You have to be able to grip it easily and comfortably. If your fingers or hands get stiff easily, or if you have arthritis, select C- or U-shaped pulls. If you like a knob, try it out in the showroom to make sure it isn't slippery or awkward when you grab it. Knobs and pulls can be inexpensive if you can stick to unfinished ones that you can paint in an accent color picked up from the tile or wallpaper. If you don't plan to buy new cabinets, changing the hardware on old ones can redefine their style. The right knob or pull can suggest any one of a number of vintage looks or decorative styles from Colonial to Victorian to Arts and Crafts to Postmodern.

Clockwise (from above): Cabinet selection will help create any decorating style you wish. The color and door style of the cabinets above evoke a Provençal style. The legs on the cabinet supporting the cooktop give the appearance of unfitted furniture. The raised panels and moldings below provide a traditional appearance to this kitchen. The cabinets, wood trim, and open shelving create a more personal style opposite. A dramatic use of color is shown above left.

COUNTERTOP OPTIONS

Selecting countertop material is not as simple as it once was because there are infinitely more choices in color, pattern, and texture thanks to new materials and applications. The trend is to use more than one, specifying types based on the functions at hand. For example, you might use a solid-surfacing material in one part of the kitchen, a marble insert at the bake center, and stainless steel next to the cooktop. Or you could pair one countertop material with the cabinetry that runs along the wall, and choose another for the island counter.

In addition to enhancing the function of your work surfaces, the countertop materials that you choose can underpin your decorating theme. Wood is a natural choice for a country-style kitchen, for example, whereas concrete looks handsome in a contemporary setting. The concrete can be poured or prefabricated into a mold on site. You can add color to it or create a one-of-a-kind inlaid design with stones, shards of glass, china, tile, shells, or just about anything else you can think of adding.

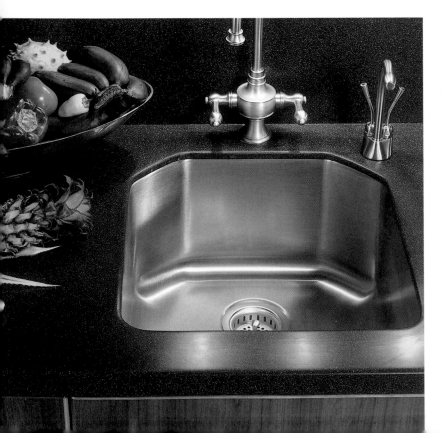

There are no hard-and-fast rules about any material you choose, but one important factor that should play a role in your selection is maintenance. Some materials demand greater care than others. Marble, for instance, must be sealed periodically because it can absorb liquids that will mar its looks. If you don't have time for the upkeep, can you live with the battle scars of everyday use?

Here's a rundown on choices for countertop material. After you've read about the attributes of each, you can decide which ones may be right for your application. Also, consider each type as a possibility for a matching or entirely different backsplash.

CERAMIC TILE

Ceramic tile is a perennial favorite. Impervious to water, it's perfect for installation at the sink. Tile is also durable, and doesn't scratch, burn, or stain. Aside from its practical attributes, ceramic tile offers the greatest opportunity

SOLID-SURFACING MATERIAL

An extremely durable, easily maintained synthetic material, solid surfacing is made of polyester or acrylic. It's expensive, costing almost as much per linear foot as luxurious granite or marble, but it wears long and well. The material is completely impervious to water, and you can repair any dents or abrasions that may occur with a light sanding.

STONE

Marble and granite are probably the most expensive materials you can choose for a countertop. Though it is stone, marble is actually a soft, porous material that can be gouged and stained easily. Considered chic today, a granite countertop is a handsome status symbol. Like marble, it has a cool surface that pastry makers favor, but it is less absorbent. This makes it less likely to stain than marble.

Left to right: Here are three of the most popular countertop materials. Solid surfacing material, opposite, comes in a wide range of colors and patterns; a variety of decorative edge treatments are also available. Granite is an elegant and durable countertop material. Ceramic tile also offers the homeowner a number of design options. Here the designer mixed tile sizes and colors to achieve this custom design.

for adding color, pattern, and texture to your kitchen. Custom designs bring personality into the room. Hand-painted, imported, and antique versions are very pricey, but you can combine inexpensive standard tiles with raised or silk-screened patterns to create unique designs and murals nonetheless.

PLASTIC LAMINATE

Made of several layers of melamine, paper, and plastic resin bonded under heat and pressure, then glued to particleboard or plywood, plastic laminate is inexpensive, relatively easy to install, and available in a vast array of colors and patterns. Plastic laminate resists stains, water, and mild abrasion very well, but it can be chipped or scratched by sharp knives, and it will scorch if you put a hot pot down on it. There is no repair option available except replacement. More expensive solid-core laminates eliminate unsightly black edges at the joints because the color goes all the way through the material.

Two other stone materials, limestone and concrete, are finding their way onto countertops in the hands of creative designers. Limestone is available as tiles, as is concrete, but the latter can be poured and molded, too. Becoming even more creative, designers are adding color to concrete, and creating inlaid designs as well.

WOOD

Wood is unrivaled for its natural warmth and beauty. But it expands and contracts, depending on environmental conditions, and may warp if exposed to water. To protect a wood countertop, apply a film finish with varnish; other alternatives include applying lacquer or oil periodically. Teak is an excellent choice for a wood countertop. Another option is butcher-block, which is actually a laminated wood product. Eastern hard rock sugar maple is the most durable wood for a butcher-block application.

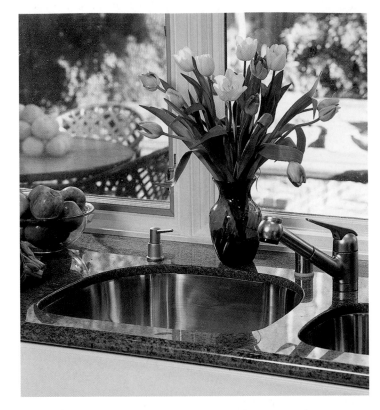

STAINLESS STEEL

Many of today's kitchens feature lots of metal, but they don't appear antiseptic or cold. That's largely because designers balance the look by introducing vibrant colors and other materials, such as ceramic tile or wood, into the room. Stainless steel used for a countertop, whether it is for the entire counter or just a section of it, can look quite sophisticated, especially with a wood trim. Stainless steel is vulnerable to scrapes, stains, and corrosion, so shop for a product with high chromium and nickel content.

SELECTING FIXTURES

What could be more basic to the modern kitchen than a sink and faucet? Yet in today's world, there's practically nothing basic about them. Style comes in all price ranges, but high-performance technology is accompanied by an equally high price tag. There are designs and finishes to suit any contemporary or traditional taste. And far from being just necessary items in a kitchen, sinks and faucets have evolved into highly decorative elements. Here's a look at what's on the market.

SINKS

These receptacles come in all sizes, shapes, and colors, and are typically fabricated from enameled cast iron, stainless steel, a composite material (solid surfacing, acrylic, or a mixture of natural quartz or granite with resins), or solid stone. They may be hand-painted or decorated with silk-screened designs, contoured, beveled, brushed to a matte finish, or polished to a mirror finish. The trend is to include the largest sink that you can accommodate within the confines of your space. Deep bowls make it easier to deal with awkward oversized items, such as large roasting pans and tall pots used for cooking pasta. A good example is the farm-style (or exposed-apron) sink that, at one time, would have been regarded as déclassé but is reemerging in glamorous solid colors or with decorative patterns. Shallow-basin sinks are also available, when there is no other place to install the dishwasher but under the sink.

Two- and three-bowl configurations are also gaining wide popularity. This arrangement allows you to separate clean dishes from dirty ones as well as from waste materials. Some sinks come with a colander and cutting board. Typically, a waste-disposal unit is installed with one of the bowls, usually the larger one. Just peel your potatoes, then whisk the skins down the disposer. Lay the cutting board over the top of the bowl for chopping, and afterwards push the potato slices into the colander for rinsing.

Clockwise (from left): Traditional cast-iron sinks complement most kitchen designs. The round bar sink opposite serves as a second sink in this kitchen. The stainless-steel sinks shown opposite above are mounted beneath a granite counter. Undermounting works with solid counter materials, such as natural stone and solid surfacing. The exposed-apron stainless-steel sink at top is an updated version of the traditional farmhouse sink.

Right: The sleek lines and single-lever operation of this faucet complements contemporary kitchens. When buying for a multibowl sink, make sure the faucet can reach all bowls.

Some designers recommend installing sinks in two separate areas. The primary sink often anchors the main food preparation and cleanup areas, while a smaller secondary sink serves outside of the major work zone. A second sink is a must when two or more people cook together routinely, but it is also handy if you do crafts in the kitchen or entertain often.

Like every other kitchen product, there are numerous choices of sinks from which you will have to make a final selection, so it won't always be easy. In terms of durability, any one of the materials mentioned above will hold up well for years, if not decades, with the right care. Enameled cast-iron sinks tend to discolor but can be cleaned easily with a nonabrasive cleanser. Stainless steel and stone should be cleaned the same way. However, composite sinks are scratch resistant, with the exception of inexpensive acrylic models, so you can use an abrasive agent on them. Expect a quality sink to last as long as 30 years. In terms of installation, there are five types of sinks to consider for the kitchen.

■ **Undermounted.** If you want a smooth look, an under-mounted sink may be for you. The bowl is attached underneath the countertop.

■ **Integral.** As the word "integral" implies, the sink and countertop are fabricated from the same material—stone, faux stone, or solid surfacing. There are no visible seams or joints in which food can accumulate.

■ **Self-rimming or flush-mounted.** A self-rimmed sink has a rolled edge that is mounted over the countertop.

■ **Rimmed.** Unlike a self-rimming sink, this type requires a flat metal strip to seal the sink to the countertop.

■ **Tile-in.** Used with a tiled countertop, the sink rim is flush with the tiled surface. Grout seals the sink to the surrounding countertop area.

FAUCETS

Faucets are no longer just conduits for water. From sleek European-inspired designs to graceful gooseneck shapes, today's selections add beauty as well as function to a kitchen. An excellent example is the pot-filler faucet, which is mounted to the wall over the cooktop. Some versions have a pull-out spout; others come with a double- or triple-jointed arm that can be bent to reach up and down, or swiveled back and forth, allowing the cook to pull the faucet over to a pot on the farthest burner. Anyone who has ever had to lug a heavy pot of water from the tap to a burner will appreciate this convenience. Just remember: You'll need additional hot- and cold-water plumbing if you install one of these faucets over your range or cooktop.

State-of-the-art technology in faucets gives you not only much more control over water use but better performance and a more extensive choice for finishes as well. Some specialty features to look for include pullout faucet heads, retractable sprayers, hot- and cold-water dispensing, single-lever control, antiscald and flow-control devices, a lowered lead content in brass components, and built-in water purifiers to enhance taste.

For a quality faucet, inquire about its parts when you shop. The best are those made of solid brass or a brass-base material. Both are corrosion-resistant. Avoid plastic components—they won't hold up. Ask about the faucet's valving, too. Buy a model that has a washerless cartridge; it will cost more, but it will last longer.

Besides selecting a spout type (standard, arched, gooseneck, or pullout), you may choose between single or double levers. Pullouts come with a built-in sprayer, if you want one. The others will require installing a separate sprayer. Until recently, a pressure-balanced faucet (one equipped with a device that equalizes the hot and cold water coming out of a faucet to prevent scalding) came only with single-lever model. Now it is available with faucets that have separate hot- and cold-water valves. You may mix your spout

with one of many types of handle styles: wrist blades, levers, scrolls, geometric shapes, and cross handles.

Chrome, brass, enamel-coated or baked-on colors, pewter, and nickel are typical faucets finishes. Make a fashion statement by mixing finishes or pair a matte, brushed, or antiqued look with one that is highly polished. Some finishes, such as chrome or enamel, are easier to care for than others—brass, for instance, which may require polishing. In terms of installation, these are the three types of faucets from which you'll have to choose:

■ **Center set,** which has two separate valves, one for hot, the other for cold water, and a spout. But all three pieces appear connected in one unit.

■ **Widespread,** which features a spout with two separate valves that appear to be three distinct pieces.

■ **Single lever,** which contains a spout and single lever in one piece for one-hand operation.

When you design your sink and faucet area, don't be sidetracked by the good looks of a product. Think about whether it works for your application. Today, good looks come in all types. Instead, compare the size of your biggest pots and racks to see whether the sink you're considering will accommodate them. If it won't and you can't install something deeper, pair the sink with a pullout or gooseneck faucet. Always make sure it directs the flow of the water into the center of the bowl and slightly to one side. A spout that is proportionately too tall for the depth of the sink will splash water; one that is too short won't allow water to reach to the sink's corners. If you plan a double- or triple-bowl configuration, the spout should deliver enough water to each of the bowls.

Thoughtful planning isn't only applied to the kitchen—it works for the bath as well, which is discussed in the next chapter.

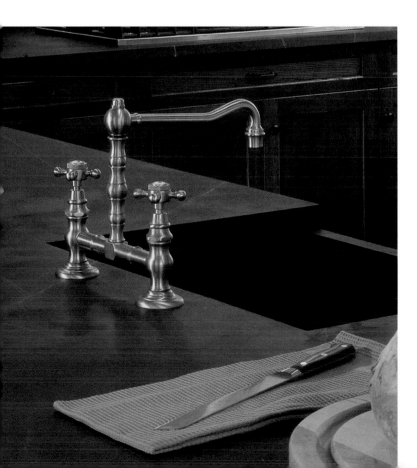

Left: Although it is traditional on the outside, this faucet is up-to-date on the inside. Brass provides corrosion-resistant performance; washerless models reduce repairs.

1. Pullout bins are one way to increase the storage capacity of base cabinets.

2. Moldings and raised-panel doors are hallmarks of traditional cabinet design.

3. A slide-out shelf holds a computer. Many kitchens contain a small office area.

4. Eating areas can come in the form of tables or snack counters, as shown here.

5. Any number of decorative edge treatments are possible with solid-surfacing material.

6. Decorative tiles are used to create a custom backsplash.

7. Shading and color distribution makes any natural stone counter a unique creation.

8. These hanging fixtures help put this traditional-style kitchen in the best possible light.

a gallery of...

5

7

6

8

...smart ideas

1 Pullout spray faucets eliminate the need for a separate spray on the sink deck.

2 Stainless-steel sinks come in multibowl configurations. This model has a decorative rim.

3 Use standard-height chairs for table-height snack counters; use stools for higher counters.

4 Explore storage options. Note the drawer for baking supplies underneath the wall ovens.

5 When planning your kitchen, don't forget to account for both natural and artificial light.

6 A gooseneck faucet with simple lever handles adds authenticity to a traditional design.

7 Place eating areas out of the main work area, as with the banquette shown here.

8 Here's a good use of space at the end of a cabinet run. A shelf for cookbooks is another possibility.

CHAPTER 10

CREATING A BATHROOM DESIGN

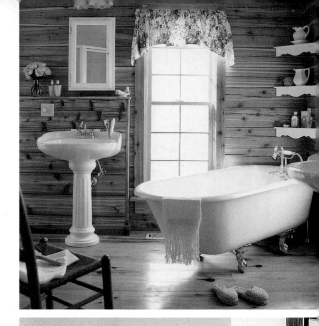

SET PRIORITIES ▪ BASIC LAYOUTS ▪ TYPES OF BATHROOMS ▪ SHOPPING FOR BATH PRODUCTS ▪ FIXTURES ▪ STORAGE FOR THE BATH ▪ SERVICEABLE SURFACES ▪ WHAT'S YOUR STYLE?

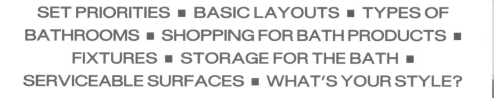

Many professionals believe that bathrooms may be the most difficult rooms in the house to design properly. The space is often small, yet it must be able to accommodate a variety of large fixtures. In addition, many homeowners tend to focus, at least initially, on the way the bathroom looks. They fall in love with the whirlpool tub that is really too large for the space or the exquisite hand-painted sink that, while beautiful, demands too much effort to keep it looking that way. Design your bath to be functional as well as beautiful.

Architect Louis Sullivan said, "Form follows function." That does not mean that style has to be subservient to function, but there must be a balance between the two. So even if you have a clear picture about how you want the new bathroom to look, put that thought on hold—temporarily— and think about how it will work.

Don't mislead yourself into believing that only a luxurious plan demands this kind of attention. Even if you are designing a modest bath, you can greatly increase its performance and your ultimate comfort by thoughtfully planning out every square inch of floor and wall space. In fact, small spaces require more attention to details than larger spaces.

Whatever the size of your investment, you should get the most out of it. Besides, if you ever decide to sell your house, potential buyers will be put off by cramped bathrooms that look like everything was designed as an afterthought. On the other hand, you can make a splash—and perhaps a tidy profit—if the fixtures are in good condition, the floor plan appears carefully thought out, the room looks bright, and there is ample storage.

SET PRIORITIES

If you will be working with a design professional, expect to be interviewed at the beginning of the planning stage. He or she will want to get to know you and whoever else will use the new bathroom. Your designer isn't being nosy. He or she simply wants to understand your likes and habits, as

Above: **Good design comes from knowing who will use the room and how they will use it. Note the large amount of storage in this family bathroom.**

well as your basic requirements and greatest expectations with respect to the new bath. The designer will also make a sketch of the existing space to get an idea of what works and what doesn't. The rough drawing may include any adjacent areas that might be considered for expansion, such as a closet, part of a hallway, or a small room.

If you will be acting as your own designer, do the same. You can't assume that you instinctively know what has to be done to transform the old bathroom into a fabulous new space just because you live there. That's acting on emotion. For the best result, approach the project in the same analytical manner as a professional who understands design and can be objective about what has to happen. To learn how to sketch a floor plan as if you were a professional, see the Smart Steps in Chapter Nine, on page 193.

BASIC LAYOUTS

If the existing floor plan works for you, all you have to think about is updating old fixtures, installing new tile, and perhaps replacing the cabinetry. Even so, you may want to play around with the idea of modifying the layout on paper. You may be surprised to discover, in fact, that a few minor changes in the floor plan can enhance your original arrangement. Just keep in mind: moving plumbing fixtures in an existing bath may significantly raise costs.

ONE: Make a new base drawing. As in the base drawing you made in the last chapter for the old kitchen, use a $1/2$-inch scale. (If you haven't made a base drawing, see the Smart Steps in Chapter Nine, on page 193.) If you are using a $1/4$-inch grid, each square represents a 6-inch square of real floor space. Begin by drawing the outer walls, and then add the windows and doors.

TWO: Make templates of the fixtures. Creating paper templates of fixtures and cabinets is an easy way to experiment with different layouts. You can draw the fixtures to scale on graph paper, or copy the templates in the Appendix of this book. Then cut them out so you can move them around your plan. If you have collected pictures and spec sheets (printed product information from the manufacturer), use the dimensions given. When cutting out templates, include both the fixtures and the required front and side clearances—that way you won't get caught short. Usually, plumbing codes require a minimum clearance for each fixture. Fixture clearances are shown in the drawings on this and the next two pages. The top number of each pair indicates the minimum required by code or function. The bottom dimension allows more room between fixtures. For an efficient but convenient layout, aim for somewhere between the two numbers when you draw your plan.

THREE: Place the fixtures. You will use some fixtures more often than others: first the lavatory, next the toilet, then the tub or shower. An efficient plan places the lav closest to the door, followed by the toilet, and finally the tub, which is located the farthest away. If there is any leeway in your plan, place the toilet so that it will not be visible when the door is open. Even in a small bathroom, the direction of the door swing can help shield the toilet from view.

Above and below: Here are the recommended clearances for sinks, toilets, and bidets. The bottom number is best, but the top will do in tight spaces.

60"
72"

30" to 32"
(Tubs)
32" to 60"
(Whirlpools)

2" to 8"

30"
48"

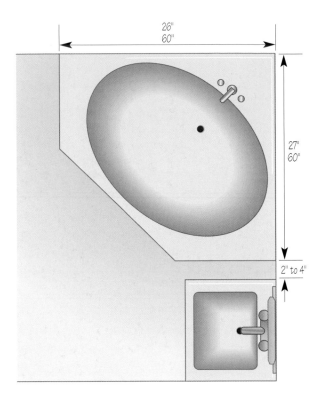

26"
60"

27"
60"

2" to 4"

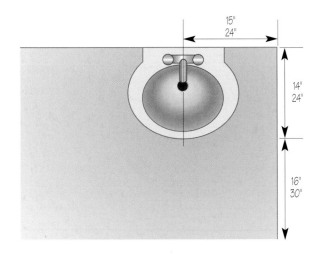

15"
24"

14"
24"

16"
30"

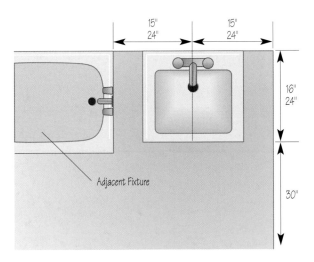

15"
24"

15"
24"

16"
24"

Adjacent Fixture

30"

30"
36"

Clockwise (from above): When measuring for clearances around lavatories, take the measurement from the center of the fixture, which is usually the drain. In these drawings of lavs, the bottom number is the preferred clearance, but the top number will do in small rooms. Note the recommended clearances in front of the lavs. Both rectangular and corner tubs should have about 48 inches of open floor space in front of them for safety.

Tub/Shower. Another easy way to place fixtures on your plan is to start with the largest ones. If you know you want a whirlpool bath and separate dual shower, pencil them in first. (Hint: position the length of the tub perpendicular to the joists to distribute the weight safely. If you don't, you'll incur the costs of adding structural support to the floor.) To make the tub the focal point of the room, put it opposite the door or within a direct line of view from the door. If there will be a separate tub and shower, locate them near each other so that they can share plumbing lines and the same sight lines. This also makes it easier to plan the space around them.

Lavatory. After placing the big items, locate your lavatory. Do you want two lavs or just one? Do you want two lavatories near each other or located on opposite sides of the room? Will two people use the room at once? Answer these questions before you pencil in the location.

Above left and right: **Showers may vary in size but the recommended clearances in front of them do not. If possible, allow 60 inches of clearance, but never anything less than 36 inches.**

Below left and right: **Location is everything. The toilet is visible from the hall in the drawing bottom left. To solve the problem, flop the toilet and lavatory and change the swing of the door.**

If you are placing two lavatories side by side, leave enough maneuvering space and elbow room. One smart way to do this is to install storage between them. Some families install two lavatories at different heights. Not only is this more comfortable and ergonomic, it defines space as adult-designated or child-designated in a bathroom shared by all.

Toilet. Once you have the lavatories in place, go ahead and locate the toilet and bidet, if you have one. (A bidet resembles a toilet but is actually a basinlike device for personal hygiene.) The bidet is another item you will want to keep away from the bathroom door and out of its sight line.

Extras. With the main elements penciled in, start adding the extras—the windows, doors, skylights, greenhouse, gym, sauna, and whatever other amenities you are considering. You can play with the design as long as you like, trying different ideas and placements, but make sure you take practical matters, such as pipes and codes, into consideration.

Customize. Although there are recommended guidelines for comfort and convenience, only you will be able to determine what will be most comfortable for you. If you happen to be 7 feet tall, you can probably forget about the height clearances and raise them! Likewise, if you are a small person, lower the counters. Don't worry about being able to resell your home later; another person of your height may appreciate the comfort of a higher or lower surface. If the need arises, installing a new vanity with standard-height countertop is not easy, but it's not a major project either.

TYPES OF BATHROOMS

The most-common-size American bathroom measures 60 × 84 inches or 60 × 96 inches. The most common complaint about it is the lack of space. The arrangement may have suited families 50 years ago, but times and habits have changed. If it's the only bathroom in the house, making it work better becomes even more important.

When planning the layout, try angling a sink or shower unit in a corner to free up some floor space. Unlike a traditional door, which swings into the room and takes up wall space when it is open, a pocket door slides into the wall. Another smart way to add function to a small bathroom is to remove the drywall and install shelves between the studs.

You can also make a small bathroom feel roomier by bringing in natural light with a skylight or roof window or by replacing one small standard window with several small casement units that can be installed high on the wall to maintain privacy.

Left: Once you have the basics sketched out in your plan, begin to add the extras that personalize your design, such as the above-counter lav and trapezoidal countertop shown here.

You can find small-scale fixtures specifically designed for the powder room, from the tiniest lavs to unusually narrow toilets. In general, however, maintain a clearance that meets code on each side of the toilet, and include comfortable reaching room for the toilet-paper dispenser. Most powder rooms measure at least 36 inches wide by 54 to 60 inches long, depending on the layout of the space.

Keep a small powder room as light and open as possible. Plan to install good lighting because the powder room is often used for touching up makeup. (For more about planing a lighting scheme, see Chapter Three, "The Right Light," on page 52.)

A carefully thought-out floor plan makes a difference in this usually small space. Make sure the door swings out against a wall, not inward, or use a pocket door for easy access. If it must be accessible for someone in a wheelchair, include a minimum 5-foot-diameter circle of space in the center of the room, which is just large enough for a wheelchair to turn around.

In the powder room, the vanity is often the focal point. The room offers the best opportunity to showcase a decorative piece, such as a hand-painted pedestal sink or a custom-made vanity. Because the powder room is often for guests and is normally located on the ground floor near the living area, take extra care to ensure privacy. If possible, the best location is in a hallway, away from the living room, kitchen, and dining area. This room can also handle stronger wall colors—either dark or bright ones—as well as larger, bolder wallpaper patterns because it is a short-stay room.

If you are adding a second or possibly a third bathroom to your house, here are a few other ideas for your consideration—and inspiration.

THE POWDER ROOM

The guest bath. The half bath. It has a lot of names, and it may be the most efficient room in the house, providing just what you need often in tight quarters. A powder room normally includes nothing more than a lavatory and a toilet.

THE FAMILY BATH

Compartmentalizing is the best way to start planning the family bath. But remember, when you separate the bathroom into smaller, distinct areas, you run the risk of making the room feel cramped. Try to alleviate this with extra natural light, good artificial lighting, and translucent partitions made of glass blocks or etched glass. Anything that divides with privacy while also allowing light to enter will help ease the closed-in feeling.

If separating the fixtures is not possible, include a sink in the dressing area within the master bedroom to provide a second place for applying makeup or shaving. Investigate building a back-to-back bath in lieu of one large shared room. Another popular option is to locate the bathing fixtures, both the tub and separate shower, in the center of the room; install the bidet, a toilet, and sink on either side in their own separate areas. To make the arrangement work, keep each side of the room accessible to the door.

Above: A decorative soffit and bright color scheme enliven this bath used mainly by the kids in the family.

Left: If possible, create separate sections for the major bath functions, such as this separate tub area.

Right: For the lav or lavs in primary or master bathrooms, be sure to provide adequate counter and storage space for toiletries and the like.

THE MASTER BATH

The concept of the master bath has come of age in the past decade. It is one of the most popular rooms to remodel and gives one of the highest returns on investment upon resale. It's where you can create that sought-after getaway—the home version of a European spa.

Some popular amenities to include in your plan are a sauna, greenhouse, exercise studio, fireplace, audio and video systems, faucets and sprayers with full massaging options, steam room, whirlpool tub, and dressing table. You are only limited by size and imagination—and some local codes.

Extras can be tempting but may require special planning. For example, you may need additional support in the floor, as well as supplemental heating and ventilation. You would not want to slip into a tub and have it fall two floors to the middle of the living room. Unfortunately, this really does happen when the weight of an oversized contemporary tub is installed on top of a 50-year-old floor. Older houses simply weren't built to accommodate the volume of water some people now use when bathing.

Some of the best floor plans for the modern adult bath also include a separate room for the toilet and bidet, a detached tub and shower, and dual sinks on opposite sides of the room with adjacent dressing rooms and walk-in closets. Modern couples want to share a master bed and bath, but they also want to have privacy and the ease of getting ready in the morning without tripping over their mates. The only way to do this harmoniously is to mingle the parts of the room that invite sharing and separate those elements that are always private.

Above right: A half wall creates an alcove for the toilet and bidet in this master bathroom.

Right: Individual lavs and separate tub and shower make this master bath attractive and functional.

SHOPPING FOR BATH PRODUCTS

The products you select to outfit your new bathroom will affect both your design and your budget. If you choose top-of-the-line products, expect a top-of-the-line bill. Factors that influence the cost of new fixtures, cabinetry, counter-tops, and flooring include updated technology and type of finish. The smarter the device, the more you'll pay for it. Likewise, the fancier the finish, the higher the price tag. But cost does not always reflect quality, nor does it equate nec-essarily with satisfaction. And quality and personal satisfac-tion are the most important fac-tors to consider when making any product selection.

So, how can you make smart choices about items such as tubs and showers, tile, and cabinets? How can you tell whether a product is reliable and will endure the daily abuse of water and moisture? Are there basic differences that make one faucet or a particular toilet better than another? To find out, you can do a little research. Shop around. Visit bath designer showrooms, read books, and don't be afraid to ask questions. Otherwise, you can take your chances on buy-ing an item that might not suit your needs. If you're not the gambling type, however, here are some steps you can take to select products and materials for your new bath with confidence.

Right: **Here's a budget saver: rather than install two lavs, the owners opted for extra storage, counter, and mirror space.**

SMART steps

ONE: Separate the product from the hype. A high price does not always mean high quality. Find out what is different about a toilet that costs $100, for example, and one that sells for $300 or even $1,000. This way you can decide whether the higher price is worth it. A knowl-edgeable salesperson will be able to tell you. If not, contact the manufacturer. Many have toll-free numbers and Web sites set up to handle consumer questions. Sometimes the price hike is because of a feature you can't see. For example, a faucet with replaceable parts costs much more than a new faucet with parts that cannot be replaced. How much do you want to gamble that the faucet you buy won't break?

Left: Stand-alone, footed tubs are extremely popular right now; they go well with casual and country decorating schemes.

FIVE: Be wary of some handmade products for the bath. You may be tempted by a handsome unglazed sink from a chic pottery shop. Certainly, it will add a unique cachet to your design, but an unglazed sink may not meet local code. Don't buy on impulse before checking out the building codes in your area. If there's any doubt in your mind, ask if you can leave a refundable deposit on the item, and then speak with your contractor, who should be familiar with the rules and can save you from a costly mistake.

TWO: Weigh your options. Analyze the benefits and the risks that come with each product. Once you have that information, a decision will be easier. If you are sprucing up an old bath or adding a new one in a house you expect to sell soon, you might install a less-expensive countertop material, for example. But if you are making a major investment in a remodeling project that you plan to live with for a long time, you might be happier in the long run with something that may cost more but gives you greater satisfaction and will be more reliable for years to come.

THREE: Seek reliable advice. Ask the manufacturer about the expected life of the product or its efficiency. Don't take advice from a store clerk unless he or she is an experienced remodeling professional. Talk to your contractor, who may be familiar with the product or can pass along critical feedback from other clients who may have purchased the same item or something similar to it.

FOUR: Don't make a choice based on style or color. It doesn't work for cars, and it won't work for building materials. Sure, style and color are important, but it's just as easy to find a first-rate fixture that looks great in your new bathroom as it is to find one that looks fabulous but performs poorly. Opt for quality.

SIX: Prorate costs. You may be dismayed by the initial sticker price, but when you divide the cost of the product or material by its anticipated longevity (how many years you expect it to last), you may be amazed at how reasonable it really is. Of course, this won't alleviate an immediate cash-flow problem, but it will ease some of the sticker shock. An expensive product that will last for 20 years may be a better choice than a cheaper one that may have to be replaced in five years. Again, weigh that decision against how long you plan to stay in the house. Are the extra benefits worth it?

SEVEN: Inquire about guarantees and service options. Some offers are definitely better than others. Look at the warranties that come from the manufacturer, as well as those offered by the place of purchase. A store may offer immediate replacement of the entire unit. While this may sound great, it isn't if you have to pay for labor or schedule time off from work for the removal and reinstallation of a fixture. Find out whether there is a better way. If all that is wrong with a faucet is a faulty washer, you may not want to yank out the entire unit. It should be your call. Find a place that offers a warranty based on the problems with the product. And always get written copies of all warranties from the store or your contractor.

Although the trend in recent years has been to increase the size of the bathroom, most are still relatively small compared with other rooms in the house. Yet this room remains the most expensive per square foot to renovate. This behooves you to invest wisely.

FIXTURES

Thirty years ago, items like tubs, toilets, and sinks were standard fare, not to mention boring. Who could have imagined they would generate the excitement they do today? As bathrooms have been elevated to symbolize status in American homes over the last couple of decades, second in prestige only to kitchens, even the most pragmatic items have become elements of design. But in addition to appearance, the workings of bathroom fixtures have become technologically more glamorous as well.

TUBS

The possibilities are nearly endless: soakers, whirlpools, classic claw-footed models, tubs for two, spas for four, contoured shapes, ovals, squares, or rounded tubs, streamlined or sculptured models, tubs with neck rests and arm rests, freestanding tubs, tubs set into platforms, and tubs you step down into. It's your soak, so have it your way.

Ask yourself: How do I like to bathe? Do I prefer a long, lingering soak or an invigorating hydromassage? A popular trend is the sunk-in whirlpool tub, which comes with an array of therapeutic and relaxing options in the form of neck jets, back jets, side jets, multiple jets, or single jets that are installed in the walls behind the tub. Other options include on-off control panels that can be reached from inside the tub (as opposed to a wall timer) and an automatic turnoff that prevents motor burnout.

EIGHT: Do a reality check. Look at your situation, and choose the best products and materials for the way you live. Don't get swept away by bells and whistles that can blow your budget. Your bottom line isn't bottomless, so compare each extra-cost feature to your real needs and lifestyle. A sumptuous shower with 18 massaging hydrojets may be your fantasy, but if your morning routine is a race against the clock to get to work on time, invest the extra money elsewhere. Besides, multiple shower outlets, as well as large tubs, may require larger water-supply lines, and that might not be an option.

NINE: Leave nothing to chance. Investigate every option and every detail for the new bathroom. Don't find yourself bemoaning what you should have done when it's too late. After you sign the final check is not the time to realize you could have installed an in-line heater to keep bath water consistently warm or a steam unit in the shower. Discover everything that's out there—before getting started on the remodeling. Don't miss any of the fun stuff, and you won't have any regrets or extra charges for changes made after work has begun.

Generally, tubs are made of one of the three following materials:

■ *Fiberglass* is a lightweight and moldable material. A fiberglass tub is the least expensive type you can buy. But it's prone to scratching and wear after about a dozen years. Some come with an acrylic finish, which holds up against wear longer.

■ *Solid acrylic* is a mid-price range product that is more durable than fiberglass and less prone to scratching because the color is solid all the way through. Whirlpool tubs are usually made of acrylic because it can be shaped easily. It's also lightweight, an important feature for large tubs that can put damaging stress on structural elements under the floor.

■ An enamel-coated *cast-iron* tub will endure as long as your house stands. It's heavyweight, though, and not recommended for a large soaking tub, even if the floor has been reinforced.

The most common size for a tub that backs up against a wall is 32 × 60 inches, but you can find models in widths of 24 to 42 inches. If someone in the family is tall, no problem: You can purchase a standard tub that's up to 72 inches long.

SHOWERS

Spectacular spray options and spa features make showering as sybaritic as the most luxuriously appointed bath. Shower units separate from bathtubs can be prefabricated from molded fiberglass or acrylic. They come in widths of 32, 36, and 48 inches, with a standard depth of 36 inches and a height of 73 inches. Custom-built showers are typically constructed of solid-surfacing, ceramic tile, or stone. Top-of-the-line features include massaging hydrotherapy sprays, steam units, a foot whirlpool, built-in seating and storage, even a CD player. Amazing technology lets you enjoy a full body massage on a miserly amount of water. Although by law, new showerheads may not deliver more than 2.5 gallons of water per minute, you can install as many as you wish.

Right: **Custom showers such as this one allow you to pick the spray heads, materials, and extras you want. This glass-block shower has multiple spray heads and built-in seating.**

The only thing limiting your shower is your imagination and your budget. If you want it, it's out there. Unless you're interested in a strictly no-frills unit, think about installing more than one showerhead and mixing and matching devices from any or all of the following three basic spray categories.

■ A *fixed spray* showerhead is mounted on the wall or ceiling, and it may or may not come with a massage option. New versions include a device that propels water into the air to give you a hydromassage. Other nifty models, called rain bars, let you close your eyes and pretend you're in a rain forest where gentle mists pamper you with a soft rinse. Or you can opt for a cascade of water that is delivered by a waterfall spout.

■ A *handheld spray* is convenient for directing water where you want it. It stores in a wall-mounted slide bar and can be adjusted up and down to accommodate the tallest or shortest bather. Combine a handheld spray with a stationary showerhead, and add a massager with as many as eight settings and a body brush, and you've created a custom shower environment that rivals any first-class away-from-home spa.

■ *Jet sprays* are housed behind the shower walls, just as those used in whirlpool tubs are. One manufacturer offers as many as 16 with its shower unit. Jet sprays can be programmed to various settings. Get a therapeutic hydromas-sage to relax stiff neck muscles or a sore back, for example. If you like, select a full body massage at whatever intensity is comfortable for you.

TOILETS

Believe it or not, you do have choices when selecting a toilet for your new bathroom. Vitreous china is still the material of preference, but there's a wide range of colors and style options to suit contemporary or traditional tastes. If you like something sleek, select a European-inspired elongated bowl. Though toilet sizes vary somewhat among manufacturers, an elongated bowl will extend about 2 inches more into the room than a standard version. The typical height of a toilet seat is 15 inches, but some come as high as 18 inches, which can be more comfortable for tall or older persons.

Another option is whether your new toilet will be a one-piece, low-profile model or a two-piece unit. There are style variations within both types, including rounded bowls, long square shapes, and vintage looks. Nostalgia lovers will be happy to know that Victorian-style high-tank toilets are still manufactured. Scaled-down toilets are available, too, for condos and apartments short on space or for tiny powder rooms, such as those tucked into a stairwell or made out of an old hallway closet.

If you are still fighting in your household about whether the seat should be kept up or down, give peace a chance. Look into these new gender-friendly features: a lid that automatically lowers when the toilet is flushed or a toilet that shines a red light in the bowl when the seat is up and a green light when the lid is down.

If that isn't enough, consider a residential urinal. One type fits into the wall; another sits on the floor next to the toilet.

Left: This low-profile one-piece toilet fits comfortably in this space. If space is tight, remember that elongated bowls extend an extra 2 inches into the room.

Besides style and type, you should be concerned about the flushing mechanism. Although appearance factors can affect cost (low-profile, one-piece, and elongated bowls being at least twice the price of standard two-piece models), the flushing mechanism may have an even bigger impact on the price tag. New toilets must conform to the government's low-flush standard, which mandates that no more than 1.6 gallons of water be used per flush. (Older model toilets used 3.5 gallons and really old models used a whopping 5 gallons per flush.) There have been many complaints about the effectiveness of low-flush toilets, especially the early models. But the technology is improving steadily.

There are three basic types of flushing mechanisms, listed in order of their cost, starting with the least expensive.

■ A *gravity-fed* mechanism is the standard device used by two-piece toilets. Press down the lever, and the force of the water that is released from the tank and into the bowl flushes waste down the drain and out through the pipes.

■ A *pressure-assisted* type uses household water pressure to compress the air in a chamber in the toilet tank. Flushing releases the compressed air, forcing the water into the trap almost instantly.

■ There is also a *vacuum-flush* toilet. In this type, two internal chambers create a vacuum that is released when you flush. The force created by the vacuum forces water into the bowl and through the trap.

BIDETS

A standard fixture in European bathrooms for decades, bidets have been slow to catch on in the American market. They are gaining in popularity, however, particularly in new construction and high-end remodeling, where they are becoming status symbols in master suites. Typically, a bidet is selected to match the toilet, and the fixtures are installed side by side.

LAVATORIES

You may find it practically impossible to select one lavatory over another because they come in so many sizes, shapes, styles, and colors. Sensuous curves, sculpted bowls, and beautiful, durable finishes can make this vessel a work of art—and an important element in your overall design. Today's lavatories can be made of vitreous china, cast iron, enameled steel, fiberglass, acrylic (solid-surfacing material), stone, faux stone, or metal. Its finish may be hand painted, contoured, beveled, brushed, or polished. A sink can be a freestanding pedestal, or it can be mounted to the wall or be part of a vanity top.

Left: Above-counter lavs such as the two shown here have a distinctive style. Other choices include pedestal sinks, wall-hung sinks, and traditional vanity-mounted units.

Vanity sinks, in pairs or as a single lav, are designed to be installed in one of four ways:

■ A *self-rimming* sink is surface-mounted. The bowl drops into the counter while the rim rests on and forms a seal with the countertop surface. This rim can be decoratively carved or hand painted.

■ An *under-mounted* sink gives a tailored look. In this instance, the bowl is attached underneath the countertop for a clean, uncluttered appearance.

■ An *integral* sink is fabricated with a countertop from the same material—stone, faux stone, or solid-surfacing. The look is sleek, seamless, and sculptural.

■ Unlike a self-rimming sink, a *rimmed model* requires a metal strip to form the seal between the top of the sink and the countertop.

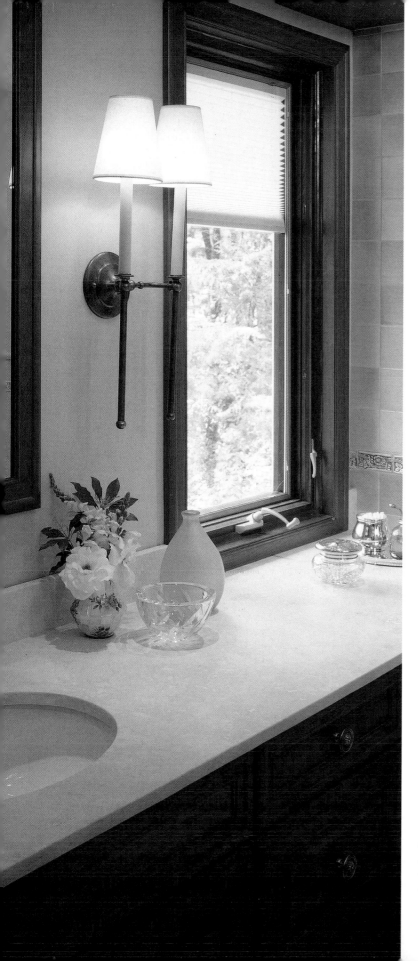

There are attractive, shapely lavs in every price range. Colored lavatories are usually a bit pricier, as are delicate hand-painted designs. If you will do anything at the sink besides washing your hands and face and brushing your teeth, consider choices in design and size carefully before you buy.

Something that is too shallow, for example, may not be practical for rinsing hair or hand washables. A pedestal sink may be pretty, but if you apply makeup, style your hair, or shave, this type may not provide surface storage for related grooming items. Hand-painted designs may look beautiful, but they may require special care to avoid wear, as well as more gentle cleaning—not the right option for an active family. Think before acting.

FAUCETS AND OTHER FITTINGS

Like showers, faucets are no longer just conduits for water. Today's faucet technology gives you much more control over your water. You can program an instrument for a pulsating effect or select the gentler rhythm of a babbling brook or a cascading waterfall; preset water temperature so that the water never gets hotter than you like; or protect young children, as well as disabled or elderly family members, from scalding.

For quality, inquire about the materials used for the faucet's innards. The best choices are solid brass or a brass-base metal, which are corrosion-resistant. Avoid plastic—it won't hold up. Inquire about the faucet's valving, too. Many faucets come with a washerless ceramic or nylon cartridge that lasts longer and is less prone to leaks. Ceramic is the better choice. Select finishes depending on your taste and other elements in the room that you may wish to coordinate with the fittings. Finishes include chrome, polished brass, enamel-coated colors, pewter, nickel, gold, and gold-plated. Handles may match the faucet or come in crystal, marble, or other materials.

Left to right: **There is such a wide variety of tub and lav faucets that you should be able to find the style, finish, and color that best suits your room. The gooseneck tub faucet, far left, is easy to reach by someone not yet in the tub. The widespread lav faucet adds flair to the room's design.**

Make a fashion statement by mixing finishes or selecting a design with inlaid stones or gems. Think of faucets as jewelry for your bathroom, and accessorize accordingly. There are three basic types of faucets for your consideration:

■ A *center-set* faucet has two separate valves (one for hot, another for cold) and a spout that are connected in one unit.

■ The *widespread* type features a spout with separate hot- and cold-water valves. All of the parts appear to be completely separate pieces.

■ The *single-lever* type has a spout and a single lever in one piece for one-hand control.

Whatever your decorating motif, you can find faucets to coordinate with the look you wish to achieve. Reproduction styles in brushed-metal finishes look good in traditional decors, as do graceful gooseneck spouts. Sleek geometrical shapes with enameled or high-gloss finishes enhance contemporary designs. And don't forget baubles. Stone, faux stone, or faux gem inserts on handles provide rich-looking details in strong architecturally inspired designs.

While you're admiring all the handsome faucet styles on today's market, remember function. Cross handles are charming, but they can be difficult to grasp for the elderly, disabled persons, or the very young. Levers and wrist blades make more sense in these cases. If you like the simplicity of a single-lever faucet, install one with a hot-limit valve so that kids can't scald themselves.

GRAB BARS AND TOWEL BARS
The first thing to remember is that grab bars and towel bars are not interchangeable items. A grab bar must be installed so that it securely attaches to wall studs or blocking behind a shower or bathtub or at the toilet. (If you are remodeling your bathroom, reinforce the walls at grab bar locations.) For quality, shop for

grab bars made of solid brass. For style, coordinate them with other hardware, such as the towel bars, faucets, shower heads, and cabinet pulls and handles.

Like faucets, towel bars can be likened to jewelry for the bath. Don't skimp on this detail: look for ones with matching toilet paper holders and door and wall hooks. Shop for quality brass or chrome construction with a finish that won't rust or tarnish when exposed to moisture.

STORAGE FOR THE BATH

Undoubtedly, an important aspect of your new bath's design is storage. Besides toiletries, grooming aids, extra linens, a hamper, and cleaning supplies, you may want to store gym equipment, books, magazines, and CDs, particularly if the room will be a place you can retreat to for adult quiet time after a day at work or with the kids. To store all these items, you'll need to be creative and utilize as much space as possible.

Above: Storage is an often overlooked component in today's baths. Note the towel and linen storage shown above.

Opposite: Bathrooms should be functional rooms, but don't overlook the opportunities for creating drama.

No matter what the size of the bathroom, it should contain a reasonable amount of storage. To get it, you'll have to thoroughly analyze the space and prioritize what items you must have handy, as well as any extras you'd like. Believe it or not, even a tiny 5- × 7-foot bathroom can accommodate spare rolls of toilet paper, additional bars of soap, a blow dryer, and curling iron, as well as a stack of clean towels, as long as you think storage issues through at the design stage of the project.

If you are working with a professional, he or she will have more than a few storage tricks to offer if you are specific about what you need. Be prepared by asking yourself some storage questions about your new bath. Is a vanity sufficient? Will it be for one or two persons? Do you require a medicine cabinet? How about a linen closet? Extra shelves? Drawers?

When you are acting on your own, think about how you intend to use the new bath. Make a list of everything you want at hand. Scale back if necessary, but start big. For

SMARTtip   Storage

A linen closet inside the bathroom is an amenity some homeowners think they can't afford if the space is small. If that's your dilemma, a little rethinking and reshuffling may yield the necessary room you thought you didn't have. First, reconsider the size of the bathroom fixtures you've been planning for your design. Would a smaller tub, shower unit, or vanity relieve the crunch? Second, think about building the closet into an adjoining room, if possible. Your designer may have other ideas, too.

You can't go wrong if you make good use of even the smallest pocket of space, like the toe-kick area at the bottom of the vanity, where you can install extra drawers or a slide-out step for kids who can't reach the sink yet. If there's a low-profile toilet next to the vanity, extend the countertop over the toilet. Ask your builder to suspend a drawer from underneath the extension. Don't forget to include a built-in shelf inside the shower or tub enclosure to hold soaps and shampoos. Use the wall space; install open shelves for extra towels, bars of soap, bubble bath, and the like. Better yet, think about opening up a wall between two studs and using the dead space for recessed shelving. One caution: don't cut the studs in case it is a load-bearing wall.

example, if your children will bathe in this room, include storage for bath toys—ideally, someplace other than along the ledge of the tub. If you'll shave, groom your hair, or apply makeup at the vanity, pencil in a place—not the countertop—to keep essentials away from the sink and protected against exposure to water. If you're tired of toting dirty clothes downstairs to the basement or ground-floor laundry room, see whether your plan can accommodate a compact washer/dryer. If you're always dashing to the hallway linen closet for towels, add shelves or, if there is space, a closet in the bathroom. These are just a few of the storage-related issues that could affect your project.

In any event, it's likely that you'll want at least a vanity and a medicine cabinet in your new bath. Like fixtures and fittings, they make important statements about how the new space will look, as well as how it will function.

VANITIES

Today there are many creative ways to approach the vanity. One is to treat the vanity as a decorative receptacle for a drop-in sink with just a countertop and legs and no attached cabinetry. If you can sacrifice the storage a cabinet provides, this option will add drama to your design, especially if the countertop is outfitted with handsome tile, stone, or colored concrete. But if you're limited by space and have to make the most of every inch, a vanity cabinet, which features drawers and shelves, is the wisest choice. Cabinets are available in three ways:

■ *Stock vanities* are factory-made in a range of standard heights, sizes, and finishes. They are usually—but not always—the most economical type. Styles are limited.

■ *Semi-custom vanities* are factory-made and outfitted with custom options upon your order. Usually midrange in price, semi-custom vanities include extras, such as pullout bins, spin-out trays, special door styles, or custom finishes.

■ *Custom vanities* are built-to-order to your bathroom's specifications. The cabinets can be designed by your architect, interior designer, or designer/builder. This is typically—but not always—the most expensive option.

A popular vanity trend is to retrofit a piece of fine wood furniture, such as an antique chest, with a lav, reproduction fittings, and an elegant countertop. But the wood surface has to be sealed with a protective coating that resists water and mildew. If you don't have the right piece of old furniture but want the same look, check out the new cabinet styles offered by manufacturers today. Look at designs created for

Above: The ornate carvings and detailing on this vanity make it a focal point in this bathroom.

Opposite: Traditionally, medicine cabinets are placed in front of the lav, but here the designer flanked the lav with two large cabinets and filled the middle of the space with a mirror.

the kitchen, as well as the bath. Some are interchangeable and display furniture details. Fluted pilasters, elegant moldings, and filigree patterns adorn many models that also come with beautiful hardware and finishes engineered to hold up to humidity and mildew. They wipe clean easily, too, so you don't have to worry about upkeep. Some are available with faux stone or wood laminate countertops, or granite or marble surfaces.

Whether you select a vanity style that is traditional or contemporary, with a plastic laminate, metal, or wood finish, give the vanity cabinet as much consideration as you would if it were meant for the kitchen. Top-of-the-line solid-wood construction may be too expensive for most budgets. However, a sturdy plywood frame combined with dovetail and mortise-and-tenon joinery is excellent, too. Make sure the interiors are well finished, however, and shelves aren't flimsy.

There are basically two construction styles for stock and semi-custom cabinetry: framed and frameless. Both styles are available from any American manufacturer.

■ *Framed cabinets* feature a full frame across the face of the unit. Hinges may or may not be visible around doors and drawers.

■ *Frameless cabinets*, often called European-style cabinets, are built without a face frame and therefore have a sleek appearance. Because the doors are mounted on the face of the box or are set into it, hinges are typically hidden inside.

MEDICINE CABINETS

You can find attractive medicine cabinets that can be wall-mounted or recessed into a nonload-bearing wall between the studs. From ultra-contemporary visions in glass and lights to designs that make bold architectural statements, there's a wide selection of stock units to match any decor or cabinet style.

When shopping for a medicine cabinet, look for one that offers room for everything from toothbrushes to shaving cream and bandages. Choose one that spans the width of your vanity or beyond it, if wall space allows. In other words, buy the largest one you can find! Look for deep shelves that accommodate objects larger than a small pill bottle. Built-in lighting, swing-out mirrors, and three-way mirrored doors are some of the other extras you may want in a medicine cabinet. In addition, some units come with a lock or a separate compartment that can be locked to keep potentially dangerous substances out of the hands of young children.

SERVICEABLE SURFACES

Even in well-ventilated bathrooms, steam and moisture can take their toll. So it's important to select materials for the walls, floor, and countertop that can hold up to water. Plastic laminate and vinyl are good choices that come in different price ranges, depending on quality. Generally they are the most affordable. Ceramic tile, solid-surfacing materials, and concrete fall into the middle to high end of the spectrum. Natural stone, such as slate, granite, and marble, are at the high end of the price scale.

LAMINATE

Consider laminate for your bathroom countertops. When installed on counters, plastic laminate resists moisture superbly and is easy to maintain. Laminate is made of melamine, paper, and plastic resin bonded under heat and pressure, then glued to particle-board or plywood. It comes in so many colors, patterns, and textures that finding one to coordinate with other elements in your design—fixtures, tile, wallcovering—is easy. Want a countertop made of slate or marble, but can't afford the real thing? Does buttery leather, cool glass, or warm wood appeal to you? A faux version in laminate may be the answer. Besides giving you a price break, plastic laminate offers a practical alternative to some natural materials that would be too delicate for such an installation. In that sense, it is versatile and practical. Plastic laminate countertop material comes in various

Above: **Choose countertop materials that can stand up to moisture, such as natural stone shown here.**

Opposite: **Ceramic tile provides so many decorating options it is one of the favorite bathroom surfacing materials.**

grades. It is generally affordable, so don't skimp by purchasing the cheapest one you can find. To get your money's worth, select the highest quality, which won't chip easily and stays looking good longer. At the very top of the line is "color-through" laminate. As opposed to laminate with color on the surface only, this type will not show a brown seam line at the edge.

With regard to flooring, the latest laminate products boast easy care, as well as moisture and stain resistance. Manufacturers now offer literally dozens of designs that are dead ringers for real wood or stone. These come in either tongue-and-groove planks or as tiles. Like sheet laminate used for countertops, laminate flooring is more economical than the natural materials it portrays, and in more cases, it installs right over old flooring.

CERAMIC TILE

Besides its practical attributes, such as imperviousness to water, durability, and easy maintenance, ceramic tile offers the greatest opportunity to bring style and personality to your bathroom. Use it to add color, pattern, and texture to the wall, floor, or countertop. Enclose a tub or shower with it. Tile is versatile. It comes in a variety of shapes, sizes, and finishes. Use decorative tiles with hand-painted finishes or raised-relief designs to create a mural or mosaic. You're only limited by your imagination. Hand-painted tile is expensive, but it allows you to do something truly unique. If cost is a factor, accent standard tiles with a few hand-painted designs. Or achieve a similar look at less cost by using mass-produced tiles with silk-screened designs. Visit a tile showroom in your area or the design department of a nearby home center to get ideas. Mix and match embossed tiles, accent and trim strips, edges, and a contrasting colored grout (the compound that fills the joints). For long-lasting wear and easy maintenance, always apply a grout sealer in areas exposed to water, such as the countertop or tub surround.

Consider the finish when you're shopping for tile. There are two kinds: glazed and unglazed. Unglazed tiles are not sealed and always come in a matte finish. If you want to use them in the bathroom, you will have to apply a sealant.

Glazed tiles are coated with a sealant that makes them impervious to water. This glaze can be matte finish or one that is highly polished. Highly glazed tile, however, can be a hazard on the floor. Instead, opt for a soft-glazed tile intended for floor installation. When shopping, inquire about the manufacturer's slip-resistance rating for the tile you are considering. It's also a good idea to make sure any tile selected for a countertop installation can handle the spills and knocks that occur typically around the sink and on the countertop surface.

SOLID-SURFACING MATERIAL

An extremely durable, easily maintained synthetic made of polyester or acrylic, solid-surfacing material is used to fabricate countertops, sinks, shower enclosures, and floors. It's not cheap, costing almost as much per linear foot as granite or marble, but it wears long

STONE AND CONCRETE

Granite, marble, and slate are probably the most expensive materials you can choose for a countertop. They are all extremely durable and rich looking. Two other stone materials, limestone and concrete, are finding their way into the creative hands of designers today, too. Unlike granite, marble, and slate, limestone has more of a primitive, textured appeal. Concrete offers flexibility, but it cracks easily. It can be colored, shaped, carved, and inlaid with objects, such as pieces of tile, glass, or shells, for a sophisticated effect.

As countertop material, any one of these materials introduces a dramatic element to the room. The only thing you have to worry about is sealing your natural countertop properly against moisture.

These materials are also heavy, so beware if you plan to use them to fabricate a tub or shower. Check with your builder or a structural engineer to find out whether you'll need additional support under the floor to carry the extra weight.

and well. It is completely impervious to water, and any dents or abrasions that may occur over time are repaired easily with a light sanding. At first, solid surfacing was available only in shades of white or pastel colors, but now its color palette has greatly expanded and includes faux-stone finishes, too.

When considering any one of these options for flooring, however, remember that they are cold underfoot and unforgiving—anything you drop that is delicate will break. Stone may pose a safety hazard on the floor, too, because it gets slick when wet. A fall on a stone floor can cause serious injury. Older persons and children are at particular risk. If ticated, high-tech finishes you can use it safely. This should come as good news to homeowners who like the incomparable warmth offered by real wood. On walls or countertops, wood requires a urethane finish. Some kinds of wood, such as teak, hold up better than other softer, porous types, such as pine.

WHAT'S YOUR STYLE?

Before locking yourself into one rigid style when choosing products for your bath, remember the first rule of thumb about decorating: please yourself. While you may want to emulate a certain look, don't become a slave to it and squash your creative spirit. The key is to build a room around a theme or a mood while carefully incorporating your personality. A favorite color is a good starting point, as is a repeated motif or an attractive pattern.

When considering style, everyone needs a little inspiration. Think about rooms you have admired and what attracted you. Was it a painted finish? A pretty fabric? Elegant cabinetry? How did the room make you feel? Restful? Energetic? Cheer? Nostalgic?

Opposite: **Sleek marble tiles create a handsome surround for this tub with distinctive waterfall faucet.**

Above: **Lush materials and extras designed to pamper turn this bathroom into a personal getaway.**

you choose one of these materials, use slip-resistant carpeting over it. Also, the task of installing a stone or concrete floor is not easy. Leave the laying, cutting, and fitting stone or pouring concrete to a professional.

WOOD

Wood has typically been taboo in the bathroom because of its susceptibility to water damage, mildew, and warping. However, if you seal it properly with one of today's sophis-

You can also take a cue from the rest of your home. Look at the style of the architecture. Is it contemporary? Colonial? Even if the architecture is nondescript, you can introduce a period flavor with reproduction fixtures, wallcoverings, molding, and accessories. You can build on these preferences in the new bathroom or depart from them entirely. Find one transitional element, such as the floor treatment or a wallcovering, to create a visual bridge from room to room.

Whatever you do, your approach to decorating the new bath should be deliberate. Let it evolve over time; don't rush your choices. Remember to let your own preferences guide you in the end.

a gallery of...

1 A glass door keeps this small custom shower from feeling cramped.

2 Separate tub and shower areas are becoming more and more popular in bath design.

3 The designer opted to forego vanity storage to achieve the sleek contemporary styling of this lav and counter.

4 Although bathrooms are usually small rooms, they still require natural light. Don't forget to arrange for privacy as well.

5 This distinctive design is made practical by the use of ceramic tile on the backsplash and the surround around the tub.

6 The pampering is in the details. Here a fireplace adds a touch of unexpected luxury to this large master bathroom.

...smart ideas

1 Custom showers often have built-in shelving. The tile pattern on the shower floor echoes the one on the main floor of the room.

2 An oval tub received a sur-round of ceramic tiles to achieve this distinctive look. Select whirlpool jets that best suit your needs.

3 Ceramic tile offers a variety of design options. Note the shower floor and borders.

4 Use the space available when designing your bath-room. Note the recessed cabinet in the wall space.

5 Creative shelving adds extra storage to this bath.

6 A pedestal sink commands the center of attention in this powder room.

CHAPTER 11

OUTDOOR LIVING AREAS

DECORATING SUNROOMS AND PORCHES ■ PATIOS, DECKS, AND GAZEBOS ■ TIPS ON LANDSCAPING

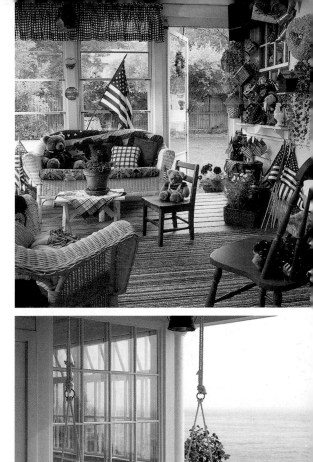

Savvy homeowners don't end their decorating at the door, they keep going to include the decks, porches, sunrooms, and patios that surround their homes. They treat these spaces as outdoor "rooms" that deserve the attention the other rooms in their homes receive. They choose the best furnishings, colors, textures, and lighting for the space. The result is additional living area that is often the favorite "room" in the house.

There are two types of outdoor spaces: those totally or partially protected from the elements, such as sunrooms, porches, or gazebos, and those areas open to the elements, such as decks, patios, or garden hideaways.

Coordinate your outdoor spaces with the exterior of your house, especially if it is located in front or on the side of the house in full view of passersby. Look at the space from the outside toward the house. Consider the scale of furnishings. Indoor/outdoor furniture comes in a variety of sizes and styles: some sleek and space-saving, some designed to visually fill up an area. Think about the difference between a folding metal bistro chair and a chair with hefty, oversized wicker arms and back, for example. The bistro chairs may look skimpy on a large deck, while a grouping of oversized wicker furniture can crowd a small porch.

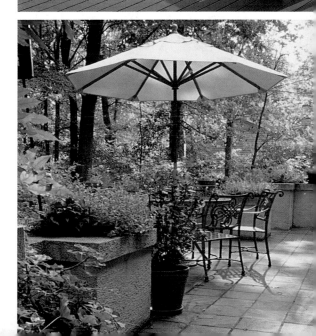

Look at your outdoor space through windows and doors, and consider extending the interior style to the outside space. Bright colors will stop your eyes at the porch, while muted ones will allow you to focus first on garden focal points, such as a magnificent bush, tree, or flower bed. Plan outside furnishings so that they augment a good view instead of blocking it.

Once you have a furniture style in mind, develop a plan that defines the function of the space and determines the furniture pieces you'll need. Consider, for instance, what's needed for conversational sitting, entertaining, dining, cooking, playing (for children), sleeping, and sunbathing.

DECORATING SUNROOMS AND PORCHES

Attached outdoor spaces that provide total or partial shelter should be considered an extension of the home's interior design. In most cases these areas embrace an entrance or serve to join two interior areas—a breezeway, for example. Traffic patterns figure importantly in overall furniture arrangements, as does the selection of furniture, durable fabrics, and other elements.

SMART steps

ONE: Document your ideas. Keep a folder full of your inspirations and any ideas you may have. Photograph the area you want to decorate from both inside the house and facing toward it from the outside. Keep clippings of similar spaces and furnishings, shades, and lighting that you like from magazines and product brochures; collect paint color chips and samples of fabric and flooring, too. Don't forget plantings, including window boxes and potted plants, and anything else influencing the design. Consider all the seasons the space is used. Will you want to add curtains to a sunroom for insulation come winter so that you can continue to use it longer into the cold weather? Will blinds or curtains add to a porch's comfort by blocking spring and fall winds?

TWO: Make a floor plan. Use the same steps for developing a grid and cutting out representative furniture pieces as recommended for inside rooms. (See Chapter One, "The Basics of Design," on page 12.) Add special features unique to your space, such as notations indicating good and bad views. You will want to arrange furniture to take advantage of a good view or to face away from an ugly one.

Indicate the sun's exposure throughout the day, and note whether it should influence furniture placement. For example, you may need shades for the southern side of a porch, or you may want to group furniture to face fabulous sunsets in the west.

Clockwise (from above): **Attached sunrooms allow you to extend the design of the rest of the house or treat the area a little more informally as above. An east-facing sunroom is a good location for a breakfast area. Choose furniture that meets your design needs but is also able to stand up to the conditions of the space.**

THREE: Make furniture templates.

Make templates of the furniture you plan to use, as well as of other elements, that require clearance space, such as planters, window boxes, or blinds. You can also use the furniture templates in the Appendix on page 268. Group them on the floor plan; try different configurations to see which is best.

FOUR: Factor in traffic patterns.

Indicate pathways to and from the house. Take into account the swing of each door because you cannot place furniture in those spaces. For sliding glass doors, indicate which side is the entrance.

Arrange furniture so that conversational areas are not interrupted by traffic to and from the house. For instance, a common problem is a porch with a central door and a stepped entrance directly opposite the door. Rather than arranging furniture in one big grouping, create smaller areas at each end of the porch. Suggestions include a table with chairs on one side and a conversational grouping on the other. A table just outside the door can double as a buffet table. Plot any other traffic aisles, and make sure that you have not blocked passages to the cords for adjusting blinds or for watering plants.

FURNISH WITH CARE

Furniture for outdoor use spans the designs made popular through the centuries. You can select benches similar to those used in Versailles, Adirondack chairs, antebellum wrought iron inspired by Victorian New Orleans, and myriad other choices. A word of caution: just as decorative birdhouses won't last outdoors, some furniture with outdoor looks may not stand up to weather. Check warranties, and read directions on the furniture for care and maintenance. Then match your choices to the possible weather exposure of the furniture itself. It may be made of one or more materials.

Wood. Naturally weather-resistant woods, such as cypress, teak, or redwood, require little upkeep and don't need staining or preservative coatings. Treated wood is decay resistant and may have a greenish-brown color; it can be painted, stained, or left natural and protected with a clear water-resistant finish. Other wood should be treated with a moisture-resistant preservative, either clear or pigmented.

Wicker and Rattan. Check that the frame is weather resistant, such as aluminum with a baked-on finish. If the location is protected, some bamboo frames are porch-suitable. Synthetic wicker and special finishes on natural wicker materials offer various levels of resistance to sun and rain.

Iron. Its weight makes iron a good choice for windy areas, but it is heavy and difficult to rearrange. Either cast or wrought iron will rust unless treated with special rust-retarding paint and touched up or repainted over the years.

Aluminum. From budget tubular furniture to wrought or cast frames, aluminum is rustproof and lightweight. Pieces designed to look like ironwork often have a baked-on enamel or textured finish. Look for finishing details such as smooth seams on welded parts. Cast-aluminum pieces and those of thick, heavy-gauge alloys are top of the line in aluminum.

Plastic and Fiberglass Furniture. Buy the best quality you can afford, because inexpensive polymer pieces that break easily will decorate the dump for decades to come. Warranties are a guide, but test pieces by sitting on them and rocking around. Tubular parts made of PVC (polyvinyl chloride) can sometimes be disassembled for storage, depending upon how they are joined. Resin pieces are molded into a variety of shapes. Both come in a range of colored plastics; some are not able to withstand direct sunlight without discoloring.

Left: **The roof of this porch provides sufficient protection for the wicker furniture. You should remove furniture during bad weather.**

Right: **Fabrics for cushions and pillows must resist rot and mildew. Check outdoor furniture stores for sources.**

FILLING IT OUT

Pillows, upholstery, slipcovers, shades and blinds, lighting, flooring, and rugs all make a sunroom or a porch lush and comfortable. What you can use depends on how rigorous the weather is on the furnishings. In a relatively moisture-free hot climate, for instance, sun resistance is the quality you want to look for, but mildew resistance is not essential. In other areas, both sun and moisture (caused by dew at night) can damage the goods. Select products specifically resistant to mold and mildew and ultraviolet rays. Choices abound for products that work well in a protected outdoor environment. Here's some guidance on which are suitable for the outdoors.

Shades and Blinds. Simple matchstick or rattan rollups can protect furnishings from some rain and sun. Other treatments might include fabulous see-through screens and blinds that block ultraviolet rays while allowing breezes to

Above: Contemporary houses rarely include a front porch, but here's an exception. The modern twist on classic furniture styles helps pull the design together.

waft through the space. Shower curtains or simply made fabric curtains are decorative solutions that add privacy as well as beauty. (Bed sheets are an inexpensive alternative to fabric.) Remember, however, if the fabric isn't sun resistant, the curtains will fade over time.

Flooring and Rugs. Tile, slate, concrete, and weatherproof painted wood are floor choices that require minimal care. Soften the look and the feeling underfoot with natural-fiber rugs, such as sisal or hemp, which by nature resist moisture damage; this type of floor covering works best in sheltered outdoor spaces. Another possibility is indoor-outdoor carpeting, which can be left outside all year long.

Fabrics. Cushions and pillows with fillings that allow water to drain through them take very little care. Add to this a wide range of new fabrics—acrylics, woven vinyl-coated polyester, laminated cotton that feels like uncoated fabric—and almost anything is possible. Look for these fabrics at tent, awning, or fabric stores, as well as the porch and patio sections of department stores and pool-supply stores. Don't overlook clear plastic to protect some fabrics, and go ahead and use conventional fabrics that catch your fancy if the area is protected. Store pillows when the weather turns foul. Fabrics treated for stain resistance are more expensive but wear better.

Clockwise (from above): In moderate climates, even an unheated sunroom provides living space into the cold-weather months. A small porch can make a design statement as shown below. Investigate period paint colors when choosing a color scheme for your porch. A sunroom warmed by the morning sun is a good place for some quiet time.

Lighting. Outdoor ground-fault circuit interrupters (GFCIs), built-in lighting, and fans make all the difference for night-time use of porches and sunrooms. Avoid conventional indoor lighting unless your space is attached to the house. And be kind to your neighbors: be sure lighting does not encroach on their space. (The same goes for any noise you create, such as from a television, radio, or stereo system.) Don't over-light, but do provide adequate transitional lighting from inside to outside, allowing eyes to adjust.

PATIOS, DECKS, AND GAZEBOS

Free-standing outdoor spaces, such as gazebos or other garden structures, differ from sheltered spaces in several ways. Generally, they are not seen from the front of the house and are usually integrated with the landscape. Gazebos provide a wonderful opportunity to let loose a little and give in to your more fanciful side.

First, consider how you will use your outdoor room. Will it be for dining and barbecues? As a place for the kids to muck about in a wading pool and sandbox? As a quiet spot to read and relax? For warm-weather parties? Or will it be all of these things? Also consider how much privacy you want.

Decks, patios, and terraces usually exist next to a wall of the house or adjoin a porch. Attached areas call for making the most efficient use of existing doors, windows, and steps. A deck or patio might also be a short walk from the protection of the dwelling or alongside a pool, pond, or playground area. In that case, you have the luxury of developing your own entrances and traffic patterns.

As with porches and sunrooms, make a plan before you start work on your patio or deck. Use the Smart Steps for porches and sunrooms as a guide in developing ideas. (See page 252.) Creating workable traffic patterns is important, as you will sometimes be carrying trays full of food, entertainment equipment, and games and toys through the space. You have to organize furnishings so that access is easy, trips to and from the house are no longer than necessary, and you can maneuver easily through the space.

Above: A slate patio tucked in the rear of the house provides space for dining and relaxing. Part of this patio is under cover for protection during bad weather.

Below: A screened porch is attached to the rest of the house by a covered walkway. When designing this type of structure, select roofing materials that match the existing house.

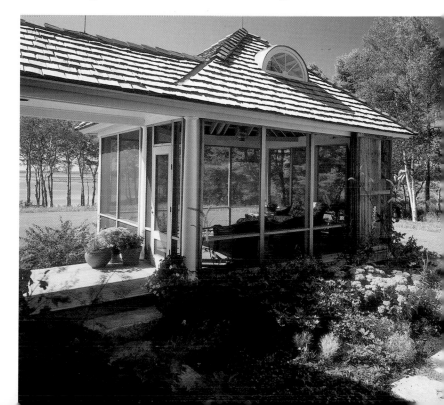

In most instances, you will want to make the patio or deck as large as possible so that it can function as a combination outdoor family room, cooking and dining area, and even a play area for kids. If space is restricted, you might consider creating an intimate area, with a small table and a pair of bistro chairs, that serves as a breakfast nook or even as a place to do paperwork in the sun.

To figure out traffic patterns, think about how you will enter this outdoor room. Will it be mostly from the house? Is the approach a path from the house or porch? Are there other areas, such as garden beds, potting sheds, bird baths, or lawn seating, that should determine exits from the patio or deck? It can be irritating to have to circumvent a deck rail or hedge to get to a frequently used destination, such as the potting shed or the barbecue grill. Figuring out potential trouble spots in advance will save you time and aggravation.

Most open spaces look best when they are defined by either hedges or fencing. Low plantings provide definition without impeding the view. Choices are nearly endless, ranging from clipped boxwood and privet hedges to low-growing junipers to a flower border of perennials or annuals. Consider what colors and fragrances you would like to have. (To learn about arranging your garden, see "Tips on Landscaping" on page 262.)

For even greater privacy—or to formalize the boundaries of a deck or patio—opt for fencing. Height depends upon your situation. A low slatted fence is a good choice for containing small children without blocking the view or interfering with the flow of air. Taller options that also allow air to flow and only partially block the view include lattice panels and alternating-board fences. Deck railing and fencing are often designed with built-in seating,

consisting of attached uprights, rails, and benches that may contain storage underneath.

Lighting defines spaces at night. It is also a safety factor. Both on-deck and in-ground systems with low voltage can be easily installed by a do-it-yourselfer. Other systems can be intricate and costly and may require a licensed electrician. Features may include fixtures for highlighting plantings or other yard features and timed sequencing that turns on and off automatically or when triggered by motion.

THE FAMILY ROOM/CONVERSATION AREA

A deck or patio is used most often as a fair-weather family room. Comfortable seating comes first, arranged for conversation as it would be in an indoor room. Add to this an area for snacking and outdoor recreation. Consider the activities of your household, how and whom you entertain,

Left to right: A covered area in the middle of a large patio protects diners and helps set the area off from the rest of the yard. Extend patio materials over the entire area for continuity as with the brick pavers used left. Sometimes the setting of your patio provides all the privacy you need. The low stone wall separates the patio from the wild.

what your hobbies are, the age of your family members, and other factors that define your needs. Remember that this is an outdoor room: the more components that can remain in place in inclement weather, the easier for you.

Decide up front whether you need shaded areas, as well as those exposed to the sun. Where you position your space in relation to the shade provided by your house, trees, or other buildings will determine how much sun it gets. Awnings, umbrellas, pergolas, and even built-in trellises are good choices for sun protection on decks and patios, which is an increasingly important consideration for many.

When the same space is used for large parties, it is likely that most of the furniture will be pushed to the perimeters

and more furniture will be added so that guests can mingle. Replot your traffic patterns and do a walk-through before the party to make sure everything is convenient for you and your guests.

ONE: Provide storage. Make your own bin with a lift-up top large enough to contain the pillows and other nonwaterproof accessories you like to have on hand, or purchase a ready-made unit designed for this purpose. A bin can keep things dry during rainstorms, but don't count on it to replace permanent storage during winter. It may not be weather resistant enough to protect outdoor furnishings. Keep ease of winter storage in mind when you are deciding on furniture, cushions, umbrellas, extra folding tables, and the like.

TWO: Invest in coverups. Vinyl slipcovers and protective cloths are available to place over large-sized pieces of cushioned furniture, and you will not have to move the cushions. They are not expensive and are easy to store.

THE KITCHEN/DINING AREA

Some people set up complete, permanent cooking centers as the focus of their outdoor spaces. Others content themselves with a simple grill. In either case, practical planning makes outdoor cooking efficient and more enjoyable, whether it is for the family or a host of guests.

Decide exactly what features you want in the cooking area. Aside from the grill, do you want an elaborate setup with a sink or a refrigerator? Perhaps a dishwasher? If so, these appliances need to be protected from the elements; place the cooking center in a sheltered location. If you prefer to keep it simple with just a grill, this option still requires some decision making. Do you want a charcoal, liquid propane (LP), or natural-gas grill? Charcoal grills are the least expensive; natural gas ones are the most expensive. The number of burners and features, such as a push-button ignition, increase the cost, too. You can also choose from a number of accessories, such as rotisseries, side burners, smoke ovens, and warming racks.

Then choose a site for the cooking area. It can be placed either nearby or far away from the house. Both locations have their advantages. A cooking area that is near the house benefits from easy access to the indoor kitchen, but one that is positioned away from the house keeps heat and smoke from diners. Remember, elaborate outdoor kitchens need gas, electric, and plumbing lines; it is easier and less expensive to run lines when the cooking area is near the house.

In general, when arranging any outdoor cooking area, make sure that all accoutrements—including serving platters, a spatula, a knife, and a pair of tongs—are readily at hand for the cook by providing plenty of surfaces and shelving. You need to accommodate both raw food and the finished product; a roll-around cart may suffice. Keep the pathway clear from the kitchen to the cooking area. A fire extinguisher nearby is an excellent safety precaution.

Any countertop material should be able to withstand varying weather conditions. Rain, snow, and bright sunlight will fade, pit, and rot some surfaces, so choose carefully. Tile, concrete, or natural materials, such as stone or slate, are good options. (Seal porous stone to prevent grease stains.) Avoid using a laminate countertop, unless it's in a well-protected area—an enclosed porch, for instance—because exposure to the weather may cause the subsurface to deteriorate. Solid surfacing is more durable, but may also need to be in a sheltered location. Think twice about using teak or other decay-resistant woods for a countertop, as they stain easily and may harbor bacteria.

Decay-resistant wood, such as redwood, cedar, teak, or mahogany, is the right choice for cabinetry, however. Other types of wood should be sealed and stained or painted. Oriented-strand board (OSB), which is made of bonded wood fiber, is also weatherproof enough for outdoor cabinetry.

Clockwise (from left): Outdoor living areas are all about comfort. On cool evenings, the large fieldstone fireplace provides the comfort for this patio. A garden pavilion shelters a small dining area. A screened-in porch can do double duty as a gathering place and a dining area. Be sure to keep traffic patterns in mind when placing furniture. Gathered fabric hanging from an awning adds a formal touch to the patio above.

TIPS ON LANDSCAPING

No outdoor living space is completely successful until it is integrated with the surrounding landscape. Just as there are principles for designing interior spaces, there are also guidelines for exterior ones. If you are choosing a site for a gazebo or a patio, it is one of the most important landscape design decisions you'll make. If the structure already exists, you can enhance it by assessing and changing the landscape. For instance, you may want to plan a garden around a gazebo, planting shrubs and flowers to highlight the beauty of the site. Or you may want to treat the gazebo as a secluded retreat. Achieving either goal takes careful planning of the site and surrounding plantings.

SMART steps | **ONE: Evaluate the site.** The landscape design should provide a framework for your outdoor living space. The views, lines, property configuration, and traffic patterns need to work together. Spend some time getting acquainted with your site and noting any special features. What are the site's assets? Are there beautiful views? Are there natural features, such as trees or streams? Consider the size and shape of your lot, the style of the house itself, as well as your own lifestyle needs and preferences.

TWO: Balance the elements. This is the process of arranging various site elements so that they are resolved and balanced. A visually heavy or large object can be balanced by a visually lighter or smaller object on the site if the smaller object is darker in color value, is unusually or irregularly shaped, has a contrasting texture, or is more elaborately detailed. All of these strategies will help to draw attention to the smaller object and thereby visually balance it with the larger object. For example, let's say you have a large clump of pine trees on one side of your yard. To visually balance the trees you might plant smaller, more colorful ornamental trees on the other side of the yard, or you might use a man-made object such as a gazebo.

THREE: Create a cohesive design. Harmony can be achieved by selecting and using elements that share a common trait or characteristic. By using elements that

are similar in size, shape, color, material, texture, or detail, you can create a cohesive feeling and relation among the various elements on the site. An example of this might be using a shape, such as a square. Imagine having a square concrete patio scored in a square (or diamond) pattern with a square table covered in a checkered tablecloth. The results can be extremely pleasing and harmonious.

FOUR: Add interest. While both balance and harmony are used to achieve unity, too much unity can be, well, boring. That's where variety and contrast come in handy. By varying the size, shape, color, material, texture, and detail, you can introduce a note of interest or a focal point into the total composition. For instance, placing a round wooden planter onto the square-patterned patio discussed in Step Three will provide a pleasing contrast of both shape and material. The contrasting object (the round wooden planter) will draw attention to itself and provide visual relief and interest to the total setting.

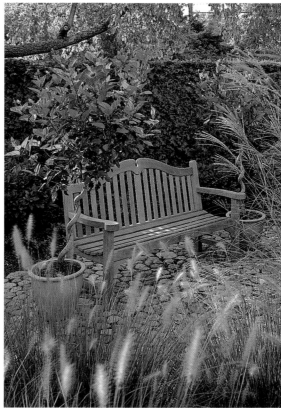

Far left: As with any room design indoors, keep scale, proportion, and balance in mind when laying out your outdoor living areas.

Left: Landscaping plays a major role in outdoor living areas. Here an inviting wood bench is tucked into a corner of a yard.

Below: Flowers and low shrubs add color and texture to this yard while defining its boundaries without hiding the view.

FIVE: Establish visual rhythm. In design terms, rhythm—or how elements are spaced relative to similar elements—can create another type of unity in a composition. Rhythm helps to establish a visually satisfying progression or sequence to a site design. For example, you can create a regular rhythm on a walkway if you place a band of decorative brick at 4-foot intervals. On the other hand, a song composed of only one sequence of notes is boring. Vary such things as the interval, color, size, shape, texture, or material of the elements.

SIX: Emphasize an element. This point assumes that within your site some of the elements have more significance than the rest and that these special elements should be emphasized. This is probably starting to sound familiar to you by now, but a special element is given its due emphasis by making it larger; by giving it a different shape (round versus square); by using a singular color, texture, or material; by shifting or rotating its orientation; by centering it within a circle or at the end of walkway; or by lighting it at night. However, if you emphasize too much, you may end up with a visually confusing design.

SEVEN: Let simplicity be your guide. Simplicity is one of the hardest things to achieve in a design because there is a tendency to use all available tools and elements. The most elegant site designs are those that begin and end with simplicity as their guiding design principle. The Zen rock gardens of Japan are a good example.

a gallery of...

1 There are a lot of ways to enjoy a porch or patio, but swinging away an afternoon in a porch swing is one of the most popular.

2 This Adirondack-style chair is one of may distinctive outdoor furniture designs.

3 A simple masonry patio and some furniture is all you need to create a welcoming outdoor living area.

4 Classic front porches often have closely spaced wood decking and painted beadboard ceilings.

5 Different flooring materials help define spaces in this long, narrow patio.

6 Built-in planters that jut out into the yard create enough space for a small alcove to accommodate a table and chairs on this attached patio.

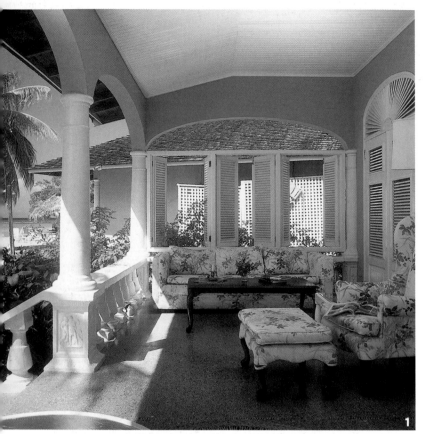

...smart ideas

1 Maintain a relationship between the interior of the house and the porch.

2 A sunroom or screened porch is the perfect spot for entertaining large groups or a private gathering.

3 Select porch furniture that is attractive and tough enough for the elements.

4 In some homes, the porch or patio is built to capture the stunning views.

5 Sleeping porches were popular before air conditioning. Create a version in a sunroom that you can use as a getaway.

APPENDIX

Window and Door Templates

Windows

Doors

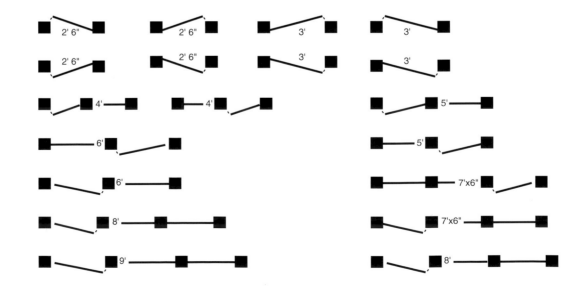

Appendix: Furniture Templates

Sofas, Love Seats, and Sofa Beds

sofa
72"x32"

sofa
72"x34"

sofa
78"x32"

sofa
78"x34"

sofa
84"x32"

sofa
84"x34"

love seat
50"x32"

sofa
90"x32"

love seat
50"x34"

sofa
90"x34"

love seat
55"x32"

sofa
96"x32"

love seat
55"x34"

sofa
96"x34"

love seat
60"x32"

sofa
102"x32"

love seat
60"x34"

sofa
102"x34"

sofa bed
70"x35"

sofa bed
82"x35"

sofa bed
75"x35"

sofa bed
92"x35"

Beds

twin bed
with
headboard
44"x75"

mattress
39"x75"

double bed
with
headboard
59"x75"

mattress
54"x75"

queen size
with
headboard
64"x80"

mattress
60"x80"

king size
with
headboard
83"x80"

mattress
78"x80"

Appendix: Furniture Templates

Chairs and Ottomans

End Tables

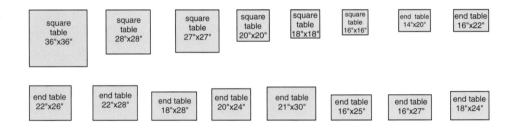

Coffee Tables and Desks

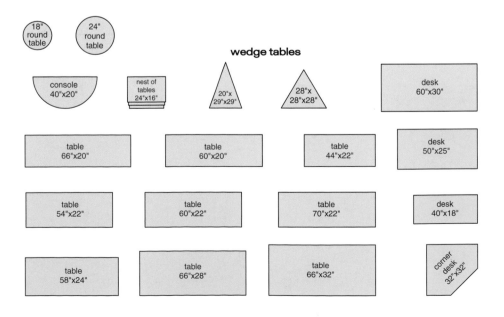

Appendix: Furniture Templates

Accessories

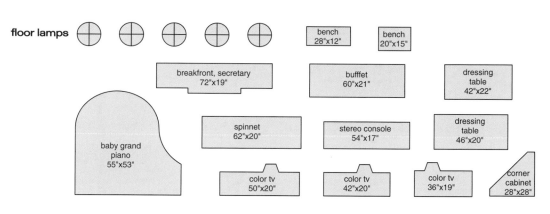

floor lamps

bench
28"x12"

bench
20"x15"

breakfront, secretary
72"x19"

bufffet
60"x21"

dressing
table
42"x22"

baby grand
piano
55"x53"

spinnet
62"x20"

stereo console
54"x17"

dressing
table
46"x20"

color tv
50"x20"

color tv
42"x20"

color tv
36"x19"

corner
cabinet
28"x28"

Appendix: Kitchen Templates

Dining and Café Tables

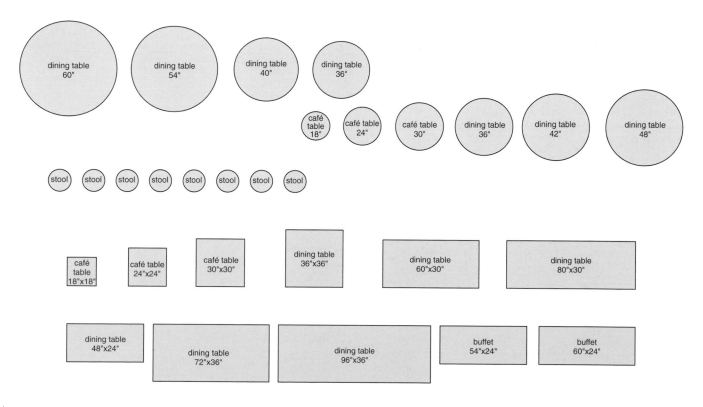

dining table
60"

dining table
54"

dining table
40"

dining table
36"

café
table
18"

café table
24"

café table
30"

dining table
36"

dining table
42"

dining table
48"

stool   stool   stool   stool   stool   stool   stool   stool

café
table
18"x18"

café table
24"x24"

café table
30"x30"

dining table
36"x36"

dining table
60"x30"

dining table
80"x30"

dining table
48"x24"

dining table
72"x36"

dining table
96"x36"

buffet
54"x24"

buffet
60"x24"

Appendix: Kitchen Templates

Countertops

Base Cabinets

desk 36"x24"	desk 30"x24"	6"x24"	base cabinet 15"x24"	base cabinet 18"x24"	base cabinet 21"x24"	9"x24"	base cabinet 39"x24"
base cabinet 24"x24"	12"x24"	base cabinet	base cabinet 30"x24"	base cabinet 33"x24"	base cabinet 36"x24"		base cabinet 18"x24"

Islands and Appliances

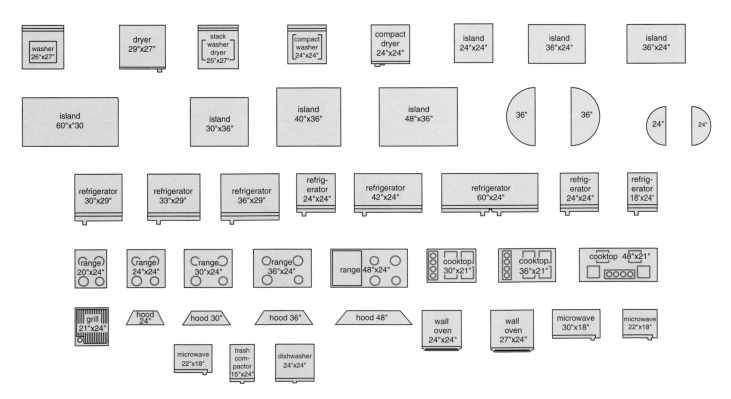

Appendix: Kitchen Templates

Sinks

Pantries

Appendix: Bathroom Templates

Lavatories

Toilets

Tubs and Shower

Appendix: Bathroom Symbols

Hardware

shower head
grab bars
12" 18" 24" 36"
corner

Appendix: Landscape Symbols

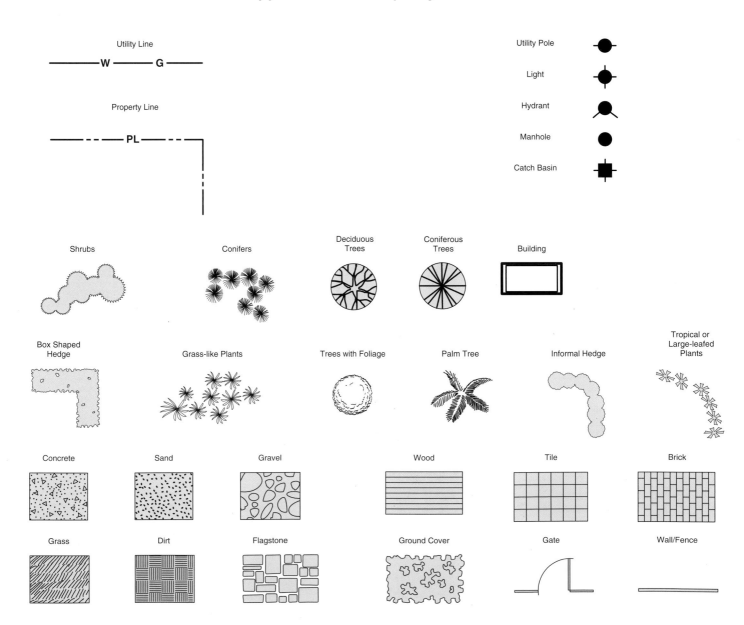

Utility Line
—W——G—

Property Line
—— · — PL —— · ——

Utility Pole
Light
Hydrant
Manhole
Catch Basin

Shrubs
Conifers
Deciduous Trees
Coniferous Trees
Building

Box Shaped Hedge
Grass-like Plants
Trees with Foliage
Palm Tree
Informal Hedge
Tropical or Large-leafed Plants

Concrete
Sand
Gravel
Wood
Tile
Brick

Grass
Dirt
Flagstone
Ground Cover
Gate
Wall/Fence

Scale: 1 square = 1 foot

RESOURCE GUIDE

The following list of manufacturers and associations is meant to be a general guide to additional industry and product-related sources. It is not intended as a listing of products and manufacturers represented by the photographs in this book.

American Furniture Manufacturers Association (AFMA) *is a trade group that provides information on American-made furniture.*
317 West High Ave.
High Point, NC 27261
Phone: 336-884-5000
www.afma4u.org

American Institute for Conservation of Historic and Artistic Works *provides information on restoring and maintaining antiques.*
1717 K St. NW
Washington, DC 20006
Phone: 202-452-9545
www.aic.stanford.edu

American Society of Interior Designers (ASID) *provides a referral service that locates designers.*
608 Massachusetts Ave. NE
Washington, DC 20002-6006
Phone: 202-546-3480
www.interiors.org

Baker Furniture, *a division of Kohler Interiors, manufactures chairs, ottomans, and other furniture.*
1661 Monroe Ave. NW
Grand Rapids, MI 49505
Phone: 800-592-2537
www.bakerfurniture.com

Bernhardt Furniture Company *manufactures sofas, chairs, and sectionals.*
P. O. Box 51, Dept. B-F
Asheville, NC 28802
Phone: 877-205-5793
www.bernhardt.com

Brewster Wallcovering Company *manufactures wallpaper, borders, and accessories.*
67 Pacella Park Dr.
Randolph, MA 02368
Phone: 800-366-1700
www.brewp.com

Broyhill Furniture Industries, Inc. *manufactures wood and upholstered furnishings.*
One Broyhill Park
Lenoir, NC 28633
Phone: 800-327-6944
www.broyhillfurn.com

Congoleum Corporation *manufactures durastone, sheet, tile, and laminate flooring.*
Dept. C
P. O. Box 3127
Mercerville, NJ 08619-0127
Phone: 800-274-3266
www.congoleum.com

Graber Window Fashions *manufacturers a line of window treatments.*
Spring Industries
P. O. Box 70
Fort Mill, SC 29716
Phone: 800-221-6352
www.springs.com (click through to Graber)

Eisenhart Wallcoverings Company *manufactures and prints designer wallcoverings.*
400 Pine St.
Hanover, PA 17331
Phone: 800-931-9255
www.eisenhartwallcoverings.com

Harden Furniture, Inc., *manufactures a wide variety of home furnishings.*
8550 Mill Pond Way
McConnellsville, NY 13401-1844
Phone: 315-245-1000
www.harden.com

Hickory Chair Company *manufactures a number of complete lines of furniture for bedrooms, living rooms, and dining rooms.*
P. O. Box 2147
Hickory, NC 28603-2147
Phone: 828-328-1801 x 7295
www.hickorychair.com

Lane Home Furnishings *manufactures home furnishings, including sectionals and tables.*
P. O. Box 1627
Tupelo, MS 38802
Phone: 662-566-7211
www.lanefurniture.com

Lexington Home Brands *manufactures home furnishings in a variety of collections.*
Attn: Consumer Services Department
P. O. Box 1008
Lexington, NC 27293-1008
Phone: 800-539-4636
www.lexington.com

Mannington, Inc., *manufactures laminate and wood flooring for home and commercial use.*
75 Mannington Mills Rd.
Salem, NJ 08079
Phone: 856-935-3000
www.mannington.com

National Kitchen & Bath Association (NKBA) *is an organization that offers information to consumers.*
687 Willow Grove St.
Hackettstown, NJ 07840
Phone: 800-652-2776
www.nkba.org

National Paint and Coatings Association (NPCA), *a nonprofit trade association, supplies information on paint and painting.*
1500 Rhode Island Ave. NW
Washington, DC 20005
Phone: 202-462-6272
www.paint.org

Paint Quality Institute *provides information on paint selection and painting.*
www.paintquality.com

Seabrook Wallcoverings *manufactures and distributes wallcoverings and borders for the home.*
1325 Farmville Rd.
Memphis, TN 38122
Phone: 901-320-3500
www.seabrookwallcoverings.com

Thibaut Wallcoverings *manufacturers wallpaper.*
480 Frelinghuysen Ave.
Newark, NJ 07114
Phone: 973-643-3777

Thomasville Furniture Industries, Inc., *manufactures living room, bedroom, and office furniture.*
P. O. Box 339
Thomasville, NC 27361-0339
Phone: 800-225-0265
www.thomasville.com

Woodard, Inc., *manufactures garden furniture.*
300 W. Washington, Ste. 500
Chicago, IL 60606
Phone: 312-423-5648
www.woodard-furniture.com

York Wallcoverings *manufactures a wide variety of wallpapers and borders.*
750 Linden Ave.
York, PA 17404
Phone: 717-846-4456
www.yorkwall.com

GLOSSARY

Accent lighting: A type of directional lighting that highlights an area or object to emphasize that aspect of a room's character.

Accessible designs: Designs that accommodate persons with physical disabilities.

Adaptable designs: Designs that can be easily changed to accommodate a person with disabilities.

Analogous scheme: See *Harmonious Color Scheme.*

Ambient lighting: General illumination that surrounds a room and is not directional.

Art Deco: A decorative style that was based on geometric forms. It was popular during the 1920s and 1930s.

Art Nouveau: A late-nineteenth-century decorative style that was based on natural forms. It was the first style to reject historical references and create its own design vocabulary, which was ornamental and included stylized curved details.

Arts and Crafts Movement: A decorative style that began in England during the late nineteenth century, where it was known as the Aesthetic Movement. Lead by William Morris, the movement rejected industrialization and encouraged fine craftsmanship and simplicity in design.

Backlighting: Illumination coming from a source behind or at the side of an object.

Backsplash: The vertical part at the rear and sides of a countertop that protects the adjacent wall.

Box pleat: A double pleat, underneath which the edges fold toward each other.

Broadloom: A wide loom for weaving carpeting that is 54 inches wide or more.

Built-in: Any element, such as a bookcase or cabinetry, that is built into a wall or an existing frame.

Cabriole: A double-curve or reverse S-shaped furniture leg that leads down to an elaborate foot (usually a ball-and-claw type).

Candlepower: The luminous intensity of a beam of light (total luminous flux) in a particular direction, measured in units called candelas.

Casegoods: A piece of furniture used for storage, including cabinets, dressers, and desks.

Clearance: The amount of space between two fixtures, the centerlines of two fixtures, or a fixture and an obstacle, such as a wall.

Code: A locally or nationally enforced mandate regarding structural design, materials, plumbing, or electrical systems that state what you can or cannot do when you build or remodel.

Colonial style: An early-American architectural and decorative style during the Colonial period that was influenced by design ideas brought by settlers from Europe, particularly England.

Color wheel: A diagram, usually circular, showing the range and relationships of pigment and dye colors.

Complementary colors: Hues directly opposite each other on the color wheel. As the strongest contrasts, complements tend to intensify each other.

Contemporary: Any modern design (after 1920) that does not contain traditional elements.

Cove: 1. A built-in recess in a wall or ceiling that conceals an indirect light source. 2. A concave recessed molding that is usually found where the wall meets the ceiling or floor.

Daybed: A bed made up to appear as a sofa. It usually has a frame that consists of a headboard, a footboard, and a sideboard along the back.

Dimmer switch: A switch that can vary the intensity of the light it controls.

Distressed finish: A decorative paint technique in which the final paint coat is sanded and battered to produce an aged appearance.

Dovetail: A joinery method in which wedge-shaped parts are interlocked to form a tight bond. This joint is commonly used in furniture making.

Dowel: A short cylinder, made of wood, metal, or plastic, that fits into corresponding holes bored in two pieces of wood, creating a joint.

Faux finish: A decorative paint technique that imitates a pattern found in nature.

Federal: An architectural and decorative style popular in America during the early nineteenth century, featuring delicate ornamentation, often depicting swags and urns, and symmetrically arranged rooms.

Fittings: The plumbing devices that bring water to the fixtures, such as faucets.

Fluorescent lighting: A glass tube coated on the interior with phosphor, a chemical compound that emits light when activated by ultraviolet energy. Air in the tube is replaced with a combination of argon gas and a small amount of mercury.

Focal point: The dominant element in a room or design, usually the first to catch your eye.

Foot-candle: A unit that is used to measure brightness. A foot-candle is equal to one lumen per square foot of lighted surface.

Framed cabinet: A cabinet with a full frame across the face of the cabinet box.

Frameless cabinet: A cabinet without a face frame. It may also be called a "European-style" cabinet.

Frieze: A horizontal band at the top of the wall or just below the cornice.

Full-spectrum light: Light that contains the full range of wavelengths that can be found in daylight, including invisible radiation (ultraviolet and infrared) at each end of the visible spectrum.

Gateleg table: A drop-leaf table supported by a gate-like leg that folds or swings out.

Georgian: An architectural and decorative style popular in America during the late eighteenth century, with rooms characterized by the use of paneling and other woodwork, and bold colors.

Gothic Revival: An architectural and decorative style popular during the mid-nineteenth century. It romanticized the design vocabulary of the medieval period, using elements such as pointed arches and trefoils (three-leaf motifs).

Greek Revival: An architectural and decorative style that drew inspiration from ancient Greek designs. It is characterized by the use of pediments and columns.

Ground-fault circuit interrupter (GFCI): A safety circuit breaker that compares the amount of current entering a receptacle with the amount leaving. If there is a discrepancy of 0.005 volt, the GFCI breaks the circuit in a fraction of a second. GFCIs are required in damp areas of the house.

Grout: A mortar that is used to fill the spaces between ceramic tiles.

Hardware: Wood, plastic, or metal plated trim found on the exterior of furniture, such as knobs, handles, and decorative trim.

Harmonious color scheme: Also called analogous, a combination focused on neighboring hues on the color wheel. The shared underlying color generally gives such schemes a coherent flow.

Hue: Another term for specific points on the pure, clear range of the color wheel.

Incandescent lighting: A bulb (lamp) that converts electric power into light by passing electric current through a filament of tungsten wire.

Indirect lighting: A more subdued type of lighting that is not head-on, but rather reflected against another surface such as a ceiling.

Inlay: A decoration, usually consisting of stained wood, metal, or mother-of-pearl, that is set into the surface of an object in a pattern and finished flush.

International style: A post-World War II architectural and decorative style that emphasized simplicity and lacked ornamentation. Smooth surfaces, an extensive use of windows, and white walls are hallmarks of this pared-down style.

Lambrequin: Drapery that hangs from a shelf, such as a mantel, or covering the top of a window or a door. This term is sometimes used interchangeably with valance.

Love seat: A sofa-like piece of furniture that consists of seating for two.

Lumen: The measurement of a source's light output—the quantity of visible light.

Lumens per watt (LPW): The ratio of the amount of light provided to the energy (watts) used to produce the light.

Modular: Units of a standard size, such as pieces of a sofa, that can be fitted together.

Molding: An architectural band used to trim a line where materials join or create a linear decoration. It is typically made of wood, plaster, or a polymer.

Mortise-and-tenon joinery: A joint in which a hole (mortise) is cut into one piece of wood to receive a projecting piece (tenon) cut into another.

Neoclassic: Any revival of the ancient styles of Greece and Rome, particularly during the late eighteenth and early nineteenth centuries.

Occasional piece: A small piece of furniture, such as an end table, for incidental use.

Orientation: The placement of any object or space, such as a window, a door, or a room, and its relationship to the points on a compass.

Panel: A flat, rectangular piece of material that forms part of a wall, door, or cabinet. Typically made of wood, it is usually framed by a border and either raised or recessed.

Parquet: Inlaid woodwork arranged to form a geometric pattern. It consists of small blocks of wood, which are often stained in contrasting colors.

Pattern matching: To align a repeating pattern when joining together two pieces of fabric or wallpaper.

Pediment: A triangular piece found over doors, windows, and occasionally mantles. It also refers to a low-pitched gable on the front of a building.

Peninsula: A countertop, with or without a base cabinet, that is connected at one end to a wall or another counter and extends outward, providing access on three sides.

Post-modernism: A term used to define the developments in architecture and interior design that originated in modernism but began to diverge from that style. Unlike modernism, it includes ornamentation and uses historical references that are often whimsically out of context.

Primary color: Red, blue, or yellow that can't be produced in pigments by mixing other colors. Primaries plus black and white, in turn, combine to make all the other hues.

Secondary color: A mix of two primaries. The secondary colors are orange, green, and purple.

Sectional: Furniture made into separate pieces that coordinate with each other. The pieces can be arranged together as a large unit or independently.

Slipcover: A fabric or plastic cover that can be draped or tailored to fit over a piece of furniture.

Stud: A vertical support element made of wood or metal that is used in the construction of walls.

Task lighting: Directional lighting that concentrates in specific areas for tasks, such as preparing food, applying makeup, reading, or doing crafts.

Tone: Degree of lightness or darkness of a color.

Tongue-and-groove joinery: A joinery technique in which a protruding end (tongue) fits into a recess (groove), locking the two pieces together.

Track lighting: Lighting that utilizes a fixed band that supplies a current to movable light fixtures.

Trompe l'oeil: French for "fool the eye"; a painted mural in which realistic images and the illusion of more space are created.

Tufting: The fabric of an upholstered piece or a mattress that is drawn tightly to secure the padding, creating regularly spaced indentations.

Turning: Wood that is cut on a lathe into a round object with a distinctive profile. Furniture legs, posts, rungs, etc., are usually made in this way.

Uplight: Also used to describe the lights themselves, this is actually the term for light that is directed upward toward the ceiling.

Valance: Short drapery that hangs along the top of a window, with or without a curtain underneath.

Value: In relation to a scale of grays ranging from black to white, this is the term to describe the lightness (tints) or darkness (shades) of a color.

Vanity: A bathroom floor cabinet that usually contains a sink and storage space.

Veneer: High-quality wood that is cut into very thin sheets for use as a surface material.

Wainscoting: A wallcovering of boards, plywood, or paneling that covers the lower section of an interior wall and usually contrasts with the wall surface above.

Welt: A cord, often covered by fabric, that is used as an elegant trim on cushions, slipcovers, etc.

Work triangle: The area bounded by the lines that connect the sink, range, and refrigerator. A kitchen may have multiple work triangles. In an ideal triangle, the distances between appliances are from 4 to 9 feet.

INDEX

A
Accent lights, 56
Accessories, 130, 135
Adaptations, 148
Alkyd paints, 103
Ambient lights, 55—56
Analogous color schemes, 36
Apartment-size furniture, 148
Appliance garages, 205
Arches, 30
Architecture
    elements in, 121, 207
    furniture choices and, 145
    lighting in, 68—69
Area rugs, 28, 90, 164
Art, 130, 131—133
    arranging, 134
    textiles as, 134
Artificial light, 55—57, 73
Asymmetry, 15, 17, 131
Atmosphere, 46

B
Backlighting, 57
Balance, 15
    asymmetrical, 15, 17, 131
    symmetrical, 15, 17, 131
Balloon shades, 115
Base moldings, 129
Bathrooms, 182—184, 221—249
    bath products for, 230—232
    fixtures for, 232—238
    focal point for, 183
    furnishings for, 183
    layouts in, 223—226
    lighting for, 184
    serviceable surfaces in, 242—245
    setting priorities, 222—223
    storage for, 238—242
    style and color for, 182
    types of, 226—229
    window treatments for, 109
Bay windows, 124
Bedrooms, 160, 176—178, 188
    focal points for, 177—178
    for children, 179—182
    furniture in, 27, 178

lighting for, 178
style and color, 176—177
window treatments for, 108
Bidets, 235
Blinds
    for porch, 255
    types of, 115
Bow windows, 124
Brocade, 43
Budget
    for flooring, 87
    for furniture, 149
    for window treatments, 111
Building codes, 65, 231
Built-in pantry units, 206—207
Butt joints, 151

C
Cabinets
    accessories and options, 205—207
    color of, 208
    construction of, 203—204
    decorative role of, 207
    hardware for, 208—209
    in kitchen design, 175, 202—209
Cambric, 43
Canvas, 43
Carousel shelves, 205
Carpeting and rugs, 82—83, 89
    adding texture with, 41
    for porch, 255
Casegoods, 154, 158
Casement curtain, 112
Casement windows, 124
Casing, 129
Cellular shades, 115
Ceramic flooring, 80—81
Ceramic tiles
    for bathroom countertops, 243
    for foyers and hallways, 164, 187
    for kitchen countertops, 210—211
Chair rail, 107, 117, 128—129
Chairs, 142—143
    reupholstering, 157
Chandeliers, 165
Children's rooms, 179—182
    furniture for, 180, 182

lighting for, 182
paint for, 102
style and color for, 180
Chimney breast, 128
Chimneypiece, 127
Chintz, 43
Clerestory windows, 124
Collection, 148
Color, 34
    altering space with, 37—38
    cultural effects of, 36—37
    developing scheme in, 42, 44
    for bathrooms, 182
    for bedrooms, 176—177
    for cabinets, 208
    for children's rooms, 180
    for dining room, 172
    for family room, 170
    for kitchen, 174—175
    for living room, 165—166
    intensity and value, 34
    light and, 38
    pattern and, 40—41
    psychology of, 36—37
Color rendition, 62
Color Rendition Index (CRI), 62
Color wheel, 34, 35—36
Combing, 97
Complementary colors, 35, 36
Concrete for bathroom countertops, 244—245
Contemporary, 146
Continuous-spectrum light, 62
Contrast, 36, 57
Conversation area, 258—260
Cool colors, 36
Corner blocks, 151
Cornices, 41, 113
    molding for, 128
Cotton duck, 43
Countertops
    bathroom, 242—245
    kitchen, 210—212
Country, 146
Cove moldings, 128
Coves, 68
Crackle, 102

Crewel, 43
Crown moldings, 128
Curtains, 112
Curved lines, 14
Custom cabinets, 204
Custom-ordered material, 148

D

Dado, 129
Damask, 43
Decks, 257—261
Decorative accessories, 121
Decorative hardware, 117
Decorative light, 57
Decorative paint techniques, 96—102
Design plan, 17—22
    basics of, 13—31
    creating, 17—22, 41—42, 44—46
    customizing, 44
    elements of, 122—130
    in notebook, 18—19, 193
    sample board in, 42
Diagonal lines, 14
Diffusion, 57
Dimmer switches, 62, 165, 170
Dining rooms, 172, 187, 188
    focal point for, 172—173
    furniture for, 27, 173
    lighting for, 58, 174
    style and color for, 172
    wallcoverings for, 107
Direct glare, 59—60
Distressing, 154
Doors, 122—123
Double complementary color
    scheme, 35
Double-dowel joints, 151
Double-hung windows, 124
Dovetail joints, 151
Dragging, 97
Draperies, 112
Dutch doors, 123

E

Eating areas in kitchen design,
    199—201

F

Fabrics
    adding texture with, 40
    choices in, 43
    for porch, 257
    for window treatments, 41, 113,
        114
    mixing patterns in, 44
    upholstery, 148—149, 157

Family bathroom, 228
Family rooms, 170—171, 258—260
    focal point for, 171
    furniture for, 26—27, 171
    lighting for, 171
    style and color, 170
    wallcoverings for, 107
Fanlight windows, 123, 139
Faucets
    for bathrooms, 237—238
    for kitchens, 214—215
Fiber optics, 63
Finishes, 154
Fireplace, 30, 167
    mantels for, 127—128, 136
Fixed windows, 124
Fixtures
    bathrooms, 232—238
    kitchen, 212—215
Floor plans
    for kitchen, 194—195
    for sunrooms and porches, 252
Flooring
    budget for, 87
    carpeting for, 82—83, 89
    ceramic, 80—81
    for porch, 255
    laminate, 78—79, 90
    natural stone, 81—82
    options for, 75—91
    picking material for, 86—87
    tile, 79—80
    vinyl sheet, 79—80, 89
    wood, 76—78, 89, 90
Flue, 128
Fluorescent bulbs, 62—63
Flush wood doors, 123
Focal points, 23—24, 28, 30
    accessories as, 135
    for bathrooms, 183
    for bedrooms, 177—178
    for dining room, 172—173
    for family room, 171
    for kitchen, 176
    for living room, 167
Fold-down mixer shelf, 205
Foyers and hallways, 164—165, 188
    furnishings for, 164
    lighting for, 165
Framed cabinets, 203
Frameless cabinets, 203
French doors, 119, 123, 139
Frieze, 128
Furniture, 141—157
    budget for, 149
    construction of, 150—151

contemporary, 146
country-style, 146
finishes for, 154
for bathrooms, 183
for bedrooms, 27, 143, 178
for children's rooms, 180, 182
for dining rooms, 26—27, 173
for family rooms, 26—27, 171
for foyers and hallways, 164
for kitchen, 27, 176
for living rooms, 26—27, 167—169
for seating, 142—143
for storage, 143, 154
groupings of, 28
identifying your, 152—153
joining methods, 150—151
judging quality in, 146—151, 155
making choices in, 144—145
placement by room, 25—27
recycling your, 156—157
templates, 21—22
traditional-style, 145

G

Gazebos, 257—261
Gingham, 43
Glazing, 99
Grab bars for bathrooms, 238
Graining, 100
Great rooms, 170
Grilles, 130
Ground-fault circuit interrupters
    (GFCIs), 257

H

Hallways, 164—165
    furniture for, 164
    lighting for, 165
Halogen, 63
Hardware, 130
    for cabinets, 208—209
Hardwoods, 76—77
Harmonious color schemes, 36
Harmony, 17
Hearth, 128
Home office, 27, 188
Horizontal lines, 14, 28

I

Incandescent bulbs, 62, 70
Indirect glare, 60
Islands in kitchen design, 198—199,
    201

J

Jabots, 113—114

Jalousie windows, 124
Jambs, 127

K

Kitchens, 174—176, 191—219
  cabinets for, 175, 202—209
  countertop options, 210—212
  eating areas in, 27, 199—201,
    260—261
  fixtures for, 212—215
  focal points for, 176
  furniture for, 27, 176
  islands and peninsulas in,
    198—199, 201
  layouts in, 196—198
  lighting for, 58, 61, 176
  set priorities in, 192—195
  style and color for, 174—175
  window treatments for, 109
  work triangle in, 195—201
Knockdown cabinetry, 204

L

Lace, 43
Lambrequin, 113
Laminate
  for bathroom countertops, 242
  for flooring, 78—79, 90
  for kitchen countertops, 211
Landscaping, 262—263
Latex paints, 103
Latex wash, 96
Lavatories, 235—237
Layouts
  in bathroom design, 223—226
  in kitchen design, 198
Lazy Susans, 205
Lifestyle concerns, 46
Light bulbs, types of, 60—63, 70
Lighting, 53—73
  accent, 56
  ambient, 55—56
  artificial, 55—57, 73
  color and, 38
  decorative, 57
  determining needs in, 63—67
  fixtures for, 67—68, 70
  for bathrooms, 184
  for bedrooms, 178
  for children's rooms, 182
  for dining room, 174
  for family room, 171
  for foyers and hallways, 165
  for kitchen, 176
  for living room, 170
  for porch, 257

  in architecture, 68—69
  natural, 54—55, 73, 109, 124
  plan for, 53, 65
  quality of, 53
  recommended ranges of, 58
  selecting levels of, 59—60
  task, 56, 57
Lighting showrooms, 66—67
Linen, 43
Linen closet, 239
Lines, 14
  curved, 14
  diagonal, 14
  horizontal, 14, 28
  vertical, 14
Lintel, 127
Living rooms, 165—170, 187, 188
  defining space for, 169
  focal points for, 167
  furniture for, 26—27, 167—169
  furniture placement in, 26—27
  lighting for, 170
  style and color, 165—166
Louvered shutters, 115

M

Mantels, 127—128, 136
Marbling, 99—100
Master bath, 229
Measurement, taking, 19
Medicine cabinets, 241—242
Mirrors, 164
Miter joints, 151
Modulars, 143, 148
Moiré, 43
Moldings, 41, 128—129, 139
Monochromatic color scheme, 35
Mortise-and-tenon joints, 151
Multipurpose space, 24—25
Muslin, 43

N

National Kitchen & Bath Association
    (NKBA), 195
Natural fibers, 149
Natural light, 46, 54—55, 73, 109,
    124

O

Objets d'art, 130
Operable windows, 124
Organdy, 43
Oriental rugs, 41
Outdoor living areas, 251—267
  landscaping, 262—263
  patios, decks, and gazebos,

    257—261
  sunrooms and porches, 252—257
Oval windows, 126
Over-draperies, 112
Overmantel, 127

P

Paint
  adding texture with, 41
  decorative techniques with,
    96—102
  for children's rooms, 102
  for foyers, 165
  for trim, 103
  for walls, 103
  instant effects with, 101—102
Palladian windows, 124
Panel doors, 123
Patios, 257—261
Patterns, 38—39
  color and, 40—41
  mixing fabric, 39, 44
Pavers, 187
Pelmet, 112
Peninsulas in kitchen design,
    198—199, 201
Physical space, 44
Picture rail, 128—129
Picture windows, 124
Plan. See also Design plan
  lighting, 53, 65
  notebook for, 18—19, 193
Plank doors, 123
Pleated fabric shades, 115
Porches, 252—257
Powder room, 226
Primary colors, 34
Professionals
  in bathroom design, 221, 239
  in kitchen design, 192
  working with, 184—185
Proportion, 14
Psychology of color, 36—37

Q

Quality
  of furniture, 146—151, 155
  of lighting, 53

R

Ragging on/off, 97
Ready-to-assemble furniture, 148
Recessed ceiling light fixtures, 57
Recycling of furniture, 156—157
Reproductions, 148
Resilient flooring, 79

Rhythm, 17
Rolltop door, 205
Roman shades, 115
Rosettes, 114
Rugs. *See* Carpeting and rugs

S
Sample board, 42, 95
Satin, 43
Scale, 14
Seating, furniture for, 142—143
Secondary colors, 34
Sectionals, 148
Shade, color, 34
Shades, 115
    balloon, 115
    cellular, 255
    for porch, 255
    pleated fabric, 115
    Roman, 115
Showers, 233—234
Shutters, louvered, 115
Silk, 43
Sinks
    bathroom, 235—237
    kitchen, 213—214
Sleeping, furniture for, 143
Slide-outs, 205
Sliding glass doors, 123
Sofas, 142
    cushions for, 148
    frames in, 147
    reupholstering, 157
    springs in, 147
    types of, 153
    upholstery for, 148—149
Soffits, 68
Softwoods, 76—77
Solid-surfacing material
    for bathroom countertops,
        243—244
    for kitchen countertops, 211
Space
    altering, with color, 37—38
    balance in, 15, 17
    defining, for living room, 169
    harmony and rhythm in, 18
    line in, 14
    manipulation of, 13
    physical, 44
    scale and proportion in, 14
Spatial effects, 40
Special details, 130—135
Special-effects artist, finding, 100
Split complement color scheme, 35
Sponging, 96—97

Stainless steel for kitchen
        countertops, 212
Stairs, 126—127
Stamping, 98—99
Stenciling, 98—99
Stock cabinets, 204
Stone
    for bathroom countertops, 244
    for flooring, 81—82
    for kitchen countertops, 244
Storage, 143
    furniture for, 143, 154
    in bathroom, 183, 238—242
    in kitchen, 201
Style
    for bathrooms, 182
    for bedrooms, 176—177
    for children's rooms, 180
    for dining room, 172
    for family room, 170
    for kitchen, 174—175
    for living room, 165—166
Sunrooms, 252—257
Symmetry, 15, 17, 131
Synthetic fibers, 149

T
Taffeta, 43
Tambour door, 205
Tapestry, 43
Task light, 56, 57
Templates in bathroom design, 223
Tertiary colors, 34
Textiles, as art, 134
Texture, 39—41
    adding, 40—41
    spatial effects with, 40
Tile flooring, 79—80
Tilt-outs, 205
Tint, 34
Toile de Jouy, 43
Toilets, 234—235
Tongue-and-groove joints, 151
Towel bars for bathrooms, 238
Traditional-style furniture, 145
Traffic patterns for sunrooms, 253
Trapezoidal window, 126
Triangular window, 126
Trim, 128—129
    painting, 103
Triphosphor fluorescent lamps, 63
Trompe l'oeil, 100
Tubs, 232—233

U
Upholstery, 148—149

V
Valances, 68, 112—113
Vanities, 240—241
Velvet, 43
Veneers, 150
Vertical lines, 14
Vinyl sheet flooring, 79—80, 89
Visual symmetry, 131

W
Wainscotting, 117, 129
Wallpaper, 105—108
    adding texture with, 41
    borders in, 117
    embossed coverings, 106
    fabric-backed vinyl, 105
    fiberglass weaves, 106
    flocked coverings, 106
    foil coverings, 106
    for foyer and hallways, 164
    natural coverings, 106
    paper-backed vinyl, 105
    vinyl coverings, 105
    vinyl-coated paper, 105
Walls
    assessing condition of, 94—95
    decorative paint techniques,
        96—102
    mirrored, 164
    painting, 103
Warm colors, 36, 50
Washing, 99
Window seats, 158
Window treatments, 108—115
    adding texture with, 41
    budget for, 111
    fabrics for, 113, 114
    full formal, 112—113
    informal, 113—114
    maintenance of, 111
    professional flair in, 111
Windows, 123—126
    materials for, 124
    sizes of, 110
    types of, 124, 126
Wood
    for bathroom countertops, 245
    for kitchen countertops, 212
Wood flooring, 89, 90
    finishing options, 77—78
    installation, 78
    maintenance, 78
    types of, 76—77
Work triangle in kitchen design,
    195—201

PHOTO CREDITS

Front Cover: Mark Samu **page 1:** Jessie Walker **page 2:** Nancy Hill **page 6:** www.davidduncanlivingston.com **page 8:** Mark Lohman **page 9:** *left* Mark Lohman. *right* Jessie Walker **page 10:** *left* Bradsimmons.com. *right* Jessie Walker **page 11:** *top left* Jessie Walker, designer: David T. Smith. *top right* Mark Lohman. *bottom right* Mark Samu, designer: Anne Tarasoff. *bottom left* Jessie Walker, architect: Thomas Swarthaut **page 12:** Mark Samu, designer: Sherrill Canet Design **page 13:** *top* Jessie Walker, designer: David T. Smith. *center* Tony Giammarino. *bottom* Jessie Walker, architect: Thomas Swarthaut **page 14:** Mark Samu, designer: Rinaldi Associates **Page 15:** *left* www.davidduncanlivingston.com. *top right* Tim Street Porter/Beateworks.com, architect: Fernan Hartman. *bottom right* Mark Samu, designer: Sherrill Canet Design **page 16:** Jessie Walker, designer: Mary De Buhr Antiques **page 17:** Mark Samu **page 18:** Jon Bouchier/Elizabethwhiting.com **page 19:** Mark Samu **page 21:** www.davidduncanlivingston.com **pages 22–23:** *left* www.davidduncanlivingston.com. *top* Jessie Walker, designer: Joan Boardman. *bottom right* Tim Street Porter/Beateworks.com, designer: Simon Potts **page 24:** both Mark Lohman **page 25:** Tim Street Porter/Beateworks.com, designer: Andrew Virtue **page 26:** *top left* Jessie Walker, designer: Jannine Wallace **page 27:** Mark Samu **pages 28 & 29:** *top* Christopher Covey/Beateworks.com, designer: Designs Two. *bottom left* Maggie Cole, designer: Morgan Interiors. *top center & top right* www.davidduncanlivingston.com. *bottom right* Mark Samu, courtesy of Hearst Specials. *bottom center* courtesy of York Wallcoverings **pages 30–31:** *left* Mark Samu, courtesy of Hearst Specials. *center* Phillip Ennis, designer: Benett Weinstock. *top right* courtesy of York Wallcoverings. *bottom right* Michael Dunne/Elizabethwhiting.com. *bottom center* Mark Lohman **page 32:** Mark Liscombe-White/Elizabethwhiting.com, designer: Laura Ashley **page 33:** *top* Brian Harrison/Elizabethwhiting.com, designer: Allen & Batson. *center* courtesy of Brewster Wallcoverings. *bottom* courtesy of Seabrook Wallcoverings **page 34:** Jessie Walker **page 36:** Brian Harrison/Elizabethwhiting.com **page 37:** Maggie Cole, designer: Dianne Lowenthal, ASID **page 38:** Nick Carter/Elizabethwhiting.com **page 39:** Jessie Walker, designer: Susan Reese Interiors **page 40:** Tim Street Porter/Beateworks.com, designer: Tom Beeton **page 41:** Mark Samu, designer: Carolyn Miller **page 42:** Mark Samu **page 43:** *top right & middle right* courtesy of Country Curtains. *bottom right* courtesy of Scalamandre. *bottom left* courtesy of Springs Window Fashions. *top left* courtesy of Thibaut. **page 44:** Tim Street Porter/Beateworks.com **page 45:** *top* Tim Street Porter/Beateworks.com. *bottom left* www.davidduncanlivingston.com. *bottom right:* Mark Samu, designer: Anne Tarasoff **pages 46 & 47:** both Jessie Walker **page 48:** Mark Samu **page 49:** *left* Bradsim-

mons.com, stylist: Cindy Martin/Fine Design. *top right* Rodney Hyatt/Elizabethwhiting.com. *middle right* Nancy Hill, designer: David Parker Interior Design. *bottom right* Nancy Hill, designer: Anne Mullin Interiors **page 50:** *top left* Neil Davis/Elizabethwhiting.com. *top right* Mark Samu, designer: Beverly Balk. *bottom* courtesy of Seabrook Wallcoverings **page 51:** *top left* Nancy Hill, designer: Stephanie Stokes. *top right* courtesy of Seabrook Wallcoverings. *bottom right* courtesy of Brewster Wallcoverings. *bottom left* courtesy of Seabrook Wallcoverings **page 52:** Nancy Hill, designer: Gillian Drummond **page 53:** *top* Jessie Walker, artist & sculptor: Diana McNich. *center* www.davidduncanlivingston.com. *bottom* Jessie Walker, designer: Donna Aylesworth **page 54:** Elizabethwhiting.com **page 55:** www.davidduncanlivingston.com **page 56:** *left* www.davidduncanlivingston.com. *right* Nancy Hill, designer: Deborah T. Lipner, LTD. www.davidduncanlivingston.com **page 59:** Nancy Hill, designer: Diana Sawicki Interiors **pages 60–61:** *left* Phillip Ennis, designer: MInico Corp./Richard Mishaan. *center* Anne Gummerson. *right* www.davidduncanlivingston.com. *bottom* Nancy Hill **page 62:** www.davidduncanlivingston.com. **page 63:** Nancy Hill, designer: Stephanie Stokes **pages 64–65:** www.davidduncanlivingston.com **pages 66–67:** *left* Tim Street-Porter/Beateworks.com, designer: Corrigan. *center* Jessie Walker, builder: Sevrono Custom Builders **page 68:** *top left* Phillip Ennis, designer: Stingray Hornsby, LLC. *bottom left* Nancy Hill. *bottom right* Mark Samu, designer: Courland Design **page 69:** *left* Mark Samu, courtesy of Hearst Specials. *right* Nancy Hill, courtesy of House Beautiful Remodeling **page 70:** *left, top right, & right center* Mark Lohman. *bottom right* Nancy Hill, designer: Deborah T. Lipner **page 71:** Mark Lohman **page 72:** Tim Street-Porter/-Beateworks.com, architect: Brian Murphy

page 73: *top left* Mark Lohman. *top right* Mark Samu, designer Richard Schlesinger. *bottom* www.davidduncanlivingston.com **page 74:** Nancy Hill, designer: Deborah T. Lipner **page 75:** *top* Maggie Cole, designer: Champa Interiors. *middle* Mark Samu. *bottom* courtesy of Congoleum **page 76:** Mark Samu **page 77:** Holly Stickley **page 78:** courtesy of Congoleum **page 79:** courtesy of Mannington **page 80:** *top* Mark Lohman. *bottom* Tim Street-Porter/Beateworks.com **page 81:** Bradsimmons.com, designer: Cindy Martin **page 82:** Mark Samu, designer: Courland Design **page 83:** Beateworks.com **page 84:** Mark Samu **page 85:** www.davidduncanlivingston.com. **pages 86 & 87:** both Bill Rothschild, designers: *left* Barbara Lembo. *right* Interior Consultants/Denise Balassi **page 88:** *top* www.davidduncanlivingston.com. *bottom left* courtesy of Congoleum. *bottom right* Jessie Walker, designer: Marilynn Davies **page 89:** *top left* courtesy of Congoleum. *top right* courtesy of Mannington. *bottom* Bradsimmons.com **page 90:** *top* Tim Street-Porter/Beateworks.com, designer: Bob & Isabel Higgins. *bottom* courtesy of Congoleum. **page 91:** *top left* courtesy of Mannington. *top right* Mark Samu, designer: Sherrill Canet Designs. *bottom* Mark Lohman **page 92:** Nancy Hill, designer: Stirling Design Associates **page 93:** *top* Phillip Ennis, designer: McIver Morgan. *center* Tim Street-Porter/Beateworks, designer: Debra Jones. *bottom* courtesy of York Wallcoverings **page 94:** Mark Lohman **page 95:** Tim Street-Porter/Beateworks, designers: Bob & Isabel Higgins **page 96:** *left* Mark Samu, faux finish by Lucianna Samu. *right* Don Wong, CH **page 97:** *left top & bottom* Mark Samu. *right* Tony Giammarino, designer: Dot Boulware **page 98:** *top* Bradsimmons.com. *bottom* Mark Samu. *bottom* Don Wong, CH **page 99:** *left* Mark Samu, faux finish by Lucianna Samu. *right* Don Wong, CH **page 100:**

Mark Samu **page 101:** Mark Samu, faux finish by Lucianna Samu. *bottom* Don Wong, CH **page 102:** Mark Lohman **page 103:** Holly Stickley **pages 104–105:** *left* Mark Samu, designer: Mayo Delucci. *center* courtesy of Jane Cornell Company **page 106:** Phillip Ennis, designer: McIver Morgan **page 107:** *top* Mark Samu, designer: Anne Tarasoff. *bottom* Tony Giammarino, decorative finishes by: Patti Ryan **page 108:** *left* Tim Street-Porter/Beateworks, designer: Bianchi. *right* Mark Lohman **page 109:** *left* Melabee M Miller, designer: Deborah Leamann. *right* www.davidduncanlivingston.com **page 110:** *top* Bob Greenspan, stylist: Susan Andrews. *bottom* Mark Lohman **page 111:** *top* Tria Giovan. *bottom* www.davidduncanlivingston.com **page 112:** *top* Mark Lohman. *bottom* www.davidduncanlivingston.com **page 113:** both courtesy of Country Curtains **page 114:** *top* courtesy of Motif Designs. *bottom right* Tony Giammarino, designer: Christine McCabe. *bottom left* Mark Lohman **page 115:** *left* Tony Giammarino, designer: Christine McCabe. *right* www.davidduncanlivingston.com **page 116:** *top left* Jessie Walker, designer: Marilyn Atkins. *top center & top right* courtesy of Thibaut Wallcoverings. *bottom* Mark Lohman **page 117:** *top* Nancy Hill. *bottom* courtesy of York Wallcoverings **page 118:** Nancy Hill, designer: Sheridan Interiors **page 119:** *top left* Jane Cornell Company. *top right* Jessie Walker, designer: Jean Goss. *bottom right* Bill Rothschild. *bottom left* courtesy of Springs Window Fashions & Graber **page 120:** Nancy Hill **page 121:** *top & middle* Mark Lohman. *bottom* Jessie Walker **page 122:** both www.davidduncanlivingston.com **page 123:** *top* Mark Samu, designer: Boccard/ Suddell. *bottom* Holly Stickley Photography **page 124:** Jessie Walker **page 125:** Mark Samu, courtesy of Hearst Specials **pages 126–127:** all Mark Lohman **page 128:** Mark Samu **page 129:** *both* Holly Stickley Photography **pages 130–131:** *top left* www.davidduncanlivingston.com. *top right* Nancy Hill, designer: Karen Houghton Interiors. *bottom right* Jessie Walker. *bottom left* Nancy Hill, designer: David Parker Interior Design **page 132:** Mark Lohman **page 133:** www.-davidduncanlivingston.com **page 135:** Jessie Walker **page 136:** *top* Mark Lohman. *bottom right* Brad Simmons/Beateworks.com. *bottom left* Jessie Walker, designer: Mary DeBuhr **page 137:** Jessie Walker **page 138:** www.davidduncanlivingston.com **page 139:** *top left* Lu Jeffrey/Elizabethwhiting.com. *top right* Mark Lohman. *bottom right* Di Lewis/-Elizabethwhiting.com. *bottom left* Mark Samu, designer: Perfect Interiors **page 140:** Nancy Hill, designer: Diana Sawicki Interior Design **page 141:** *top* courtesy of Baker Furniture. *middle* Holly Stickley Photography. *bottom* Jessie Walker, architect: Thomas Swarthaut **page 143:** Brad Simmons/Beateworks.com, architect: Mark L. Brown, designer: Harker Design **page 143:** Mark Lohman **page 144:** Mark Lohman **page 145:** Nancy Hill, designer: Diane Burgoyne Interiors **page 146:**

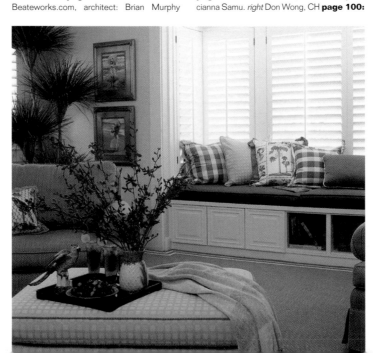

top Mark Lohman. *bottom* Bradsimmons.com **page 147:** *all* Brian McNiell **page 148:** American Furniture Manufacturers Association, courtesy of Bassett Furniture **page 149:** Maggie Cole, designer: Sandra Morgan Interiors **pages 150–151:** *left to right* courtesy of Baker Furniture. Mark Samu. Mark Lohman. American Furniture Manufacturers Association, courtesy of Palecek **page 154:** Mark Lohman **pages 155–157:** *all* Jessie Walker, artist, *155 bottom* Kathleen McCann **page 158:** *top left* courtesy of Baker Furniture. *top right* Mark Lohman. *bottom right* Mark Samu. *bottom left* American Furniture Manufacturers Association, courtesy of Stanley Furniture **page 159:** *top left* Maggie Cole, designer: Lynn Hoffman Interiors. *top right* Mark Lohman. *bottom right* Mark Lohman **page 160:** *top & bottom* Mark Lohman **page 161:** *top left* Jessie Walker, designer: Carol Knott, ASID. *top right* Mark Lohman. *bottom* www.davidduncanlivingston.com **page 162:** Maggie Cole, designer: Elaine Koufman Interiors **page 163:** *top* Mark Lohman. *middle* Nancy Hill, architect: Robert Davis, A.I.A. *bottom* Jessie Walker, designer: Susan Chastain **page 164:** Mark Lohman **page 165:** Nancy Hill, designer: Diane Burgoyne Interiors **pages 166–168:** *all* Mark Lohman **page 169:** *left* www.davidduncanlivingston.com. *right* Mark Lohman **page 170:** Nancy Hill, designer Karen Houghton Interiors **page 171:** Mark Lohman **pages 172–173:** Nancy Hill, designer Deborah T. Lipner, L.T.D. *center* Mark Lohman. *right* Mark Lohman, designer: Lynn Robinson **page 174:** *top* Mark Lohman. *bottom* Neil Davis/Elizabethwhiting.com **page 175:** *top* Jessie Walker. *bottom* Robert Harding Picture Library **page 176:** Nancy Hill, architect: Robert Davis, A.I.A. **page 177:** *top* Maggie Cole, designer: Champa Interiors. *bottom left* www.davidduncanlivingston.com. *bottom right* Jessie Walker, designer: Joan Babb, The Potting Shed **page 178:** Mark Lohman **page 179:** *top* Jessie Walker, designer: Kathy McDonald. *bottom* Mark Lohman **pages 180–181:** *center* Jessie Walker. *top right* Bradsimmons.com, stylist: Joetta Moulden/Sheltersville.com. *bottom right* Bill Rothschild, designer: Sue Wenk Interiors **pages 182–183:** *left* Jessie Walker. *center* Jessie Walker, architect: Bill Bauhs. *right* Mark Lohman **pages 184–185:** *center* Bill Rothschild, designer: Ellen Dunn ASID. *right* Nancy Hill, designer Karen Houghton Interiors **page 186–187:** *top left* Jessie Walker. *top center* Jessie Walker, designer: Rachel Samet. *top right* Nancy Hill, designer Stephanie Stokes, Inc. *right center* Tony Giammarino. *bottom right* Maggie Cole, designer Sandra Morgan Interiors. *bottom center* Jessie Walker. *bottom left* Mark Lohman **page 188:** Mark Lohman **page 189:** *top left & top right* Mark Lohman. *middle right* Jessie Walker. *bottom right* Maggie Cole, designer: Elaine Koufman Interiors. *bottom left* Jessie Walker **page 190:** Mark Lohman. **page 191:** *top* courtesy of Wilsonart International. *center & bottom* courtesy of Merillat Industries. **page 192:** Brian Vanden Brink, architect: Mark Hutger and Associates. **page 193:** Brian Vanden Brink, architect: Sholz and Barclay **page 201:** James Bennett/Beateworks.com **pages 202–203:** *left* Phillip Ennis, architect: Mojo Stumer. *center* Phillip Ennis, designer: Sandra Oster Interiors **page 204–205:** *all* www.davidduncanlivingston.com **page 206–207:** *left* Philip Clayton-Thompson, designer: Chris Tosdevin. *top center* Bradsimmons.com, builder: Yankee Barn Homes. *bottom right* www.davidduncanlivingston.com. *bottom left* courtesy of Wellborn Cabinet, Inc. **page 208:** Philip Clayton-Thompson, designer: Ann Palmer **page 209:** *top left* www.davidduncanlivingston.com. *top right* Bradsimmons.com, designer: Todd Hall, builder: Yankee Barn Homes. *bottom right* Phillip Ennis, designer: M&S Associates. **page 210–211:** *bottom left & top* www.davidduncanlivingston.com. *bottom right* Holly Stickley, architects: Pratt & Larson. **pages 212–213:** *all* www.davidduncanlivingston.com **page 214:** www.davidduncanlivingston.com **page 215:** Brian Vanden Brink. **page 216:** *top left* courtesy of Kraftmaid. *top center & right* courtesy of Wellborn Cabinetry. *bottom* Jessie Walker **page 217:** *top left* courtesy of Wilsonart International. *top right, bottom right & bottom left* www.davidduncanlivingston.com **page 218:** *top left* Brian Vanden Brink, builder: Morning Star Marble and Granite. *top right* courtesy of Elkay Manufacturing Company. *bottom right* courtesy of Jenn-Air. *bottom left* www.davidduncanlivingston.com **page 219:** *top left* www.davidduncanlivingston.com. *top right* courtesy of Ann Sacks Tile. *right center & bottom right* Phillip Ennis, designer: John Buscarello **page 220:** Mark Lohman **page 221:** *top* Bradsimmons.com. *middle* courtesy of Grohe Plumbing. *bottom* courtesy of Kohler **page 222:** Mark Lohman **page 226:** James Shanks **page 227:** Mark Lohman **page 228:** *top* Tony Giammarino. *bottom left & right* Mark Lohman **page 229:** *top* Philip Clayton-Thompson. *bottom* Brian Vanden Brink, architect: Dominic Mercadante **page 230:** Phillip Ennis **page 231:** Elizabethwhiting.com **page 232:** courtesy of Jacuzzi **page 233:** www.davidduncanlivingston.com **page 234:** Melabee M Miller **page 235:** Brian Vanden Brink, architects: Mark Hutger & Associates **pages 236–237:** *left* Bradsimmons.com. *right* Mark Samu **page 238:** courtesy of Kohler **page 239:** courtesy of Imperial Home Decor Group **page 240:** Mark Samu **page 241:** Mark Lohman **page 242:** Brett Drury, builder: Dakota Builders **page 243:** Bill Rothschild **page 244:** Carolynbates.com **page 245:** Bill Rothschild **page 246:** *top left* Mark Lohman. *top right* Elizabethwhiting.com. *bottom right* Tria Giovan. *bottom left* www.davidduncanlivingston.com. *bottom* Elizabethwhiting.com. *bottom* www.davidduncanlivingston.com **page 248:** *left* Mark Lohman. *right* Carolynbates.com **page 249:** *top left* Mark Lohman. *top right* Brian Vanden Brink, architects: Mark Hutger & Associates. *bottom right* Robert Perron. *bottom left* Mark Lohman **page 250:** Mark Lohman **page 251:** *top* Bradsimmons.com. *middle* Brian Vanden Brink, designer: Weatherend Estate Furniture. *bottom* Tony Giammarino, designer: Shipp & Wilson Landscape design **page 252:** Jessie Walker, designer: Barbara Metzler **page 253:** *top* Jessie Walker. *bottom* Tony Giammarino, architect: Willow Pond Farm Inn **page 254:** *both* Tony Giammarino, designer: Shane Miller **page 255:** Tim Street-Porter/Beateworks.com **page 256:** *top* Bradsimmons.com. *middle left, bottom left & bottom right* Jessie Walker **page 257:** *top* Tria Giovan. *bottom* Brian Vanden Brink, architect: Rob Whitten **page 258:** Mark Lohman **page 259:** *left* Jessie Walker. *right* Brian Vanden Brink, archi-

tects: Mark Hutger & Associates/Wheaton **page 260:** *top* Jessie Walker. *bottom* Tria Giovan **page 261:** *top* Tria Giovan. *bottom* Mark Lohman **page 262:** Tim Street-Porter/Beateworks.com **page 263:** *top* Brian Vanden Brink, architects: Mark Hutger & Associates. *bottom* Brian Vanden Brink, designer: Weatherend Estate Furniture **page 264:** *top* Mark Lohman. *bottom* Brian Vanden Brink. *top right* Jessie Walker **page 265:** *left* Brian Vanden Brink, architects: Weston & Hewitson. *top* Mark Lohman. *bottom* Tony Giammarino, architect: Steve Berg **page 266:** *top* Tim Street-Porter/Beateworks.com. *bottom* Brian Vanden Brink **page 267:** *left* Brian Vanden Brink, architects: Mark Hutger & Associates. *top right* Tim Street-Porter/Beateworks.com. *bottom right* Jessie Walker **page 286:** Mark Lohman **page 287:** Jessie Walker **Back Cover:** *top* Bradsimmons.com. *left top & bottom* Mark Lohman. *right* Christopher Covey/Beateworks.com.

SOURCES

Photographers & Stylists: Beate Works, Inc., Los Angeles, CA; Beateworks.com. 310-558-1100. Brian Vanden Brink, Camden, ME; 207-236-4035. Philip Clayton-Thompson, Portland, OR; 503-234-4883. Maggie Cole, Meriden, CT; 203-494-8763. Phillip H. Ennis, Bedford, NY; 914-234-9574; phillip-ennis.com. Tony Giammarino, Richmond, VA; 804-320-23235. Tria Giovan, New York, NY 212-533-6612. Robert Harding Picture Library, London, G.B., 207 4784 000. Nancy Hill, Ridgefield, CT, 203-431-7655. David Duncan Livingston, Mill Valley, CA; 415-383-0898; davidduncanlivingston.com. Mark Lohman, Los Angeles, CA; 323-933-3359. Bill Rothschild, Wesley Hills, NY, 845-354-4567. Mark Samu, Saratoga Springs, NY, 518-581-7026. James Shanks; 212-780-0031; Jamesshanks.com. Brad Simmons, Perryville, KY; 859-332-8400. Holly Stickley, Portland, OR; 503-283-1016. Jessie Walker Associates, Glencoe, IL; 847-835-0522. Elizabeth Whiting & Associates, London, G.B., 242 1700 08.

Designers, Architects, & Manufacturers: Ann Sacks Tile, 800-278-8453. Beverly Balk Design, 516-759-3198. Sherrill Canet Design, 516-676-7611. Country Curtains, Stockbridge, MA; 800-937-1237. Mark Hutger & Associates Architects, Vineyard Haven, MA; 508-693-3344. Jacuzzi, 800-288-4002. Jenn-Air, 800-688-1100. Kohler, 800-456-4537. Kraftmaid Cabinetry, 888-562-7744. Dominic Mercadante, Belfast, ME; 207-338-4089. Carolyn Miller Interiors, 516-491-3010. M & S Associates, Roslyn Heights, NY; 516-484-5837. Ann Palmer, Beverly Hills, CA; 310-276-5055. Lucianna Samu, Blue Point, NY; 516-363-5902. Scalamandre, Long Island City, NY; 718-361-8500. Anne Tarasoff Interiors, 516-944-8913. Wilsonart International, 800-433-3222. Yankee Barn Homes, 800-258-9786

Have a home decorating, improvement, or gardening project? Look for these and other fine **Creative Homeowner books** wherever books are sold.

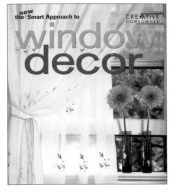

Design advice and industry tips for choosing window treatments. Over 425 photos & illustrations. 208 pp.; 9"x10"
BOOK #: 279438

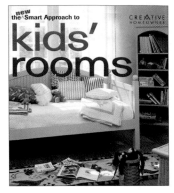

Original ideas for great kid's rooms. More than 260 color photographs. 208 pp.; 9"x10"
BOOK #: 279478

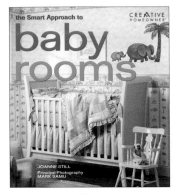

Create a beautiful and safe environment for your baby. 260+ color photos. 208 pp.; 9"x10"
BOOK #: 279482

Fill your home with the spirit of country: fabrics, finishes, and furniture. Over 200 photos. 176 pp.; 9"x10"
BOOK #: 279685

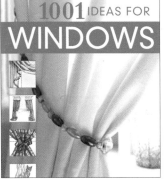

Guide to all possible window dressings. Over 1000 illustrations and photos. 240 pp.; 8$\frac{1}{2}$"x10$\frac{7}{8}$"
BOOK #: 279408

A guide to paint techniques and faux finishes. More than 300 color photos. 240 pp.; 8$\frac{1}{2}$"x10$\frac{7}{8}$" w/flaps
BOOK #: 279020

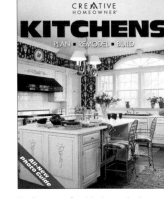

Reference for kitchen design and renovation. Over 550 color photos, illustrations. 256 pp.; 8$\frac{1}{2}$"x10$\frac{7}{8}$"
BOOK #: 277061

Complete bathroom remodeling guide. Over 650 color photos and illustrations. 256 pp.; 8$\frac{1}{2}$"x10$\frac{7}{8}$"
BOOK #: 278627

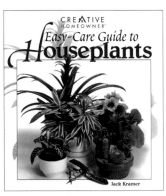

Complete houseplant guide. 200 readily available plants; more than 400 photos. 192 pp.; 9"x10"
BOOK #: 275243

An impressive guide to garden design and plant selection. More than 950 photos. 384 pp.; 9"x10"
BOOK #: 274610

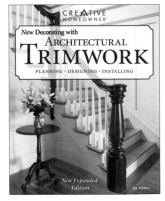

Transform a room with trimwork. Over 550 color photos and illustrations. 240 pp.; 8$\frac{1}{2}$"x10$\frac{7}{8}$"
BOOK #: 277500

The ultimate home improvement reference manual. Over 300 step-by-step projects. 608 pp.; 9"x10$\frac{7}{8}$"
BOOK #: 267855

For more information and to place an order, go to www.creativehomeowner.com